CHARLES BUKOWSKI

LOCKED IN THE
ARMS OF A
CRAZY LIFE

CHARLES BUKOWSKI

LOCKED IN THE ARMS OF A CRAZY LIFE

Howard Sounes

drawings by Charles Bukowski

GROVE PRESS
New York

First published in Great Britain in 1998 by Rebel Inc.,
an imprint of Canongate Books Ltd., Edinburgh, Scotland
Published simultaneously in Canada
Printed in the United States of America

FIRST AMERICAN EDITION

Library of Congress Cataloging-in-Publication Data

Sounes, Howard, 1965–
    Charles Bukowski : locked in the arms of a crazy life : the
biography / by Howard Sounes ; drawings by Charles Bukowski. — 1st
American ed.
        p.   cm.
    Includes bibliographical references (p.   ) and index.
    ISBN 0-8021-1645-0
    1. Bukowski, Charles. 2. Authors, American—20th century—
Biography. 3. Los Angeles (Calif.)—Intellectual life. 4. Beat
generation—Biography.   I. Title.   II. Title: Locked in the arms of
a crazy life.
PS3552.U4Z88   1999
811'.54—dc21
[b]   99-12772

Design by James Hutcheson

Grove Press
841 Broadway
New York, NY 10003

99 00 01 02   10 9 8 7 6 5 4 3 2 1

CONTENTS

CONTENTS

AUTHOR'S NOTE

Charles Bukowski died before I started work on this biography, and I never had an opportunity to meet him. So in order to tell the story of his life and work, hopefully the definitive account, I have interviewed people he was close to: his friends, his many lovers, his drinking partners, work colleagues, fellow writers, publishers and members of his family. Happily, I can report that virtually everybody of significance co-operated with this project.

There were additional important sources of information: Bukowski was a prolific correspondent and I obtained copies of hundreds of his previously unpublished letters together with the often intimate letters of his friends and lovers.

Bukowski's friends and relatives were kind enough to give me dozens of previously unpublished personal photographs which tell a story of their own. There are two extensive photographic sections in the book.

In Germany, where Bukowski was born, and in the United States of America, I hunted down documents relating to Bukowski's family and employment history, his draft record, and criminal convictions, in order to clarify the many myths about his life.

Finally I referred to the print and filmed interviews Bukowski gave and, of course, his writing in more than forty-five books of poetry and prose, not to mention the hundreds of magazines his work has appeared in.

Once I had accumulated this mass of information – boxes and

boxes of files and documents and tape-recorded interviews piled up around me as I write this – I found I had ample evidence not only as to what Bukowski did and said throughout his life, but evidence as to what he and people close to him were *thinking* at the time (letters were particularly revealing in this respect). There was so much strong material that I decided to try and weave a narrative which could be read, first and foremost, as a good story – because Bukowski's life is a terrific story, sometimes sad, often very funny, and ultimately a wonderful example of an underdog overcoming adversity – without stopping to justify and explain every piece of information in footnotes and parentheses.

There is a need to explain sources, however, and I have done this in an extensive section of source notes at the end of the book. Here the reader will find a full account of every source used to back up every assertion in each chapter of the main body of the book, often several independent sources, together with the provenance of the information and additional background.

So, if while reading this biography, you find yourself pausing and thinking, 'Hey! How on earth could he know *that*?', the answers are in the source notes.

Also, I would like to point out that I have deliberately refrained from commenting on Bukowski's lifestyle, and from making judgements about aspects of his behavior. I see my job as presenting you, the reader, with the true facts of Bukowski's life – drawn from those people who knew him best, from letters and documents I have found – and I have tried to do this dispassionately. It is up to you, once you have read the evidence, to make up your mind about what sort of man you think Bukowski was.

Howard Sounes
London, 1998

if you see me grinning from
my blue Volks
running a yellow light
driving straight into the sun
I will be locked in the
arms of a
crazy life

('one for the shoeshine man')

PROLOGUE

Charles Bukowski raised himself up from his chair and got a beer from the refrigerator behind him on stage. The audience applauded as he drank, tipping the bottle until it was upside down and he had drained the last golden drop.

'This is not a prop,' he said, speaking slowly with a lilt to his voice, like W.C. Fields. 'It's a necessssssitty.'

The crowd laughed and clapped. A young girl in front exclaimed that he was a 'funky old guy'. Indeed, at fifty-two, Bukowski was old enough to be the father of most of the kids who had come to hear him read, and his behavior was all the more amusing because of it.

Bukowski looked odd, as well as speaking in a peculiar way. He was a tall man, a quarter-inch under six feet, heavyset with a beer belly, but his head seemed too big for his body and his face was alarming, like a Frankenstein mask: a long jaw, thin lips, sad slitty eyes sunk into hollows; a large boozer's nose, red and purple with broken veins; and a scraggly grey beard over greasy skin mottled with acne scars, skin so bad he looked like he'd been in a fire.

He had been flown up to San Francisco, in September, 1972, by his publishers, City Lights Books, because of the success of a collection of his short stories, *Erections, Ejaculations, Exhibitions and General Tales of Ordinary Madness*. The book was dedicated to his young girlfriend, Linda King:

who brought it to me
and who will take it
away

Eight hundred people paid to get into a gymnasium on Tele-
graph Hill, eager to see the author of *Life in a Texas Whorehouse*
and the other outrageous, apparently autobiographical stories. The
idea of appearing before them terrified Bukowski. Although he
looked intimidating, he was chronically shy and hated himself for
hustling his ass in the home town of the beat writers, a group he
neither liked nor considered himself part of.

He'd been drinking all day to get his courage up, on the
morning flight from Los Angeles, in the Italian restaurant where
he and Linda King had lunch, and behind the curtain while
waiting for his cue to go on. His face was grey with fear, and
he vomited twice.

'You know it's easier working in a factory,' he told his friend,
Taylor Hackford, who was filming a documentary. 'There's no
pressure.'

The crowd knew him for his short stories, but Bukowski read
poetry. Poems about drinking, gambling and sex, even going to
the crapper – he knew that the title alone, 'piss and shit', would
make them laugh.

'Listen, some of these poems are serious and I have to apologize because I know some crowds don't like serious poems, but
I've gotta give you some now and again to show I'm not a
beer-drinking machine,' he said. He chose a poem about his
father, whom he had hated with a passion. It was called 'the
rat':

> with one punch, at the age of 16 and ½,
> I knocked out my father,
> a cruel shiny bastard with bad breath,
> and I didn't go home for some time, only now and then
> to try to get a dollar from
> dear momma.
>
> it was 1937 in Los Angeles and it was a hell of a
> Vienna.

. . .
me? I'm 30 years older,
the town is 4 or 5 times as big
but just as rotten
and the girls still spit on my
shadow, another war is building for another
reason, and I can hardly get a job now
for the same reason, I couldn't then:
I don't know anything I can't do
anything.

It seemed he might cry as he finished the last sad lines. But he snapped out of it and began playing the wild man again.

'Do I know you?' he asked a fan who called out a request. 'Don't push me around, baby . . .' he threatened, breaking into a grin. 'One more beer, I'll take you all.' He threw his head back, showing ruined teeth, and cackled. 'Ha Ha Ha. Watch out!'

Another fan tried to get up on the stage.

'What the hell you want, man? Get away from me,' said Bukowski, as if talking to a dog. 'What are you, some kinda creep?' The crowd whooped with laughter.

Somebody asked how many beers he could drink. Others were less impressed, demanding that Bukowski stop wasting time; they had paid to hear poetry, not to watch a drunk.

'You want poems?' he teased the college kids, disliking their expensive clothes and untroubled faces. 'Beg me.'

'Fuck you, man!'

'Any other comments?'

The more drunk he became, the more hostile he was towards the audience and the more hostile the audience got. 'It ended up with them throwing bottles,' recalls beat poet Lawrence Ferlinghetti, owner of City Lights Books, who had Bukowski hustled out back for his own safety.

There was a party afterwards at Ferlinghetti's apartment in North Beach. The place was packed with poets, musicians, actors, members of the audience, and almost everybody was drunk or stoned. Bukowski had little time for drugs, but he was roaring drunk. He asked every woman he met whether they wanted to have sex with him, and snarled at Taylor Hackford when Hackford tried to film a close-up:

'What do you want, mother-fuck?'

Bukowski was talking to his friend John Bennett when a fan came over to compliment him on a great show. They told him to get lost.

'Fuck you, and your mother!' said the fan.

Bukowski didn't mind people insulting his mother – he had disliked her himself – but Bennett took offence at the remark and threw the man down the stairs.

'Oh God, here we go!' exclaimed Linda King as she watched a chair smash through a window in the fight that ensued. Bennett put his fist through another window, gashing his hand, and soon half the men in the room were throwing punches at each other.

Bukowski grabbed Linda's hand and pulled her after him into the kitchen. She assumed he wanted to protect her, or maybe give her a kiss, but he accused her of flirting with John Bennett, saying she was no better than a whore, and tried to hit her over the head with a frying pan.

'I looked in his eyes and it was like a creature who was not Bukowski at all,' says Linda, who had been the victim of his jealousy many times in the year and a half they'd been together. 'I always claimed he got possessed when he was drunk. I could see he was really going to get me.'

He blocked her in a corner with his left arm, and was brandishing the frying pan in his right hand, ready to bang her on the head. She bit him hard on the hand, ducked and made a run for it. He lunged after her with the pan, but tripped and cut his face on the stove as he fell.

'To hell with you, bitch, you're out of my life,' he screamed.

Linda heard the familiar sound of police sirens wailing towards them through the city. This often happened when they went to a party, even though Bukowski promised to behave. In her frustration, she kicked a panel out of the door and clattered down the stairs into the street where a crowd was gathering. The police soon showed up, but Linda stayed back, knowing it was better not to get involved.

Marty Balin, leader of the rock group Jefferson Airplane,

wanted to make a movie out of Bukowski's short stories and came to the party to meet him. 'The windows were broken and glass was all over the floor,' says Balin who arrived just after the fight. 'Bukowski was on a mattress on the floor with no other furniture in the place, broken glass all over, bottles. His face was all cut up.'

When he saw Marty Balin's girlfriend, Bukowski scrambled to his feet and squared up to the couple.

'You know, I could take that woman away from you like that!' he said, snapping his fingers in Marty Balin's face.

The poet Harold Norse turned up to find Ferlinghetti outside on Upper Grant Avenue, apparently appalled at the goings on. Norse asked what had happened and the mild-mannered Ferlinghetti replied that Bukowski and Linda King were wrecking his place.

'Didn't I warn you?' asked Norse. He knew Bukowski of old and that, when he was sober, Bukowski was quiet and polite, even deferential. But when he got drunk – especially in sophisticated company, which made him uneasy – he became Bukowski the Bad: mischievous, argumentative, even violent. They could hear him up there now being Bukowski the Bad. He was howling like a lunatic.

'FUCK ALL THIS!' he bellowed.

Morning broke with beautiful warm autumn sunshine, a fresh breeze blowing in from the bay, and the sound of broken glass being swept up. Lawrence Ferlinghetti and Harold Norse came back to the apartment and picked their way upstairs, through the shards of glass and splintered wood, until they found Bukowski. He was sitting on the floor, still dressed in the clothes he had on the day before, his face smeared with dried blood, drinking a beer for breakfast. He had been in residence for only one night, but, as Ferlinghetti says, the place 'looked like a nest of junkies had been living there a month.'

Ferlinghetti greeted Bukowski remarkably affably, considering the state his home was in, and told him he had brought his money for the reading. His share was $400.

'And to think I used to work for 35 cents an hour,' said Bukowski in genuine wonder. He was talking about the factory jobs he had worked at nearly all his adult life, most recently as mail clerk in Los Angeles, sorting letters while the supervisor yelled at him to hurry up. He held that terrible job almost twelve years before leaving, when he was forty-nine, to become a writer. Everybody said he was mad – what about his pension? – but this proved he had been right. He held the money to his face.

'Poetry, I love poetry,' he said, kissing the bank notes. He meant it seriously, but couldn't help making a joke that lived up to his image. 'It's better than pussy,' he added, 'almost.'

TWISTED CHILDHOOD

1

Bukowski claimed the majority of what he wrote was literally what had happened in his life. Essentially that is what his books are all about – an honest representation of himself and his experiences at the bottom of American society. He even went so far as to put a figure on it: ninety-three per cent of his work was autobiography, he said, and the remaining seven per cent was 'improved upon'. Yet while he could be extraordinarily honest as a writer, a close examination of the facts of Bukowski's life leads one to question whether, to make himself more picaresque for the reader, he didn't 'improve upon' a great deal more of his life story than he said.

The blurring of fact and fiction starts with the circumstances of Bukowski's birth.

'I was born a bastard – that is, out of wedlock,' he wrote in 1971, and he repeated this story many times both in interviews and in his writing.

His parents met in Andernach, Germany, after World War One. His father, Sgt Henry Charles Bukowski, was serving with the US army of occupation and Bukowski's mother, Katharina Fett, was a local seamstress. She didn't like Henry at first, ignoring him when he called to her in the street, but he ingratiated himself with her parents by bringing food to their apartment and by speaking with them in German. He explained that his parents had emigrated to America from Germany so, by ancestry, he was German too.

Henry and Katharina started dating and Henry soon made her pregnant.

There was a delay before they got married because Henry had to get demobbed from the army first. But Andernach city records show that they did marry, on 15 July, 1920, before their child was born.

They rented an apartment at the corner of Aktienstrasse, near the railway station, and it was here Katharina gave birth to a boy at 10 p.m. on 16 August. A few days later the child was baptized at the Roman Catholic cathedral, at a font decorated with a bird very much like a black sparrow. The priest named the child Heinrich Karl Bukowski, like his dad.

They stayed in Andernach for two years while Henry worked as a building contractor, and then moved to nearby Coblenz where they lodged for a while with a family named Gehrhardt on Sclostrasse. Gehrhardt family letters reveal that Katharina shocked them by telling sexy jokes, and that Henry kept postcards of nude girls hidden in the wash stand in his room.

Henry and his bride probably would have settled in the town if it hadn't been for the collapse of the German economy in 1923. Everyday life became so difficult after the crash that Henry had little choice but to return to the United States, and so they set sail from Bremerhaven, on the SS *President Fillmore*, on 18 April, 1923.

When they arrived in Baltimore, Bukowski's mother started calling herself Kate, so she sounded more American, and little Heinrich became little Henry. They also changed the pronunciation of their surname to *Buk-cow-ski*, as opposed to the harder European pronunciation which is *Buk-ov-ski*. Henry worked hard and they soon saved enough to move out to California where he had been born and raised.

His father, Leonard, had done well in the construction boom but had turned to drink and was separated from Henry's mother, Emilie, a strict Baptist. She lived alone in Pasadena, matriarch of a quarrelsome, bad-natured tribe described as 'the battling Bukowskis' by cousin Katherine Wood 'because none of them got along'. The siblings, in particular, couldn't stand each other. Henry had no time for his brother, John, who drank and was often out of work. He also disliked his brother, Ben, who was confined to a sanatorium. Neither was he keen on his sister, Eleanor, being jealous of the little money she and her husband had saved. Emilie Bukowski made things more difficult by showing favoritism to Henry and his wife. 'My grandmother thought Kate was really something,' says Katherine Wood. 'She thought she was kind of above us. It was a snob thing.'

They moved to nearby Los Angeles in 1924, first to a small house on Trinity Street, not far from downtown, and three years later to a two-bedroom bungalow on Virginia Road in the Jefferson Park area. Apart from his travels around America in the 1940s and early '50s, Bukowski lived his whole life in and around LA and the city became an integral part of his writing. Indeed, few writers of literature have been so closely associated with, or so lovingly described the city, a place often dismissed as ugly, dangerous and culturally desolate.

LA was quite beautiful in 1924, almost a paradise; the sky was unclouded by smog, and there were still orange groves between the boulevards. The neighborhoods were safe enough for Angelenos to leave their doors unlocked, and for children to ride bicycles to the beach after school. It was a city of just over a million people, a fraction of what it became, and there was a heady boom town atmosphere, partly because of the film studios in Hollywood. Henry wanted his share of the good life. But the best job he could find was with the LA Creamery Company, delivering milk by horse and cart.

Henry and Kate dressed their son in velvet trousers and shirts with frilly collars, in the German style. 'Isn't he sweet?' Kate wrote home on the back of a photograph. 'When you ask him who he likes the best, he says, "I like mother as much as father and father as much as mother".'

Kate called her husband 'my biggest treasure' in her letters, but dropped hints he was not an easy man to get on with. One set of photographs she sent home to Germany was from a day at Santa Monica beach. Kate wrote that Henry wanted her to send these pictures to *prove* they were having fun in America. Included was a snap of Bukowski, sitting on the sand with a Stars and Stripes flag. He looked thoroughly miserable.

In his autobiographical writing, in interviews and letters to friends, Bukowski made it plain that his childhood was joyless and frightening and, about this part of his life, at least, he seems to have told the unvarnished truth. 'A twisted childhood has fucked me up,' he wrote. 'But that's the way I am, so I'll go with it.' He said he was forbidden to mix with other children because, in their snobbery, his parents considered themselves better than the neighborhood where they lived. They didn't even like him playing on his own in case he spoilt his clothes. Not surprisingly, the local children jeered at the prissy boy, calling him 'Heinie', and they sniggered at his mother's 'Kraut' accent.

Bukowski was also set apart from other children by dyslexia. As he later described in his poem, 'education', his mother wept when she was summoned to school to be told about the problem, chiefly because she was scared of what his father would say.

> 'oh, Henry,' my mother said,
> 'your father is so disappointed in
> you, I don't know what we are
> going to do!'
>
> father, my mind said,
> father and father and
> father.
>
> words like that.
>
> I decided not to learn anything
> in that
> school.
>
> my mother walked along
> beside me.
> she wasn't anything at
> all.
> and I had a bellyache
> and even the trees we walked
> under
> seemed less than

trees
and the more like everything
else.

It was while he was attending Virginia Road Elementary that his father beat him for the first time, because he had been sent home with a note for fighting. Many punishments followed. 'My ass and the backs of my legs were a continual mass of welts and bruises,' Bukowski wrote. 'I had to sleep on my belly at night because of the pain.' Henry also beat Kate. He had affairs and once abandoned the family, taking a room on West Adams Boulevard where he entertained his mistress.

Worse was to come when they moved to 2122 Longwood Avenue, what Bukowski later called, 'the house of agony, the house where I was almost done in'. It was an unremarkable bungalow, one of thousands being thrown-up in the mid-city suburbs – built in the Spanish style, covered in stucco and painted white. There was a yard at the back, car porch at the side, and a small front lawn. The house was a step up for Kate and Henry, slightly bigger and nicer than their previous homes, and each weekend they cleaned it from top to bottom. Their son was excused chores at first and seized this rare opportunity to mix with other children, kicking a football about in the street. The boys awarded him a proper American nickname: Hank, the name his friends would use the rest of his life.

Then one Saturday his father called for him and Bukowski turned to see him standing in front of the house in that peculiar way of his, with one foot in front of the other. He seemed almost excited. He wanted Bukowski to cut the grass, which normally would have been the work of no more than an hour because the lawns were not large. But his father made a sadistic game of it. He wanted the lawns manicured, front and back, so he would not find 'one hair' sticking up.

Bukowski toiled all through the afternoon as his friends played football, knowing he would never get to the game. Finally his father came to check.

'I found a hair!' he shouted triumphantly.

The house smelt of polish and detergent. It was cool inside after working in the garden. Into the bathroom, his father ordered. It was a small room with white tiles, like a torture chamber. He was told to take his pants and shorts down. He bent over next to the tub with his head under the window. His father took the leather strop, which hung beside the mirror, and belted him three times. Next Saturday he would do it right.

The weekend manicuring of the lawn, and the inevitable punishments that followed for his failure to do the job properly, and for many other reasons too, became part of the routine of childhood. It was one of the reasons Bukowski came to talk so slowly – he learned to think before speaking in case he upset his father. He claimed to have been punished almost daily, receiving up to fourteen lashes while his mother stood impassively in the doorway. Her failure to stop the beatings, or show compassion afterwards (she didn't even hug him) made Bukowski lose all respect and affection for her. He did not trust or like her. His mother became nothing to him.

'You can't help screaming especially when you are six years old, seven years old,' he said. But after a couple of years of this brutal treatment he decided not to give his father the satisfaction, and remained silent while he was being thrashed. 'The last beating I got I didn't scream at all. I didn't make a sound and I guess that terrorized him because that was the last one.'

If the cruelty of his father was the primary influence on Bukowski's character, the second was the disfiguring acne which erupted when he was thirteen. The acne was not simply spots, but a pestilence of boils 'the size of apples' he said. They erupted on every surface, and in every crevice, of his head and upper body: they were on his eyelids, on his nose, behind his ears and in the hair follicles on his head. They were even inside his mouth. 'The poisoned life had finally exploded out of me. There they were – all the withheld screams – spouting out in another form.'

He was taken downtown to the gleaming new Los Angeles County Hospital where his condition was diagnosed as *acne vulgaris*, the worst the doctors had seen. Almost a freak case. The boils were to be lanced with an electric needle and drained of pus and blood. Bukowski endured the treatment without complaint, although it was painful. A nurse squeezed the pustules dry afterwards, and put him under an ultra-violet lamp before dressing the wounds. He developed a crush on the kindly girl who was so much more sympathetic than his parents. 'They were ashamed of him. They were repulsed,' says Katherine Wood. 'It was a horrible thing they did to him, and that's probably what shaped him into what he became.'

The only time he felt safe was when he was alone in his bedroom, lying on the counterpane, following the patterns of sunlight on the ceiling. Bukowski, who had already demonstrated a talent for creative writing at school where one of his essays had been read to the class, listened to airplanes droning overhead on their way to Los Angeles airport and was inspired to invent stories about fliers, writing them up in a yellow notebook for his own amusement. One of his first stories was about the daring adventures of a World War One German air ace.

In January, 1936, Bukowski graduated from Mount Vernon Junior High with a mention in the student magazine, the *Minute Man*. In its look forward to what the alumni of '36 would be doing in twenty years, the editors predicted he would be a doughnut baker 'trying to make more profit by putting bigger holes in the doughnuts'. The flip humor was in keeping with the cheerful faces of the boys and girls who lined up for their graduation photograph. They radiated confidence. Bukowski, in contrast, squatted in front, unsmiling, his arms wrapped tightly about himself.

At first the depression was something Henry and Kate saw at the movies on the news reel, before Henry's favorite Wallace Beery pictures – footage of Okies and Arkies with their belongings heaped on the back of ancient Fords. Then people they knew started to lose their jobs. Henry's elder brother, John, was out of work for many months, and, in January, 1936, Henry lost his job, too.

Soon many of the men on Longwood Avenue were out of work. The once proud and busy fathers of Bukowski's schoolmates mooched around their yards, unshaven and cantankerous, or sat smoking endless cigarettes. They drove to the local bars to get drunk, until they ran out of money for gasoline and beer, and then sold the cars and took the last of their money into the alleys to play seven-up and twenty-one. Shorn of the virility of work, they lost the respect of their sons who ran wild. A mood of stagnation pervaded the neighborhood, inspiring one of Bukowski's most evocative poems about childhood, 'we ain't got no money, honey, but we got rain':

> the jobless men,
> failures in a failing time
> were imprisoned in their houses with their
> wives and children
> and their
> pets.
> the pets refused to go out
> and left their waste in
> strange places.
>
> the jobless men went mad
> confined with
> their once beautiful wives.
> there were terrible arguments
> as notices of foreclosure
> fell into the mailbox.

Kate went out to work and they lived thriftily on makeshift meals, eating plenty of bologna, peanut butter sandwiches on day-old bread, fried eggs, canned beans, and stews made with what Bukowski joked was an 'invisible chicken'. These meals were washed down with watery coffee. In a letter home to Germany for Christmas, 1936, Kate described how difficult life was. 'I won't forget the first eight months of 1936 in a hurry,' she wrote. 'We have suffered a lot. We nearly lost our house (and) couldn't make any payments for a whole year.' She added that Henry was depressed by his lack of work and felt he was 'not a worthwhile man', and that they had been reading with admiration how Hitler was returning Germany to virtually full employment.

Henry pretended to the neighbors he was working as an engineer, driving off each morning as if he was going to a job and then walking the streets until 5 p.m. when he drove home again. Bukowski knew about the deception and thought it pathetic. He

looked to outlaws like John Dillinger, Machine Gun Kelly and Pretty Boy Floyd as heroes, men who were not afraid to take what they wanted. He would always admire strong men, from writers like Hemingway to prize fighters, and champion jockeys, men he saw as the antithesis of his pitiful father.

The acne was so severe and needed such intensive treatment that he was excused the first semester of high school. From February through September, 1936, he stayed home alone while his mother was at her low-pay job and his father was at his imaginary job. He peeped through the drapes at the porch across the street where a woman sometimes sat with her skirt riding up around her thighs. Bukowski fetched his father's binoculars and tried to see what magic thing was up there, masturbating himself.

He started visiting the public library at the corner of La Brea Avenue and Adams Boulevard, taking armfuls of novels home. He read Sinclair Lewis' *Main Street*, D.H. Lawrence, John Dos Passos' *USA*, Sherwood Anderson's *Winesburg, Ohio* and the early stories of Ernest Hemingway. There was a lot of time to read with no school to go to, and practically no friends to distract him, so he began reading the Russian novelists, too, sitting up until his father – whose own literary tastes stopped at Edgar Allan Poe, appropriately enough – came in and snapped off the bedroom light to save electricity.

The books which first excited Bukowski influenced his literary tastes for the rest of his life. He never got over his youthful passions and prejudices: loving Hemingway's early stories, for instance, but having no time for his later novels; enjoying Turgenev, but never getting to grips with Tolstoy. Also, as an adult, he mispronounced words and names he had read in adolescence, but had never heard spoken. It was a trait noticed by friends like the poet Miller Williams. He says that if Bukowski came to understand that he had made a mistake he would pretend it was on purpose. 'It would have been a source of embarrassment, but he would hide that embarrassment by saying, "this is how I pronounce it, god-damnit, if you don't like it, you pronounce it your own fucking way."'

When his parents went to bed at 8 p.m., as they did most nights, Bukowski climbed out his bedroom window and walked up to the bars on Washington Boulevard where his acne scars made him look old enough to be served alcohol. One night he was too drunk to get back in through his window, so he came to the front door. His parents were horrified at his condition, and refused to let him in, so Bukowski burst the lock. He staggered into the living room and vomited on the rug. Henry came up behind him and pushed his head down.

'Do you know what we do to a dog when it shits on the rug?' he asked, forcing the boy's head lower. 'We put his nose in it.'

Bukowski had never retaliated before, but warned his father to stop. Henry continued to push his face down into the sick, so Bukowski spun round and punched him.

'You hit your father! You hit your father!' Kate exclaimed, clawing his face with her nails. Apparently it was OK for the father to beat the child, but not the other way round.

Henry's snobbery was the reason Bukowski enrolled at Los Angeles High, the élite school of the city, after transferring from another high school which was nearer their home. LA High was built in the style of an Ivy League university on the outskirts of fashionable Hancock Park, and its students invariably went on to university and professional life. Bukowski had seen many of them at Mount Vernon; they were the same children who made fun of him in the *Minute Man* magazine, not because they were necessarily spiteful but because he seemed such an oddball. He later scorned these teenagers as 'untested by life', but confessed he often heard them snigger when he came into class.

The girls at LA High looked beautiful in their fashionably casual clothes, and the boys handsome and healthy. The in-crowd lived what appeared to be a golden life, catching the Big Red street cars to the beach after school, and borrowing automobiles for weekend dates. They went dancing at the Biltmore Bowl, or to a drive-in and on to Hugo's hot dog stand. The school was so perfect it was used for the filming of a Jackie Cooper comedy, *What a Life*.

Bukowski hated LA High. His father made him join to fulfill a social fantasy, but he was never going to fit with the Hancock Park set. His family had significantly less money than most of the students. His skin problem made him look strange at a time in life when looks are so important and, at this age, he was unable to overcome these handicaps with the force of his personality.

'His acne was very noticeable,' says former pupil Roger Bloomer. 'He had a bad case and that was tough for a kid. That was why he was so quiet and a loner. He would be around, and say hello, but he never really joined in the circle. He wasn't particularly happy. He wasn't outgoing.'

Scared the other boys would see the boils on his back if he stripped for gym class, Bukowski opted to take ROTC (Reserve Officers' Training Corps), a form of military training. Stephen Cavanaugh, the student who led Bukowski's ROTC battalion, says he was neither rebellious nor troublesome. In fact, he got on well in their pretend army, being promoted to sergeant, just like his old man, and even won a drill competition.

Bukowski graduated high school in the summer of 1939. He hadn't intended to go to the senior Prom, partly because he didn't have a date, but found himself crouched in the bushes outside the gymnasium on the night, peering in at his fellow students. The roof beams had been decorated with blue and white crêpe paper and hundreds of balloons were suspended in a net over the stage where a band was playing the tune, 'Deep Purple'. A mirror ball revolved slowly, reflecting lights onto the happy faces.

He had never had a girlfriend, or any sexual experience, apart from masturbating and weekend visits to the burlesque shows at The Follies and The Burbank on Main Street, so the sight of the girls in their ball gowns made a big impression on him. They all looked so beautiful and sophisticated, like grown women. As he explained in his novel *Ham on Rye*, he knew he would never be able to speak to one of them, let alone dance. He was amazed the other boys knew how. They had learned things he was ignorant of, and part of him craved to be included. Then he caught his reflection in the glass, and was shocked by how ugly and desperate he looked in comparison. There was no way a guy like him would ever be part of that normal world. It made him angry to be excluded. He hated them for it, but told himself that one day he would be just as happy.

THE BARFLY YEARS

2 FARM LABOR MARKET

The Los Angeles Public Library, on West 5th Street, became a sanctuary for Bukowski when he was downtown looking for a job – a grand, richly ornamented building with all the books he might want to read. There were even girls to peek at. He went as often as possible, hoping to find something which expressed how he felt as an unhappy and restless young man. Then one day he discovered a book that became so significant in his life he likened finding it to discovering 'gold in the city dump'.

John Fante's novel, *Ask the Dust*, is written in a strikingly spare and lucid style with short paragraphs and short chapters, but it was the subject matter that was, at least initially, more interesting to Bukowski. The hero, Arturo Bandini, is a twenty-year-old would-be writer, the son of immigrant parents, who feels cut off from society. He wants to write about life and love, but has little experience of either so he goes to live in a flophouse at a place called Bunker Hill where he meets and falls in love with a beautiful girl.

Bukowski was enthralled by the story – seeing himself in Arturo Bandini – and incredibly excited by the fact that Bunker Hill was a real place, a shabby district of rooming houses directly across the street from the library where he sat with the book in his hands.

The specific place Fante romanticized in *Ask the Dust* was Bunker Hill, but more generally he wrote about downtown Los Angeles which was very different to the drowsy LA suburbs where Bukowski had grown up. Downtown bustled with garment makers, jewellers, street vendors, paper boys, cops, prostitutes, thieves and hawkers, all busy with some mysterious and important task. There were ethnic restaurants with crashing kitchens; back alleys where stock boys shared cigarettes; seedy bars; hotels both grand, like the Biltmore, and dives where the hookers worked. The funicular railway, Angel's Flight, climbed Bunker Hill and then racketed down again, spilling him across the street into Grand Central Market.

When he had a few dollars, Bukowski drank in the local bars and imagined himself part of Fante's world, inspired to try and become a writer himself. 'Fante was my god,' he later wrote, describing the intoxicating effect of *Ask the Dust*. 'He was to be a lifelong influence on my writing.'

Bukowski made a perfunctory attempt to live the conventional life his parents expected, taking a job at Sears Roebuck, on Pico Boulevard. The department store was close to LA High and Bukowski was fired after he got into a fight with a student who came in and made fun of him. He'd hated the job, anyway, being contemptuous of the wage-slave mentality of the staff.

In September, 1939, he enrolled as a scholarship student at Los Angeles City College to study Journalism, English, Economics and Public Affairs with the vague idea he might become a newspaper journalist. LA City College had a more metropolitan feel than LA High, being in the heart of the city, on Vermont Avenue near Santa Monica Boulevard, and the curriculum was designed especially for students like Bukowski who wanted vocational courses, but he got poor to average grades, being put on 'scholarship warning' in February, 1940, and on 'scholarship probation' in June.

There was much talk of the war in Europe and of joining the army, but Bukowski upset his fellow students by speaking up for Hitler and Nazism. He wrote to newspapers expressing his extreme views, making his parents fear for their safety because he was still living at home, and he attended meetings of a neo-Nazi group. He later excused his behaviour, saying he simply enjoyed being controversial.

In 'what will the neighbors think?' he wrote:

> . . . I wasn't aligned
> with any group or
> ideology.
> actually the whole idea of
> life and people
> repulsed me
> but it was easier to
> scrounge drinks off the
> right-wingers
> than off old women
> in the bars.

Bukowski was basically apolitical, throughout his life, but he also enjoyed doing and saying outrageous things to shock and draw attention to himself, and was attracted to extreme characters.

'He saw that Hitler was like fire,' says FrancEyE, a girlfriend of his adult life, who remembers Bukowski talking about Hitler as an adult. 'It was that fire that attracted him.'

On another level, he had heard his mother saying what a great man Hitler was, and some of it sunk in; Kate Bukowski openly admired Hitler, calling him a champion of 'all us working class', a leader whom she believed had made life better for ordinary German people like her parents.

Having failed to hold a job, and now fast becoming a failed student, there was increasing tension at home. When his father discovered he had been writing stories on the typewriter they bought to help with his college work, Henry tossed the manuscripts, the typewriter and his son's clothes out onto the lawn. Bukowski took $10 from his mother and caught a bus downtown where he rented a room on Temple Street before moving to a 'plywood shack' on Bunker Hill. He dropped out of college soon afterwards, in June, 1941, and, after working manual jobs for six months, in the Southern Pacific railroad yards and at the Borg-Warner factory on South Flower Street, he set out to explore America so he could write about 'the real world' of rooming houses, factory jobs and bars, like John Fante.

He caught a bus to New Orleans and worked in a warehouse there, saving his money until he had enough to quit the job and pay his rent in advance so he could stay in his room all day and write. When he ran short of money, he tried to live on candy bars to postpone getting another 'eight-hour job of nothingness'. The only friend he made in New Orleans was a near-senile old man, and the only place he went was a depressing bar near Canal Street, 'the saddest bar I was ever in' as he wrote in his poem, 'drink'.

In Atlanta, Georgia, he lived in a tar-paper shack lit by a single bulb. He was still trying to write, but the stories kept coming back from the New York magazines and he allowed himself to starve rather than get a regular job, believing that writing would save him, like the deluded hero of Knut Hamsun's *Hunger*, another favorite novel. Atlanta was the nadir of Bukowski's time on the road, almost the end of him. Sick with hunger, he wrote to his father asking for money and, after getting a long letter of admonishment by reply, he considered committing suicide by touching a live electric wire. Then he noticed the blank margins on his newspaper and began writing in them. Looking at his life in retrospect, he said this was the moment that proved he was a writer. Although nobody would ever read what he had written, he felt compelled to scribble something.

He traveled west through Texas as part of a railroad gang. In the El Paso public library he read Dostoyevsky's *Notes From Underground*, one of the dozen or so novels which made a lasting impression. He empathized with the wretched narrator, who considers himself to be hideous, and yet yearns to be loved, and the descriptions of Czarist St Petersburg with its social élite reminded him of LA High.

By the spring of 1942 he was in San Francisco, driving a truck for the Red Cross. It was the most agreeable job he had yet had with good pay, easy duties and the company of young women. He had comfortable lodgings, too, in a boarding house overlooking Golden Gate bridge. The landlady gave him beer and allowed him to use her gramophone to play records he bought second-hand. Most people his age were interested in dance music or jazz, but Bukowski preferred symphony music.

He dutifully registered for the draft for World War Two and wrote to his father that he was willing to serve. He passed the physical examination, but after a routine psychiatric test he was excused military service for mental reasons and classified 4–F or, as he put it, 'psycho'. Bukowski later recalled that the psychiatrist had written on his draft card that he was unsuitable for service partly because of his 'extreme sensitivity'.

Fired from the Red Cross for arriving late at a blood donor center, he drifted on across the country, sometimes choosing his destination by randomly pointing at places on a map. In this haphazard way he found himself in St Louis, Missouri, where he packed boxes in the basement of a ladies sportswear shop.

Bukowski resented it when his co-workers volunteered for overtime, so they had money to take their wives and girlfriends on dates. He did meet girls who were interested in him, but was too shy and awkward to form a relationship. He expressed his alienation in his autobiographical novel, *Factotum*, where a girl tries to strike up a conversation with the hero: 'I simply couldn't respond. There was a space between us. The distance was too great. I felt as if she was talking to a person who had vanished, a person who was no longer there, no longer alive.'

Instead of going out, he locked himself in his room and wrote stories which he mailed to prestigious magazines like *The Atlantic Monthly*, not knowing any other way of getting published. ' . . . and when they came back I tore them up. I used to write eight or ten stories a week. All I'd do was write these stories and drink as much as possible.'

Whit Burnett was a magazine editor known as a patron of new talent. He had famously discovered William Saroyan, first publishing him in *Story* magazine. Bukowski was greatly impressed by Saroyan's *The Daring Young Man on the Flying Trapeze*, so he submitted one of his own pieces to the magazine. *Aftermath of a Lengthy Rejection Slip* was an autobiographical account of having a submission rejected by Burnett and, possibly by merit of his cheek, it was accepted with a payment of $25. The byline he chose for this, his début as a writer, was Charles Bukowski, dropping his first name because it reminded him of his father.

He went to New York in the spring of 1944 to see his name in print and excitedly bought the magazine for forty cents in a Greenwich Village drug store, but his story was not among the main body of the magazine. It appeared in the end pages as a novelty item and he was crushingly disappointed, feeling he had been made a fool of.

He took a job as a stock room boy in Manhattan so he could rent a room, but didn't find the city to his liking. He was cold in his lightweight clothes. His landlord ripped him off. And he was alarmed by the el' train that ran past his window. Intimidated by the city, and so angry with Whit Burnett that he never submitted to *Story* again, Bukowski left New York deciding he wanted to live in a 'nice, shady, quiet city where everything is calm, where people are decent, where there's no trouble'. He chose Philadelphia because it was known as The City of Brotherly Love.

It was lunch time when he walked into the bar on Fairmount Avenue, near downtown Philadelphia. A bottle whistled past his head.

'Hey, you sonofabitch,' said the man beside him, talking to another man down the bar. 'You do that again, I'm gonna knock your goddamn head off.'

A second bottle spun towards them, and the men went out back to fight. Bukowski was thrilled by this action. He decided to stay in the neighborhood, and drink in this bar.

He rented a room at 603 North 17th Street in the Spring Garden district where there were many Irish and Polish families and a fellow named Bukowski could fit in, and he worked briefly as a shipping clerk at Fairmount Motor Products. When he wasn't working, which was most of the time, he hung around the bar. He was the first customer in the morning, drinking the sops from the night before, and the last out the door at night. 'I'd go home and there'd be a bottle of wine there. I'd drink half of that and go to sleep,' he said.

In exchange for free beer or a shot of whiskey, he ran errands for the other customers, laying bets and fetching sandwiches. Sometimes he and the bar man, burly part-time laborer Frank McGilligan, 'a big ox with a cruel streak', went out back to see who was toughest. Mostly Bukowski got thrashed, but that always earned him a couple of drinks. 'I was hiding out,' he said of the two and half years he spent in the bar. 'I didn't know what else to do. This bar back east was a lively bar. It wasn't a common bar. There were characters there. There was a feeling. There was ugliness. There was dullness and stupidity. But there was also a certain gleeful high pitch you could feel.'

One Saturday evening in July, 1944, he was resting up in his room, drinking port wine, with Brahms' 2nd Symphony on the radio, when two FBI agents barged in wanting to know why he hadn't reported for the draft. He told them he was 4–F. But why hadn't he kept in touch with the draft board? They suspected he was a draft-dodger and took him to jail.

Although it looked impressive with its castellations and granite walls, Moyamensing was a low-security prison holding men awaiting trial, and men serving short sentences for non-payments of fines. But it was the first prison Bukowski had been in and he wrote about the experience many times afterwards, giving the impression of having been in a veritable Alcatraz.

The guards took him to a whitewashed nine-by-thirteen-foot cell, with a single barred window, occupied by a chubby fellow who looked like an accountant and introduced himself to Bukowski as Courtney Taylor, 'public enemy number one'. Bukowski introduced himself, saying he had been accused of draft dodging and Taylor tried to menace the new boy saying draft dodgers were the one type of criminal cons didn't like. Bukowski presumed this is what was meant by honor among thieves.

'What d'you mean?' Taylor asked.

'Just leave me alone.'

Taylor was thirty-six, a fraudster who had operated under more than fifty aliases and spent literally half his life in jail. From 1941 to 1943, he was incarcerated in Wisconsin. When he was released, he moved to a basement off Fairmount Avenue where he was arrested in June, 1944, for manufacturing and passing bad checks and, ironically, considering what a hard time he gave Bukowski, for forging draft cards. As for being public enemy number one, he did feature on the FBI's 'ten most wanted' list but not until years later.

It seems they were put in the same cell because the authorities wanted to keep the mental cases together. Bukowski was 4–F, which put a question mark against his sanity, and Taylor was an oddball who demanded to be seen by a psychiatrist and, when he was sentenced, asked the judge for an extra eight years.

Taylor cheerfully explained to Bukowski that if he wanted to kill himself – as many try to do on their first night inside – he could stand in the slopping out bucket and jam his hand in the light socket. That would do it. Bukowski thanked him, because he had been thinking about it, but perhaps not right now. Instead, they spent a convivial evening betting dimes on who could capture the most bed bugs. Taylor, the veteran swindler, won by breaking his bugs in half and stretching the pieces to double his score.

Bukowski was released from prison as soon as he failed a second psychiatric test, and went back to the 'good old scum bar' on Fairmount Avenue. McGilligan welcomed him home by asking him outside for a fight.

'The schtick, of course, was to let him beat me up for the entertainment of the customers,' said Bukowski. 'I got tired of that game and decked the bastard and they promptly 86'd me. There I was, on the streets, and out of a job just like that.'

He claimed that for the next ten years of his life he abandoned writing to become a drunk, a barfly, but the truth is he continued to work on short stories and successfully submitted to magazines.

His most notable success came in the spring of 1946 when he received a letter from the socialite, and patron of the arts, Caresse Crosby, who together with her husband had founded the Black Sun Press, publishing many of the greatest names in modern literature including James Joyce and Henry Miller. Bukowski had submitted a short story, *20 Tanks from Kasseldown*, to Crosby's *Portfolio* magazine. It was about a man in prison awaiting execution and Crosby was sufficiently intrigued to write asking who Bukowski was. He claimed to have replied, enigmatically:

> Dear Mrs Crosby,
> I don't know who I am.
> Yours sincerely, Charles Bukowski

The story was accepted for publication in the third issue of *Portfolio* which appeared in the spring of 1946. The contributors, who included Jean Genet, Garcia Lorca, Henry Miller and

Jean-Paul Sartre, were given space for a biographical note and Bukowski emphasized his blue collar credentials by writing: 'I am employed sandpapering, puttying and packing picture frames in a warehouse. This is not as bizarre as it sounds, but it almost is.'

Influenced by reading the work of poets including Walt Whitman and Robinson Jeffers, he decided that 'poetry is the shortest, sweetest, bangingest way' to express what he wanted to say. Two of his earliest efforts were accepted by *Matrix*, a Philadelphia mimeographed magazine, and published in the summer of 1946 along with a short story. The poems are interesting in that they deal with the subject matter which became his stock-in-trade: rooming house life, bar life and unfaithful women. They also have the distinction of being his first published poetry, appearing a full nine years before he generally said he started writing poems.

> Rex was a two-fisted man
> Who drank like a fish
> And looked like a purple gargoyle.
> He married three
> Before he found one.
> And they hollered over cheap gin,
> Were friendless
> And satisfied.
> and frightened the landlord.
> She hollered plenty
> And he would listen dully,
> Then leap up red with choice words.
> And then she began again.
> It was a good life.
> Soft and fat like summer roses.

('Soft and Fat Like Summer Roses')

The short story, *The Reason Behind Reason*, features a principal character named Chelaski, similar to the name Henry Chinaski which Bukowski used for the hero of most of his later prose. *Matrix* readers were promised another 'slightly wacky sketch by Charles Bukowski' in the next issue and, sure enough, he appeared that winter with a short story and two more poems. The story dealt with a mean-spirited father who bills his son for living at home, charging him for laundry, room and board. It was told simply with short paragraphs, plenty of dialogue and what can be seen in retrospect as a classic Bukowski title, *Love, Love, Love. Matrix* readers were unimpressed, however, one writing in to complain about Bukowski's 'puzzling' style.

Returning to LA, Bukowski lodged with his parents and, for the best part of the next two years, he worked at the Merry Company, downtown. Apart from a brief return trip to Philadelphia, he stayed home all this time and seems to have been trying to get back to a conventional way of life. A remarkable set of photographs taken at Longwood Avenue in July, 1947, bear this out. Two years into his supposed ten-year drunk, Bukowski is seen smartly dressed in a suit and tie, with hair neatly cut, and shoes shined, posing happily with his parents in their back garden. He looks like he is going for a job interview.

When Henry saw *Portfolio III*, with his son's name alongside Sartre and Lorca, even he could not fail to be impressed. He took it into the LA County Museum, where he was working as a guard, to show his work mates. A father might be excused for boasting about the achievements of his son, but Henry Bukowski must have had a devious mind indeed because he pretended to be the author of the article (a simple deception as they had the same name) and his bosses were so impressed they promoted him. Bukowski was disgusted when he found out, imagining the people at the museum looking at his father and saying, admiringly: 'There goes the writer Charles Bukowski.' It was too terrible to live under the same roof as 'the beastly little prick', so he left home and rented a room downtown, off Alvarado Street in the red light district.

He was drowning his sorrows in The Glenview Bar one night when he met Jane Cooney Baker.

Jane inspired much of Bukowski's most powerful work: the poetry book *The Day Run Away Like Wild Horses Over the Hills* is suffused with her memory; she became Betty in his first novel, *Post Office*; and Laura in his second novel, *Factotum*. Most famously she became Wanda, the character played by Faye Dunaway in the film *Barfly*, for which he wrote the screenplay. With *Barfly*, and other pieces he wrote, Bukowski transformed Jane into a stock character of his fiction, second only to Henry Chinaski and his father. She died before Bukowski became famous and was never interviewed. Her picture has not previously been published. The only information about who she really was has come from the few biographical details Bukowski provided in interviews. He said she was a half-Irish/half-Indian orphan, raised by nuns after being abandoned by her parents, and that she married a wealthy Connecticut attorney. This colourful story was entirely fictitious.

Jane was the youngest daughter of well-to-do St Louis doctor, Daniel C. Cooney, who contracted pneumonia in 1919, when Jane was nine. He moved his family to New Mexico where he hoped the dry air would be good for his health, settling in Glencoe, 170 miles south-east of Albuquerque. He died soon afterwards. Jane's mother, Mary, was obliged to move the family to a more modest house in nearby Roswell where she went to work for the First National Bank.

At Roswell High School, Jane was known by the nickname 'Jacques' and for her catch-phrase: 'Isn't that atrocious!' Although not outstandingly pretty, being short with mousy hair and slightly boss-eyed, she had many boyfriends and managed to scandalize the town. 'She liked to go out and party, drink and dance,' says Orville Cookson, who knew the family. 'But Mary was a devout Catholic and she was against all that.'

Jane graduated high school in the spring of 1927 and almost immediately became pregnant by one of her boyfriends, twenty-one-year-old Craig Baker from the nearby hick town of Artesia. They married on 25 January, 1928, the licence having been granted the night before, and left for El Paso in the morning, soon returning with a young son, Jo. In 1931, Jane had a second child, Mary.

Far from living in luxury, as Bukowski said, Jane and Craig moved in with her mother because Craig was doing so poorly in business. There were arguments and Craig started to drink heavily. The night before Mary Cooney's funeral, in 1947, Jane and Craig had dinner with neighbors who recall the condition he was in. 'Craig was royally drunk. Jane wasn't drinking, but he got stinko,' says Lavora Fisk. 'She begged him to eat, but he wouldn't because he was so stowed-up with liquor.' Craig died shortly afterwards, in an automobile accident for which Jane blamed herself, and she began to drink heavily, too.

It was a year later that she met Bukowski in LA. Jane was thirty-eight, an alcoholic who had lost touch with her family. She was also getting a little crazy, and had a reputation for attacking men she took a dislike to. But she allowed Bukowski to drink with her and they left The Glenview together, picking up two fifths of bourbon and a carton of cigarettes before going back to his place.

'Say, I don't know your name. What's your name?' asked Bukowski, when they were in bed.

'What the hell difference does it make?' she said.

Although Bukowski was twenty-seven, Jane was his first serious girlfriend, only the second woman he had slept with (the first being a Philadelphia prostitute when he got out of prison). He was initially attracted by her looks, particularly her legs which she liked to show off, but he probably would have fallen for Jane whatever she looked like because she was the first woman who had ever paid him any attention and, once he had 'cured' her of smashing a glass in his face when the urge took her, he found they had much in common. 'She had a strange mad kind of sensibility which knew something, which was this: most human beings just aren't worth a shit, and I felt that, and she felt it,' he said. Then there was the booze. If anything, Jane hit the bottle harder than he did, so they were drinking partners as well. 'I thought I really had something,' he said. 'I did, I had lots of trouble.'

They lived together in a succession of apartment houses around Alvarado Street. The first place, 521 South Union Drive, was on a hill round the corner from MacArthur Park. The landlady welcomed them as a respectable married couple (they had to pose as such to get a room), gave them a new rug and fussed over their comfort. It was exciting having a writer in the place – Bukowski always made sure to tell them he was a writer – and more than once Jane's beer belly was mistaken for her having a baby on the way, but it wasn't long before they smashed the place up in a drunken fight and found themselves evicted.

Another place they stayed was The Aragon apartment building on South West Lake Avenue, a block over from Alvarado Street. It had once been quite a grand residence, four storeys high with an ornamental fountain out front to give it class, but had degenerated into a dive. There was no air-conditioning and in the summer, when the windows were open, everyone could hear everything that went on, including the fights in the room Mr and Mrs Bukowski were renting. One day Bukowski found a note under their door:

Notice to Quit
Apartment occupied by Mr and Mrs C Bukowski.
Said apt to be vacated for reasons: excessive drinking, fighting and foul language, disturbing other tenants.

Most of the fights started because Jane flirted with men whom she thought would buy her drinks, and this made Bukowski jealous. He decided she was little better than a whore, and was not above slapping her around. When the fights got really vicious, dangerous to themselves and others, the police took him to the drunk tank. He was arrested for drunkenness in 1948, 1949 and 1951, and held in the cells overnight each time.

The hangovers were monumental. The worst he ever had was one morning after they'd been drinking cheap wine, many bottles of it, at a room overlooking MacArthur Park. Bukowski was at the window trying to get some air. He felt like a steel band was around his head. Then he saw a body, a man fully dressed even wearing a necktie, fall past him in an apparent suicide attempt.

'Hey, Jane. Guess what?' he called out.

'What?' She was in the bathroom, throwing up.

'The strangest thing just happened. A human body just dropped by my window.'

'Ah, bullshit.'

'No. It really happened. Come on out here. Come to the window and stick your head out the window and look down.' She took some persuading, but she came and looked down.

'Oh God Almighty!' she exclaimed, and ran back to the bathroom where she puked and puked.

'I told you so, baby,' he said. 'I told you so.'

He worked as shipping clerk at places where he could slip down the back alley to a bar between orders. He worked for a

while at Milliron's, a department store at the corner of 5th and
Broadway, and in various small factories in the garment district,
'shit jobs' where he connived to waste as much time as possible
before he was fired, jobs which became material for the novel,
Factotum, and for poems like 'Sparks' which is about working
for The Sunbeam Lighting Company:

> and after ten hours
> of heavy labor
> after exchanging insults
> living through skirmishes
> with those not cool enough to
> abide
> we left
> still fresh
>
> we climbed into our old
> automobiles to
> go to our places
> to drink half the night
> to fight with our women
>
> to return the next morning
> to punch in
> . . .
>
> those filthy peeling walls
>
> the sound of drills and
> cutting blades
> the sparks
>
> we were some gang
> in that death ballet
>
> we were magnificent
>
> we gave them
> better than they asked
>
> yet
>
> we gave them
> nothing.

When there was money, he didn't work at all but hit the bars with Jane. Many of his best stories and poems are based on the adventures they had, including the richly comic poem, 'fire station', which he dedicated to her. It describes a day when the narrator and his girl wander into a fire station. She starts flirting with the firemen, and he settles down to play blackjack. The firemen slip upstairs to take turns having sex with the girl, and the boyfriend takes $5 from each man when they come back down. Then the alarm goes off.

> she stood there waving goodbye to the
> firemen but they didn't seem
> much interested
> any more.
> 'let's go back to the
> bar,' I told
> her.
>
> 'ooh, you got
> money?'
>
> 'I found some I didn't know I
> had . . .'

The inference in this poem, and other pieces he wrote, is that Jane was a woman of such loose morality she was virtually a prostitute. Whether this was the case or not, the relationship left Bukowski with a very poor opinion of women. He often called his girlfriends 'whores' or 'bitches' and described sex in brutal language, frequently using 'rape' as a synonym for intercourse. Linda King believes he expected all his girlfriends to behave as Jane had. 'It sounded like she was an absolute sleep-around what-ever,' she says. 'She was an alcoholic and she went out and fucked whoever would give her some booze. If he didn't get home, his woman would be gone. He talked about her a lot.'

Bukowski first worked for the post office as a temporary mail carrier for two weeks over Christmas, 1950. As he would later write in his novel, *Post Office*, it began as a mistake when the drunk up the hill told him they would take just about anybody.

Fifteen months later he was taken on as a full-time carrier at $1.61 an hour and he held this job for the next three years.

When he got back to the court on South Coronado Street, where he and Jane were living, she was often gone, the bed unmade and dirty dishes in the sink. Sometimes he found her in one of the bars on Alvarado Street, sitting with a man who had been buying her drinks. Maybe she went out back with him, too. When he couldn't find her, he drank on his own, imagining her in bed with some sailor or salesman she was calling 'daddy'.

Sometimes he invited the barflies back to his room to drink and keep him company, and one night he awoke to find a body in bed with him. He decided to take the opportunity to fulfill a long-held fantasy of having anal sex. 'You know, I thought I screwed a woman in the ass one night, and I screwed a man in the ass,' he said years later. 'It was a friend of mine staying there, and I thought it was a girl called Mystery and, uh, you know, I was kinda drunk, laying there, and I tried a few motions, and I thought, "Well, she doesn't seem to mind," you know. I gave her a little more (I don't have too much, you know), and pretty soon I gave her it all, and I heard . . . uh . . . I looked at the back of the head, and this was my friend, B—! I said, "God Almighty!" I drew that thing out.'

He had been drinking hard for more than ten years, cheap wine, green beer, whiskey when he could get it, not always eating well and smoking heavily. He was still a young man, but he had never been particularly healthy and in the spring of 1955 he paid the price for this dissolute life. He was at work at the post office when he began to feel ill, and went home to their new apartment on North Westmoreland Avenue. By morning he was vomiting blood and, as he had no medical insurance and no savings, the ambulance took him to the charity ward of LA County. He had a bleeding ulcer and needed a transfusion, but if he couldn't establish any blood credit with the hospital, he was told he couldn't get any blood. It seemed they were waging a war of attrition against him. Without blood, he would die. Once he was dead, he would cease to be a problem. Ironically, the one member of Bukowski's family who did have blood credit was his father and it was because of Henry that Bukowski was given the transfusion which saved his life.

He went back to Jane afterwards and told her the doctors said if he ever drank again it would kill him, which was good straight advice, and maybe it was even true, but what the hell else was there to do?

'We'll play the horses,' she said.
'Horses?'
'Yeah, they run and you bet on them.'
She found some money on the boulevard. We went out. I had 3 winners, one of them paid over 50 bucks. It seemed very easy.

(From: 'Horsemeat')

Hollywood Park was the track, a huge arena in Inglewood near Los Angeles airport. The crowd put Bukowski off at first; so many people and all apparently mindless, drunk, yelling like maniacs. Then he began to get interested in the psychology of gambling and factored the stupidity of the crowd into a system of laying bets. He figured that whichever way they betted was probably wrong and, if he watched the odds changing on the tote board in the final minutes before the race, he might pick the winner. It was a system, one of many he tried over the years.

The horses leapt from the gate and began pounding the dirt track, the crowd roaring them on, louder and louder as the horses turned into the final furlong and charged to the post – a crescendo of excitement – then a collective sigh of disbelief, of being gypped, because the crowd never won. But Bukowski found he held a winning ticket and, like many people trapped in low-paid work, he came to see racing as a way of getting free from everything that oppressed him. 'I piss away time and money at the racetrack because I am insane. I am hoping to make enough money so I will not have to work any longer in slaughterhouses, in post offices, at docks, in factories,' he said, explaining his love of the sport. 'The track does help in certain ways – I see the faces of greed, the hamburger faces; I see the faces in early dream and I see the faces later when the same nightmare returns. You cannot see this too often. It is a mechanic of life.'

The great dream was that, if he studied the form and perfected his system (it was never exactly right), maybe he could quit the 8 to 5 and make it at the track. He tried it a couple of times, once enjoying a winning streak so long he walked off his job and followed the races round southern California, eating steak dinners in different restaurants each night, nice quiet places by the ocean, and then resting up in comfortable motels. He started to drink again, cautiously at first, diluting wine with milk in case the doctor had been telling the truth. But he didn't die. So he had a beer, and then a whiskey. Soon he was drinking like old times. Even better, he was drinking and making it at the track. What did the doctors know?

But winning streaks always end and gamblers wind up broker than before. Rent money gone. Gas money gone. Busted. Things got so bad Jane had to get a job so they would have food on the table. But she began to suspect Bukowski was cheating on her, seeing another woman when she was out at work, so she left him. Now he had no money, no job and no woman. At least it helped his writing, as he explained: 'After losing a week's pay in four hours it is very difficult to come to your room and face the typewriter and fabricate a lot of lacy bullshit.'

DEATH WANTS MORE DEATH

3

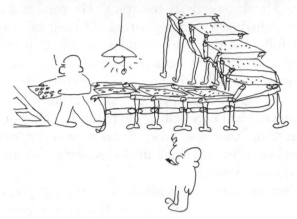

There was a period of time in the early 1950s when Bukowski had trouble getting anything published, and became so desperate he stooped to using emotional blackmail. 'He wrote to me and said to please publish his poems, else he was going to commit suicide,' says Judson Crews, who edited literary magazines in New Mexico. 'I simply turned around and sent his poems right back. He obviously didn't mean it, or else he didn't *really* mean it.'

So when Barbara Frye, the editor of *Harlequin* magazine, advertised that she wanted poems from new writers, Bukowski promptly sent a bundle of material to her address in Wheeler, Texas. And he was delighted when she wrote back saying she accepted the poems for publication and, moreover, considered Bukowski the greatest poet since William Blake.

A correspondence developed that quickly became intimate. Barbara wrote that she was a single woman with a slight physical deformity, a problem with her neck which she feared might prevent her finding a husband. She repeated this sad story in a number of letters, becoming quite plaintive on the subject of being left on the shelf, and Bukowski couldn't help feeling sorry for her, especially as she had been so kind about his work. One night he dashed off a letter to Texas telling Barbara to relax, for Christ's sake, and stop worrying about not finding a husband. She sounded like a really nice girl and, in fact, come to that, he'd marry her himself! He forgot about it the next day, but Barbara replied that she accepted.

She wrote to say she was quitting her job in Wheeler and catching a bus to Los Angeles, giving details of when Bukowski should meet her at the bus terminal. In the meantime, she sent photographs of herself, and when Bukowski saw the photographs he really started to worry.

Barbara had two vertebrae missing from her neck which, together with a slight curvature of the spine, gave the impression she was permanently hunching her shoulders. It also meant she couldn't turn her head. She looked very odd indeed, as her cousin Tom Frye explains: 'Hers was an obvious deformity because you could tell it as far as you could see her. Her chin sat right on the ribs of her chest. She was a plain girl, short with no neck.'

Bukowski prepared himself for the worst, but when Barbara stepped down from the bus he didn't think she looked that bad, certainly attractive enough to go to bed with. So he took her back to his apartment on North Westmoreland and that evening they tried to make love.

He worked away for what seemed hours, but no matter what he did, or what fantasy images he conjured up, he couldn't come and it was a relief when Barbara climaxed and fell asleep. Bukowski lay awake afterwards, smoking cigarettes, wondering what the hell was wrong. Finally, he decided that Barbara had 'a big pussy'. This was the real reason no man would marry the poor creature. It was nothing to do with her neck. Her pussy was so big a fellow couldn't feel what he was doing.

'Barbara, I understand,' he said, when she woke the next morning. 'But we'll go through with it. I won't back out.'

'What do you mean?'

'Well, I mean, you've got this big pussy. You know, last night.'

'What?' she said. 'You weren't even in there.'

'But what in the hell? You were moaning and groaning. I think you climaxed.'

'I thought that was a new way of doing things . . . I didn't know.'

'You mean I wasn't even inside of you?

'No.'

Bukowski later confessed he was so sexually naïve that, unless a woman placed his penis inside her, he was not at all sure what to do. They tried again, with Barbara guiding him in, and he was relieved to find the fit was snug and he was able to ejaculate. Satisfied everything was as it should be, they drove across the desert to Las Vegas, Nevada, where they married on 29 October, 1955.

Like most of the women in Bukowski's life, Barbara became the subject of many poems and works of prose – most notably she was Joyce in *Post Office* – but little he wrote about her matched up with reality.

Barbara's great-grandfather was a pioneer settler of the west who arrived in the Texas panhandle in 1877 to claim eight thousand acres as The Frye Ranch. The family ran cattle, bred horses and struck oil, although that was not the limit of their achievements. Barbara's cousin Jack Frye invented an airplane called The Frye Interceptor, and co-founded TWA with Howard Hughes. Another cousin made a fortune training pilots. Barbara Nell Frye was born on 6 January, 1932, making her eleven years younger than Bukowski. Her parents divorced when she was two, leaving her to be raised by her grandparents, Lilly and Tobe Frye, whom she called Mummy and Daddy Tobe just as Joyce in *Post Office* calls her father 'Daddy Wally'. Bukowski writes: 'Silly bitch . . . he wasn't her daddy.' She graduated high school, went to college and, through Daddy Tobe's influence, was elected Wheeler court clerk.

Barbara had never had a regular boyfriend and she told no one of her decision to marry Bukowski, just taking off for California with the little money she had in her savings account and, despite Bukowski persistently referring to her as 'the millionairess', this was the only money she had all the time they were together. Her father said she was crazy to marry a man she didn't know, but other members of the family were more understanding. 'It didn't surprise me too much because I guess that was her only chance,' says her cousin, Sunny Thomas.

In *Post Office*, Bukowski writes about Chinaski visiting Joyce's home town and the impression given is that they settled in Texas for a while. Although Bukowski and his bride did visit after getting married, it was only for a couple of weeks when her grandparents, who didn't approve of the marriage, were on vacation. Bukowski arrived in his regular city clothes and had to be fitted out in a set of Daddy Tobe's cowboy duds, which made him look ridiculous. His next shock was discovering that Wheeler was in a dry county.

When they got back to LA Barbara published a special issue of *Harlequin* featuring eight of Bukowski's poems, including the accomplished 'Death Wants More Death', and they co-edited issues of *Harlequin* with Bukowski dealing out rough treatment to contributors he didn't like, which was most of them, and getting his own back on poet-editors who had rejected his work. One of his first victims was Judson Crews whose poems he rejected as pay-back for the snub he'd received. Another victim was Leslie Woolf Hedley, a poet who had responded to Barbara's advertisement. Bukowski thought Woolf Hedley's poems awful and told Barbara they couldn't publish them, even though they were already accepted. 'She wrote me a letter that she wasn't going to use the poems because Bukowski refused to do so. He was against it,' says Woolf Hedley, who considered taking legal action against them. 'Mine were not quite as avant-garde as he would like. He was a professional alien, a person who liked to be alienated, and I think he played that to the hilt.'

Barbara was not content to live in a downtown apartment building, so they moved to a little house in the LA suburb of Echo Park. She also made it clear they wouldn't be living on her family's money, telling Bukowski she intended to prove to the folks back home they could make it on their own. Bukowski, who had been forced to resign from the post office after his hemorrhage, would have to start thinking about a career. He was working at a typical 'shit job' at the time, shipping clerk at the Graphic Arts Center on West 7th Street. He despatched consignments of ink, paper and pens from the warehouse to trucks that pulled up in the alley and spent a good part of each shift swigging beer in the Seven-G's bar round the back. It was the same old routine and he liked the people at Graphic Arts, but Barbara said it wouldn't do at all and got it into her head he might become a commercial artist. He had a modest talent for drawing and, with some schooling, maybe he could get himself a job in an advertising agency, or with a newspaper. She persuaded him to enroll in classes at Los Angeles City College, and started taking him out to galleries.

The college work involved designing Christmas advertisements for Texaco gas stations and Bukowski's idea, which he thought a good one, was to have a Christmas tree with the Texaco star at the top. The teacher told him he didn't want designs featuring Christmas trees because Christmas trees were passé. Although he had been doing reasonably well until then, scoring a B average, he lost interest after this and eventually dropped out of the course. But when Christmas rolled around, he was amused to see Texaco stations had posters with a star on a tree.

'Look, baby, my drawing,' he said. 'Aren't you proud of me?'

'You're always laughing at yourself,' Barbara replied, exasperated with his lack of ambition.

She was unable to understand how a man who had been published in a magazine with Jean-Paul Sartre could laze round the house drinking beer and reading the racing form, and was less than impressed when Bukowski went back to work for the post office as a trainee distribution clerk for $1.82 an hour.

'You didn't turn out the way I thought you would,' she told him when they were several months into the marriage. 'I expected you to be more fiery, more explosive.'

For his part, Bukowski was becoming irritated by what he perceived as Barbara's phoniness. He noticed she affected a fake English accent to answer the telephone. She never knew when he was being funny. Conversely, she thought he was joking when he was serious. In fact, the more he thought about her personality, the less he liked it. She was a 'cold, vindictive, unkind, snob bitch'.

'He was a screwball,' says Barbara's aunt, Leah Belle Wilson, who received a visit from the couple in San Bernardino. Bukowski was surly and uncommunicative and, when she tried to engage him in conversation about his work, just chit chat – did he like his job? – he grunted that he didn't want to talk about it and began reading a comic book instead. Barbara attempted to excuse her husband saying he was a writer, a dreamer, 'a child who has never grown up'. But Aunt Leah Belle thought him plain rude. It certainly wasn't the way folks carried on back in Texas. 'He wasn't very friendly,' she says. 'He was like an outsider.'

When they had first got married, sex was so good Bukowski decided Barbara was a nymphomaniac. Then she frightened him by saying they should be thinking about having children. He was set against the idea and began to withdraw before ejaculation, the only form of contraception he was willing to try. It wasn't easy to get the timing right and he worried Barbara would trick him into coming inside her. When she did become pregnant, she miscarried their baby. Bukowski blamed himself, believing the amount of alcohol he had drunk over the years had damaged his sperm in some way. Barbara blamed him, too. She took a lover and began divorce proceedings, accusing Bukowski of subjecting her to mental cruelty, a charge which upset him because, whatever his shortcomings, he didn't feel he'd mistreated her.

The divorce was finalized on 18 March, 1958, two years and four months after their wedding. It seemed he wouldn't be getting his hands on those Texas millions after all, as he wrote in one of his most sardonic poems, 'The Day I Kicked Away a Bankroll':

> . . . you can take your rich aunts and uncles
> and grandfathers and fathers
> and all their lousy oil
> and their seven lakes
> and their wild turkey
> and buffalo
> and the whole state of Texas,
> meaning, your crow-blasts
> and your Saturday night boardwalks,
> and your 2-bit library
> and your crooked councilmen
> and your pansy artists –
> you can take all these
> and your weekly newspaper
> and your tornadoes,
> and your filthy floods
> and all your yowling cats
> and your subscription to *Time*,
> and shove them, baby,
> shove them.

Triple X cinemas. Cocktail lounges. Apartment courts with cracked swimming pools. Boulevards lined with diseased palm trees sagging in the smog. This was the other Hollywood, what Bukowski called East Hollywood, the area he moved to after leaving Barbara. It was only a couple of miles from the mansion homes of the movie stars in Beverly Hills and West Hollywood, but had more in common with the seedy end of downtown where he had lived with Jane, and which it was also near to.

The 1600 block of North Mariposa Avenue cut north–south from Hollywood Boulevard to the broken down, busted-out east end of Sunset Boulevard in the rotten core of the district he adopted as his new home. He parked his '57 Plymouth and went into the Spanish-style rooming house at number 1623: two dozen cold water apartments arranged like prison cells along three landings. There was no elevator and no air conditioning. He took room 303 on the second floor. There were a couple of old chairs, a lamp with dented shade, chipped dining table, cockroaches in the kitchenette, a Murphy bed that folded out of the wall and a shared bathroom down the hall.

Ned's Liquor Store, at the corner of Hollywood and Normandie, was a short walk away. Bukowski stocked up on Miller High Life beer, boxes of White Owl cigars and cartons of Pall Mall cigarettes, went back to his room, turned his transistor radio to a classical station, pulled the shade, flipped the top from a beer and sat at the typewriter, thinking of the other losers who had lived there before him. Then he began to type whatever came to mind, experimenting with putting down what Black Sparrow Press publisher, John Martin, calls a 'series of images', as opposed to his mature work which mostly consisted of stories.

'Hank's room was filthy,' remembers Jory Sherman, a poet from St Paul, Minnesota, who became a close friend at this time. 'He never cleaned up. Dishes in the sink and cigarette butts everywhere.'

Grim though the surroundings were, Bukowski was free from his failed marriage, and the expectations of his ambitious wife. He was doing what he wanted, and had his job at the post office to keep him from starving. '. . . at the best of times there was a small room and the machine and the bottle,' he wrote. 'The sound of the keys, on and on, and the shouts: "HEY! KNOCK IT OFF, FOR CHRIST'S SAKE WE'RE WORKING PEOPLE

HERE AND WE'VE GOT TO GET UP IN THE MORNING!"
With broomsticks knocking on the floor, pounding coming from
the ceiling, I would work in a last few lines . . .'

The landlord told him he would have to stop typing at 9.30
p.m. because the other tenants were complaining. That was precisely the time Bukowski was getting into the swing of it, with a
few beers inside him, a cigar going and maybe some Mozart on
the radio, if he lucked it. He put up with the noise of the other
tenants: the canned laughter from their television sets, and 'the
lesbian down the hall' who played jazz records all evening with
her door open. Why couldn't he be allowed to write? But the
landlord had made his mind up. It was a new rule. So Bukowski
developed a system. He typed until 9.30 p.m. and finished his
work silently in hand-printed block capitals. He became so skilful
he could hand-print almost as fast as he could type.

For several years, contact with his parents had been limited to
asking for money when he was broke, and it got so that they barely
saw each other. Kate and Henry moved out of LA to the suburb of
Temple City, buying a new bungalow on Doreen Avenue and often
complained to their neighbours, Francis and Irma Billie, about their
wino son. By Francis Billie's account, Henry was the same bullying
braggart Bukowski had always despised, remembering that he tried
to boss the neighbors around and exaggerated his importance at the
LA County Museum, describing himself as Art Director although
he had never risen higher than a preparator, and that by posing
as the author, Charles Bukowski.

Kate started to drink heavily. She ordered deliveries of wine
from the corner liquor store when Henry was at work and Irma
Billie says that, when Henry came home, he often found Kate
passed out drunk.

The last time Bukowski saw his mother she was in the
Rosemead Rest Home, dying of cancer. Kate said he should
have more respect for his parents, especially his father. 'Your
father is a great man,' she told him.

Henry decided their son would make no further visits, and
stopped giving him news of Kate's condition. 'Henry said it
wouldn't do any good anyway,' says Irma Billie. 'He would

just come down there drunk, so he didn't bother to tell him.' On Christmas Eve, 1956, Bukowski went out and bought a rosary as a gift for his mother and drove over to the home. He was trying to open the door to her room when a nurse told him she had died the day before. To what extent the bereavement caused him pain is impossible to say for certain because Bukowski never dwelt on his feelings for his mother, either in his writings or in private conversation, but it seems to have made little impression on him. 'It's a very veiled sort of thing, barely there,' says his widow, Linda Lee Bukowski.

Henry lost no time looking for a new wife. First he tried to seduce Anna Bukowski, widow of his late brother, John, but she didn't want to know, so he got engaged to one of the women who worked at the Billies' dry-cleaning business. Late on the afternoon of 4 December, 1958 – nine months after Bukowski's divorce – Henry's fiancé came by the house and found him dead on the kitchen floor having apparently suffered a heart attack. If Bukowski failed to grieve for his mother, the death of the father was positively a cause for jubilation. '. . . he's dead dead dead, thank God,' he wrote.

The old man's corpse lay in a Temple City funeral parlor where his girlfriend wept over the casket. 'No, no, no,' she wailed. 'He can't be dead!' He had only been sixty-three, she said, a fit and strong man, with many years ahead of him. Bukowski, his Uncle Jake and Aunt Eleanor stood together looking at the corpse. Bukowski remembered his father beating him with the razor strop, telling him he would never amount to anything; trying to push his head down into the vomit on the rug; beating him while his mother stood by doing nothing; beating Kate until she screamed. He had a powerful compulsion to push the girlfriend aside and spit on his face.

A substantial block of granite marked the family plot at the Mountain View Cemetery in Altadena – BUKOWSKI etched in capital letters. The older ones were almost all dead: Henry and Kate; Henry's brothers, John and Ben, both broken by the depression; Grandfather Leonard, the drunken veteran of the Kaiser's army; and Grandmother Emilie, the hard-shell Baptist who cackled she would outlive them all. But Henry Charles Bukowski Jnr was left, whiskey on his breath and an uneasiness in his stomach as he listened to the prayers said for his namesake.

Back at Doreen Avenue, friends of his parents looked over bits of furniture and talked about lawn mowers and hedge clippers, and other oddments borrowed or promised over the years, things 'Henry and Kate would have wanted us to have'. Bukowski told them to take whatever they wanted, giving away pictures from the walls, silverware, anything they asked for. Women were practically fighting over his mother's home-made preserves in the kitchen, and so much stuff was taken that the contents of the house was valued at only $100 when it was sold.

There was a perverse pleasure lounging around in the empty bungalow while 'the old man was down in the dirt' and Henry's attorney totted up what he would inherit. Bukowski remembered his father saying a family could get rich if the sons of each generation bought property and willed it to their heirs. It had seemed a stupid idea and he felt vindicated in his disdain for his father's lifestyle when the attorney informed him that Henry had less than $300 in savings and still owed $6,613 to the Bank of America on his mortgage. Apart from the equity in the house, the only real assets were a pension fund, a painting by Erich Heckal and a four-year-old Plymouth. Still, when everything was settled, Bukowski received a little more than $15,000. After he became famous, he claimed to have drunk and gambled away the inheritance, but he never revealed he had inherited $15,000, a substantial amount in 1959, and it's unlikely he frittered it all away. Friends remember him having thousands of dollars in savings within a few years of his father's death, and the truth is that, from this point on, he became careful with money.

As Bukowski produced and submitted a greater volume of work – never bothering to keep carbons so he had no copies unless the poems were published or returned – his poems appeared more frequently in the little magazines. This was partly because he was writing darker, more realistic poems reflecting his recent experiences of loss and death. In 1959, he had poems accepted by magazines including *Nomad*, *Coastlines*, *Quicksilver* and *Epos*. Success fired up his ambition, as Jory Sherman recalls: 'He said, "I want to beat them all, beat every one of them." He wanted fame, he really did.'

His first chapbook was published in October, 1960, two months after his fortieth birthday. E.V. Griffith, a small press editor from Eureka, California, who had already published broadsides of two Bukowski poems, spent two years sweating over *Flower, Fist and Bestial Wail*. 'There were numerous delays in getting the book into print and the correspondence that ensued between poet and publisher was often testy,' says Griffith. 'But any ill-will dissipated quickly when copies were at last in Bukowski's hands.'

Flower, Fist and Bestial Wail is little more than a pamphlet, twenty-eight pages long and only two hundred copies printed, a good proportion of which went to friends of the publisher and author, yet it had a special significance for Bukowski being his first book.

Many of the poems, like 'soirée', were dark and introspective:

> in the cupboard sits my bottle
> like a dwarf waiting to scratch out my prayers.
> I drink and cough like some idiot at a symphony,
> sunlight and maddened birds are everywhere,
> the phone rings gamboling its sounds
> against the odds of the crooked sea;
> I drink deeply and evenly now,
> I drink to paradise
> and death
> and the lie of love.

Also in his fortieth year, Bukowski was show-cased in *Targets*, a New Mexico quarterly whose editors turned over an entire section of the magazine to 'A Charles Bukowski Signature'. This included a number of his most accomplished early poems, like 'The Tragedy of the Leaves' which again is a gloomy, claustrophobic poem. It concludes with a confrontation between the poet and an angry landlady in a rooming house not unlike the place Bukowski was living:

> and I walked into the dark hall
> where the landlady stood
> execrating and final,

sending me to hell,
waving her fat, sweaty arms
and screaming
screaming for rent
because the world had failed us
both.

A further step towards what Judson Crews calls the 'Hank persona' came with the chapbook, *Longshot Pomes* (sic) *for Broke Players*, published in New York. There were poems about prostitutes, the race track and classical music, not the best work Bukowski ever wrote on these subjects, but getting closer to what he would become famous for. The change of direction was indicated by the cover art of a man playing cards at a table while a woman waits in bed. Inside was a brief biography giving the salient points of the emerging Bukowski mythology: his unhappy childhood; the years bumming around the country, living in rooming houses and working at menial jobs, crazy jobs like being the oven man in a dog biscuit factory and 'coconut man' in a cake factory. These jobs may have been invented to add colour, as they are not recorded on the very detailed work experience forms Bukowski later completed for the post office.

Of all the small press publishers Bukowski dealt with in these early years the most significant, by far, were Jon and Louise 'Gypsy Lou' Webb and their extraordinary Loujon Press.

As a young man, Jon Webb took part in the hold-up of a jewellery store in Cleveland, Ohio, and served three years in a reformatory. It was whilst he was inside that he developed a passion for literature, editing the reformatory weekly and writing crime stories. Upon being paroled, he returned to Cleveland where he met and married an Italian girl who came to be known as Gypsy Lou because of her colorful clothes and long dark hair. In 1954 they moved to the French quarter of New Orleans where Jon Webb decided to become a publisher of avant-garde writing. He contacted William Burroughs, Lawrence Ferlinghetti, Henry Miller and other leading underground figures urging them to submit work to *The Outsider*, a journal he and Gypsy Lou were setting up. Jory Sherman was appointed West Coast editor and suggested they might also publish Bukowski. The Webbs loved his work. As Gypsy Lou says, they were greatly impressed with, 'the realness, you know, not phony at all. He was just very honest and down to earth.'

The Webbs published eleven Bukowski poems in the first issue of *The Outsider*, some of the best he had written, alongside work by fashionable beat writers. The Bukowski selection was all the more impressive because Webb took a professional approach to being an editor, rejecting much of what Bukowski submitted as sub-standard. The best Bukowski poem in the issue was 'old man, dead in a room', which he meant as his own epitaph:

> and as my grey hands
> drop a last desperate pen
> in some cheap room
> they will find me there
> and never know
> my name
> my meaning
> nor the treasure
> of my escape.

At times it seemed the poem might be prophetic. Bukowski was drinking hard, hitting the cocktail lounges night after night, getting into fights, and often waking up in city drunk tanks with the other 'silverfish', as he called his cell-mates. He retched so hard in the morning he saw blood in the toilet pan. Maybe he would die as the doctors had predicted, ripped apart by another hemorrhage. His drinking caused him to suffer small injuries and unpleasant ailments: he jammed a shard of glass in his foot when he was stumbling about drunk one night; and developed hemorrhoids to beat a world record. Thoughts of killing himself returned and he made an abortive attempt at gassing himself in his room one afternoon.

Once again, he started seeing something of Jane who was in an even more desperate state than when they were living together. She was working as a maid at The Phillips, a dive hotel in Hollywood, in exchange for a room rent-free and a few dollars drinking money.

Her legs had lost their shapeliness and her pot belly had grown to a grotesque size. Bukowski referred to her as 'the old woman' and they enjoyed the companionship of fellow alcoholics, as he wrote in 'A Nice Place':

> I uncap the new bottle
> from the bag and she sits in the corner
> smoking and coughing
> like an old Aunt from New Jersey

Sometimes they had sex, but Jane was so far gone that intercourse repulsed him. He wrote to his pen friend, the Louisiana academic John William Corrington, that it made him think of a film he had once seen of a Cesarian operation.

There was a sense of impending tragedy about Jane, that nothing much could help her. In *Post Office*, Chinaski visits Betty at her hotel a few days after the Christmas holidays and the scene Bukowski describes is probably an accurate description of how low Jane had fallen by January, 1962: it is early in the morning when Chinaski calls at her room, but Betty is already drunk, surrounded by bottles of liquor given as Christmas gifts by the tenants, all cheap brands. Chinaski fears she will keep drinking until the bottles are empty, or until she is dead.

> 'Listen,' I said, 'I ought to take that stuff. I mean, I'll just give you back a bottle now and then. I won't drink it.'
> 'Leave the bottles,' Betty said. She didn't look at me. Her room was on the top floor and she sat in a chair by the window watching the morning traffic.
> I walked over. 'Look, I'm beat. I've got to leave. But for Christ's sake, take it easy on that stuff!'
> 'Sure,' she said.
> I leaned over and kissed her goodbye.

A couple of weeks later, on a Saturday, Bukowski went back to see her. There was no answer when he knocked at her door, so he went in and saw the bottles were gone, the bed covers had been pulled back and, when he came closer, he saw blood on the sheet.

Frenchy, the landlady, told him an ambulance had taken Jane to Los Angeles County Hospital.

Her body was riddled with cancer; she also had cirrhosis of the liver. She had suffered a massive hemorrhage, and was in a semi-coma when he arrived, in a ward with three other women, one of whom was laughing loudly as she entertained her visitors. Bukowski pulled a curtain round Jane's bed for privacy and sat beside her holding her hand, saying her name over and over. He got a rag and wiped away some blood from the corner of her mouth.

'I knew it would be you,' she said, rousing herself for a moment.

Jane died on the evening of 22 January, 1962, while Bukowski was trying to place a telephone call to her son in Texas. She was fifty-one.

After the funeral at the San Fernando Mission, north of LA, Bukowski went on a five-day drunk and, when he couldn't stand his own company any longer, drove over to see Jory Sherman in San Bernadino. They worked their way through a six-pack of Miller High Life as he talked about how it had only been 'half a funeral' because there had been a mix up about whether Jane was a bona fide Catholic – the priest didn't want to do the full service. Bukowski said more of Jane's family should have been there. Just because she was a scrub woman in a cheap hotel didn't mean she was nothing. He said he wished he had telephoned her more often; maybe if he had called after he saw her that morning, with the bottles, it might have made a difference. 'Hank felt he had lost someone that he allowed himself to get very close to, which was rare for him,' says Sherman. 'I have seldom seen a person so grief-stricken. He was weeping and he was drinking heavily and his world had just crashed.'

In the morning, Bukowski drove to the races where he picked up a girl he knew from the post office, but he was unable to have sex when they got back to her place because he imagined Jane was watching. He returned to his room on North Mariposa where he still had some of her belongings: black beads which he moved through his fingers like a rosary while listening to the silence of the telephone, the telephone he used to pack with a matchbook cover so he wouldn't be disturbed when he was working. The closet door was half open, more of her things hanging there – blouses, skirts and jackets, the lifeless fabric her body had given shape and movement to. When the hangover cleared on 29 January, he began to write a series of grief poems which are among his most affecting work.

> . . . and I speak
> to all the gods,
> Jewish gods, Christ-gods,
> chips of blinking things,
> idols, pills, bread,
> fathoms, risks,
> knowledgeable surrender,
> rats in the gravy of 2 gone quite mad
> without a chance,
> hummingbird knowledge, hummingbird chance,
> I lean on this,
> I lean on all of this
> and I know:
> her dress upon my arm:
> but
> they will not
> give her back to me.

He called the poem, 'for Jane, with all the love I had, which was not enough—'

CONVERSATIONS IN CHEAP ROOMS

4

BUK

For months after Jane's death, Bukowski was profoundly depressed, and unable to get her out of his mind. Women he saw in the street reminded him of Jane. He saw her face in his mind's eye when he woke, and she was there again at night when he tried to sleep.

'Even though he hadn't been living with her at the time, he mourned her. He really had an attachment,' says Ann Menebroker, a poet from Sacramento who began corresponding with Bukowski at this time. He felt so depressed he hid knives, scissors and razors out of sight, saying he couldn't remember the last time he'd suffered such a serious attack of his suicide complex, and Ann believes the desire to kill himself was real enough. 'I'm sure he felt he wished he was dead sometimes, with his drinking and his going back and forth to jail. It was a terrible existence. I think the writing and the drinking was all that he had to keep things going and, yes, I think he meant it. His whole life was an extended suicide.'

He drank to try and forget his problems and spent hours touring the bars of East Hollywood, sometimes visiting the burlesque shows on Sunset Strip where he yelled at the go-go girls.

'SHAKE IT IN MY FACE, BABY!' he would holler, the beads on the girl's top flicking up an erotic wind of promise as she bent down and jiggled herself for Bukowski, hoping he would tip her well.

'YEAH, SHAKE IT!'

After a while, management gathered, correctly, that he was mocking the performance and kicked him out.

When he woke in his room the following morning, with a pounding head and dry mouth, Bukowski discovered the $450 he had won at the track the previous afternoon had gone from his pocket. Another calamity: Jane's goldfish, which he had taken from her room at the Phillips Hotel after she died, was not in its bowl on the table. It was on the floor having apparently leapt out during the night, either trying to catch a fly, he presumed, or in an attempt at suicide. Looking at its discoloring body, he was reminded of Jane and all the regrets he had about her death.

He was so upset he called Jory Sherman to tell him what had happened. 'It crushed him; he couldn't stand to see animals die. He was just emotionally overcome because that was a part of Jane,' says Sherman, who was a little put out by the call because Bukowski hadn't been much of a friend to him during a recent crisis. 'He was a very tender-hearted guy – not towards people necessarily, but towards goldfish . . .'

Bukowski wrote an extraordinary poem about the death of the fish, 'I thought of ships, of armies, hanging on . . .', describing how he tried to revive the fish by putting it back in the water, but it floated dead so he had to flush it down the toilet. The tone is so sombre, it becomes comical, although that was almost certainly not his intention:

> I put the bowl in the corner
> and thought, I really can't stand
> much more of this.

There were many sad, hung-over days like these when he stayed in his room watching the birds in the trees on North Mariposa, laying on the bed with a bottle in his hand listening to classical music. Late in the afternoon the other tenants returned from what he assumed were their miserable jobs, and began scampering up and down the concrete stairs like rodents. He was convinced he would die alone in that '1623 place', his stomach ripped apart after a heavy night drinking, gobs of blood staining the sheets round his head, empty bottles in the wastebasket, the yellow bathrobe Jane had worn hanging like a shroud in the closet, flies shuttling about on the screen. Aunt Eleanor and Uncle Jake were his next of kin, now both parents were dead, but what would they care about his work, his chapbooks and collection of magazines? They would probably throw the mags out with the garbage, along with the racing forms and old newspapers.

He tried to write himself out of his depression, firing off submissions to editors all over the country, including newspaper journalist, John Bryan, who recalls how amazingly productive Bukowski was: 'He started sending me boxes of material. He sent cartons, a couple of hundred poems, thirty or forty short stories. I could pull anything I liked out of it, which was a nice choice, and I would send back the rest.'

John Bryan visited Mariposa three months after Jane died and found Bukowski in a dreadful state, broke, hungover and suffering all manner of ailments. 'He had a waste basket full of hemorrhoid Preparation-H tubes. He apparently had the worst case of hemorrhoids in the world.' Bukowski gave him some more poems, four of which Bryan printed in his magazine, *Renaissance*. The work was punk-like in its nihilism. The poem 'an empire of coins' concludes with the words 'fuck everybody', and 'the biggest breasts' ends with these sneering lines:

> the waiter came smiling with his watery mouth
> but I sent him running right off
> for a couple of motherfucking
> drinks.

This sort of provocative material added to his growing notoriety and a number of editors, critics and academics began to champion Bukowski as a fresh new voice. Small press publisher R.R. Cuscaden wrote an essay in *Satis* magazine likening Bukowski's estrangement from society to that of Baudelaire. It was Cuscaden who also published the third limited edition Bukowski chapbook, *Run with the Hunted*, dedicated to John William Corrington, the Louisiana-based poet and English teacher who wrote a thank-you letter so effusive it made Bukowski cringe: 'I just got immortal: at least a footnote when they write up Charlie.'

The sound of Bukowski bashing out all these poems on his manual 'typer' continued to irritate his neighbors, even when he tried to work within the hours agreed with the landlord, and the old woman downstairs began thumping the ceiling with her broom again. This made him very angry because *he* had to listen to the canned laughter coming from her television. He didn't think those television shows were funny, anyway, except *The Honeymooners* which he enjoyed whenever he caught an episode in a bar. He took a page of a letter he'd been writing to the Webbs and scrawled his neighbor a note which he took downstairs and slid under her door:

You knock on my floor when I type within hours. Why in the hell don't you keep your stupid t.v. set *down* at 10.30 tonight? I don't complain to the managers, but it seems to me that your outlook is very one-sided.
H Bukowski.
Apt 303

He wrote to Ann Menebroker: 'Doesn't she know I am the great Charles Bukowski? The bitch!'
The old woman in 203 replied:

Sir:
It is not my TV set you hear, I don't have it loud at any time.
I was told you work from 5.30, but your machine is going day and night and Sunday. It is like living beneath an arsenal.
This is an apartment house not a business establishment . . . It sounds as if you have all kinds of machinery up there.
You would not be allowed all that noise and racket in any apt house where people live for peace and quiet.
I have been in this house 26 years, and have inquired from many people, and you are out of line.
Apt 203.

He took a month's unpaid leave from the post office to play the horses, but they were 'running like salami' and he lost his money. He became so low that suicide seemed the only logical solution to his problems. He began putting his affairs in order: mailing Jane's bobby pin to Ann, boxing up the letters he had received from Corrington and mailing them back to Baton Rouge 'before something happens', as he explained.

He had always hated Christmas, appalled by the behavior of what he called 'amateur drunks'. Bukowski believed it was a time of year when professional drinkers like himself should stay indoors. 'I hate to go out on the streets on Xmas day. The fuckers act like they are out of their minds,' he wrote to the Webbs. But a few days before Christmas, 1962, when he was particularly low, he broke his rule and downed three fifths of Scotch in the local bars before passing out on a neighbor's lawn. The police locked him up for the night in the drunk tank and, when he came to, Bukowski found himself frightened by his own excesses, as he wrote on 18 December to Ann:

> Have been laying here in horrible fit of depression. My drinking days are over. This is too much. Jail is a horrible place. I almost go mad there.
>
> I don't know what is going to become of me. I have no trade, no future. Sick, depressed, blackly, heavily depressed.
>
> Write me something. Maybe a word from you will save me.

Most evenings around 6 p.m. he had to stop work and drive along Sunset Boulevard to his post office job. The setting sun bled the sky in the rear view mirror as he rolled east out of Hollywood, past Echo Park, across Alvarado Street and into downtown, forking left on Alpine Street to the Terminal Annex – the 'post office' made famous in his novel of that name – a gigantic sorting office ornamented with carved eagles and US Postal Service decals.

'How're you doin' tonight?' called out assign clerk, Johnny Moore, when Bukowski punched on for the graveyard shift.

'Alright, Big John,' he shouted back.

The work floor was the size of a football field, floodlit and busy with hundreds of clerks sticking mail, sorting parcels and lugging sacks while the supervisors yelled for them to keep moving. The noise was incredible. Cancelling machines clattered, huge conveyor belts moved an endless river of mail and there was muzak playing from speakers high up in the roof. It was hot, too, even when Bukowski arrived in the evening, a heat generated by the toil of human beings.

Johnny Moore assigned Bukowski to one of the many booths that made up Sanford Station Letters* or to Parcels where two men together worked tossing boxes around like basketballs. Parcel work was rotated and, if Bukowski had a hangover when it was his turn, he would ask to work on letters because sorting letters was easier.

'He used to come in loaded sometimes,' says Johnny Moore. 'That was dismissal right there, but we took care of it.' He would assign Bukowski to a place where the supervisors were unlikely to find him, because the clerks thought of themselves like family, and Bukowski was one of them. 'We knew the ropes, see, we was there a long time, and we don't want no supervisor firing nobody when they're a friend of ours.'

There were ten black workers to every white worker on the night shift, which was the most unpopular shift of all at the Annex. 'The whites saw it as beneath them,' says former clerk Grace Washington. Bukowski could have moved to a day shift, if he wanted, but he stayed on nights for years, coming in around 6.30 p.m. and leaving around 2.30 a.m., because it gave him time during the day to write and go to the track and, perhaps surprisingly, his former co-workers say he was one of the least prejudiced whites in the whole building.

The mail clerks worked in booths leaning on a rest bar made of wood. 'What you did, you rested your butt on this thing,' says David Berger, Bukowski's union rep. 'That would keep you in a permanent position so you weren't actually standing on your feet, you were at an angle. It kind of took the weight off your feet and made it easier to work.' The mail arrived in long trays

---

* Sanford is the name of the postal district of LA that Bukowski had learned by rote.

which had to be sorted within a time limit or else the clerks were 'written up' by the supervisors. There were other rules: clerks were only allowed to use their right hand to throw mail, and the mail had to go into the relevant cubby holes so the stamps were 'up' and the return addresses 'in'. Bukowski was not exaggerating when he described in *Post Office* how this system ground the clerks down over the years. It was a brutal régime and many, including Bukowski, suffered chronic back and shoulder pains.

'KEEP MOVING!' called the supervisors as they marched along beside the rows of clerks. 'PICK IT UP NOW!' they yelled, as new mail came down the conveyor belts. Up above in what the clerks called 'the spy gallery' other supervisors watched for pilfering. Bukowski knew that if he took one stamp home he would be fired.

The clerks chattered incessantly to pass the time, about sport mostly, football games and baseball scores. They also bet to see who could clear their trays fastest, each throwing a dollar in a pot and then sticking mail as fast as possible until one clerk finished. But there was no way of beating the clock, as David Berger says: 'Just about the time you figure you had cleaned up what was in front of you, here came somebody with another tray, so it never ended.'

Bukowski was unusual because he didn't talk while he was working. He didn't joke or race the other clerks or try and get the trays that seemed to have less mail. He worked steadily, without joy or complaint, with the stoicism he had learned as a boy. 'He wasn't grumpy, he just never started any conversation,' says Berger. 'If you talked to him, he would probably answer you, but he would never really carry a conversation.' Grace Washington actually wondered if he was retarded.

In his break, Bukowski either went downstairs to the cafeteria or across the street into Chinatown where the clerks could get a late night beer at Mama's Bar. Sometimes when he was in Mama's, he would tell the clerks he was a writer, but this only confirmed their opinion that he was a way-out fellow and Johnny Moore says they never believed him anyway. Then it was back to the Annex until 2 a.m., or later in the run-up to Christmas.

For the best part of twelve years Bukowski held this back-breaking job, working two weeks straight and then taking a four-day weekend and, as the years went by, he became convinced it would kill him.

It was a Friday night in the spring of 1963, the start of a long weekend after working ten days at the post office, and Bukowski was drinking in his room. Not having had any female company to speak of since Jane died over a year ago, and feeling lonely, he decided to call a woman who had written to him saying she loved his work. She was from somewhere back east but had recently come to stay with her mother in Garden Grove, a suburb of LA.

'I have to see you right now,' Bukowski insisted, when he got her on the line. 'You have to come at once.'

She said she would love to, but had no transport because her mother was using the car.

'How about tomorrow?'

'No, come *now*.'

There was a Greyhound leaving Anaheim around midnight. If she walked to the station, she might catch it. But she wouldn't be in LA until at least 2 a.m. Bukowski said he would be up.

His new friend was born Frances Elizabeth Dean in San Rafael, California, in 1922, but later changed her name to FrancEyE. Her father was an electrical engineer from a well-to-do family who made a fortune inventing a type of boiler. He died when FrancEyE was eight and she was brought up in Lexington, Massachusetts, home of her paternal grandparents. She went to Smith College where she joined the poetry club and started to write about what she describes as 'my bitterness and despair'. She married a soldier and settled in Michigan, raising a family of four daughters, but continued to write poetry and to correspond with other poets.

One of her pen friends was Stanley Kurnik who ran a writers' workshop in LA and knew Bukowski. He would go over to North Mariposa and look at his poems, the pile of old work he kept in the closet, and pick out some good ones to read to his workshop group. Sometimes Kurnik sent copies to FrancEyE and she was so thrilled by them that she wrote to Bukowski expressing her admiration. When her marriage ended, and she moved to Garden

Grove, FrancEyE wrote again, this time asking to meet him. It was this letter Bukowski was turning over when he called her on the telephone.

'Of course he was drunk,' she says. 'He was drunk out of his mind. I didn't realize this at the time. But I do remember thinking in the cab that brought me from the bus station, I hope he does follow through because I don't have enough money to pay this cab driver.'

The next thing FrancEyE knew she was at North Mariposa in the still of the early morning with Bukowski, sobered up a little, coming down the steps with the money for the driver. 'Bukowski seemed like this giant, this gorgeous giant,' she says. 'His hair was all slicked back . . . His gaze was very direct. He had a very symmetrical face. His nose was kind of smashed, but I just thought he was gorgeous.'

He was not supposed to have female visitors in his room out of hours, so they sneaked up to 303 and whispered together until dawn. 'We would sit and not say anything and he would get nervous because he could never stand silence. He would always say something to start the conversation again.' They discussed their mutual feelings of depression and isolation. 'I was desperately lonely and grief-stricken and on the edge of suicide all the time because I didn't have my kids,' she says. 'I didn't have a life. And he was in much the same situation.' Bukowski spoke about Jane's death, and all the guilt and grief he felt, and how much he regretted being cruel to a dog they had, when he was drunk one time. When they had worn each other out with their misery, they climbed into the Murphy bed.

The following afternoon Bukowski took FrancEyE to Santa Anita to watch the horses. An incorrigible spendthrift herself, she noticed that, although he was clearly addicted to gambling, he was cautious with the amount of money he spent. 'His rent was paid. His savings were in his savings account and he would gamble what he had left,' she says.

They began to see each other regularly and she moved into Los Angeles to be near him, taking a cheap room on North Vermont Avenue, a couple of blocks up from the Phillips Hotel. The Hollywood Freeway ran under the apartment building and when she opened her window in the morning she was engulfed in a cloud of exhaust.

FrancEyE was a moderate drinker, nothing like Jane had been, but this didn't stop Bukowski from boozing. She remembers he kept his drinking more or less under control during the week, when he had to get to his job, but 'drank non-stop' at the weekends, benders which often ended with some accident, or with him spending the night in jail followed by a court appearance. He had a newspaper clipping about Alcoholics Anonymous stuck to the wall and would occasionally talk about whether he fitted the profile of an alcoholic. On balance he decided he didn't because he could stop drinking if he wanted, if only for a day or so, and because he carried on writing however much he drank. This remained his opinion throughout his life.

Despite the indifference he later showed FrancEyE, she says the relationship began as a love affair. 'We both had such a need for love and we both received love from each other,' she says. Bukowski did not write very much about FrancEyE, and there are no love poems comparable to those he wrote about Jane. Indeed, the closest he ever came to admitting love was in the poem, 'one for old snaggle-tooth', written years after they'd split, in which he acknowledges they 'were once great lovers'. However, in a letter to Corrington, he described FrancEyE as a grey-haired old woman (she was forty-one when they met) who loved him, but whom he did not love.

FrancEyE explains this by saying Bukowski had difficulty expressing love. 'He wrote about the negative emotions more,' she says. 'He used to be really embarrassed by positive feeling.' This was not limited to feelings for her, but extended to all human relationships. As an example, she recalls Bukowski confessing he admired some people who had recently been to visit him. He thought they were wonderful, but he said these feelings of admiration for other human beings made him feel sick.

The visitors were probably photographer Sam Cherry and his teenage son, Neeli. Bukowski was becoming close to the family, whom he had met through Jory Sherman, admiring Sam Cherry for the hard life he'd led during the depression: riding the box cars as a hobo, working as a longshoreman and living on San Francisco's Skid Row.

When Sam Cherry visited North Mariposa, Bukowski tried to establish his own tough guy credentials, by boasting that he'd killed five men.

'Come on, don't give me that shit, Bukowski,' Cherry replied. 'How many men did you really kill?'

Bukowski took a drink, looked at the crack in the wall, and said he had killed four men. Cherry guffawed and there was another pause before Bukowski revised this to three men.

'After about twenty or thirty minutes it got down to zero,' says Cherry. 'He was full of bullshit.'

Apart from the love and support of FrancEyE, and the friendship of people like Sam Cherry, it was Jon and Gypsy Lou Webb who lifted Bukowski out of his long period of depression by writing to him that they liked his work so much they had decided to make him their first Outsider of the Year. He would get an inscribed plaque to hang on his wall and, more importantly, they would publish an anthology of his best poems. Bukowski was overwhelmed by the Webbs' generosity of spirit, people he still had not met. He knew it would be a crippling task for them financially, with no money other than what they could raise through friends like book dealer, Ed Blair, and sympathetic writers like Henry Miller, as well as being a massive time commitment.

The proposed book was to be an infinitely more substantial publication than the chapbooks previously brought out. It would be a beautifully produced hard-cover volume, properly bound, and sold commercially through stores. The Webbs selected Bukowski's best work since 1955 – poems like 'the tragedy of the leaves', 'conversation in a cheap room' and 'old man, dead in a room' – and then set about making the design so remarkable that anyone walking into a store would feel compelled to pick the book up, even if they'd never heard of Bukowski. The poems were printed on expensive deckle-edged paper in a range of colours and bound in an elaborate cork cover. Jon Webb wanted to sell autographed copies so he mailed unbound pages to Bukowski to sign with a silver deco-write pen, giving precise instructions on how hard he must press, how long the ink took to dry, which side of the paper to work on and how many inches in from the margin he should write. A bemused Bukowski reflected it was a wonder the book didn't walk and talk the amount of trouble they were taking with it.

In the colophon, Webb described the arcane conditions in which the book was produced, writing that he and Gypsy Lou hand-fed the pages into an ancient Chandler & Price letterpress, working through the humid summer of 1963 in a workshop behind a sagging mansion in the French Quarter of New Orleans. 'The workshop's windows gaping out into a delightful walled-in courtyard dense to its broken-bottled brims with rotting banana trees, stinkweed and vine.' Rats ran about in the roof sending showers of plaster over completed pages and they had to share the workshop with 'cockroaches big as mice'. There were myriad hitches to contend with, including bugs in the ink, blown fuses and wiring that twice caught fire. The press broke down three times, and the Louisiana humidity burst the composition rollers, but finally the job was done.

John William Corrington wrote the introduction identifying one of Bukowski's main achievements as his use of 'a language devoid of the affections, devices and mannerisms that have taken over academic verse'. This style, he wrote, was 'the spoken voice nailed to paper'.

The title of the book, *It Catches My Heart in Its Hands*, was taken from a line in a poem by Robinson Jeffers, Bukowski's favorite poet at the time. 'Jeffers, I suppose, is my God,' he wrote to Jory Sherman, 'the only man since Shakey to write the long narrative poem that does not put one to sleep.' He also liked Conrad Aiken and Ezra Pound, 'but Jeffers is stronger, darker, more exploratatively (*sic*) modern and mad.'

The finished book, which was published in October, 1963, was a work of art and, although only 777 copies were made, the extraordinary craftsmanship could not fail to draw attention to Bukowski and his poetry. The arrival of the first copy at North Mariposa was THE DAY. 'My God, you've done it, you've done it!' Bukowski wrote to the Webbs in high excitement. 'Never such a book!' The years of misery, the depression, the feelings of loss had been worth enduring to see something so wonderful.

'That made him,' says Gypsy Lou. 'Of course he made a lot of money later in life, but we helped him get going.'

FAMILY LIFE AT DE LONGPRE AVENUE

5

When FrancEyE became pregnant she didn't tell Bukowski straight away, but considered having a termination because her circumstances were not ideal for having a child. She had little money. She was living in a rooming house, and Bukowski had made it very clear he didn't want a family. The only reason they hadn't used contraception was that he hated condoms and, at forty-one, FrancEyE believed she was too old to get pregnant. Yet despite all the problems, she decided to have the baby. 'I thought, well, I'll go to Bukowski and, if he doesn't want to help, I'll go to my mother. Somewhere I'll get help.'

When she did tell him, Bukowski unexpectedly asked FrancEyE to marry him, not because he particularly wanted to repeat an experience that had ended so unhappily with Barbara Frye, but because he wanted to do the right thing. FrancEyE thanked him, but said she never wanted to marry anyone again and they compromised by agreeing to live together as a family with Bukowski paying the bills. They found a suitable home on De Longpre Avenue, where Bukowski would stay for the next nine years and where he wrote some of his best work.

The 5000 block of De Longpre Avenue runs parallel with Sunset Boulevard in East Hollywood, still within walking distance of Ned's liquor store. There is a Ukrainian church, a scattering of modest family homes and a few low-rent apartment courts, one of which was owned by a middle-aged couple named Crotty who worked as extras at the nearby film studios. Theirs was not exactly 'the last Skid Row court in Hollywood' as Bukowski was fond of describing it, but it had seen better days. It consisted of four bungalows built on one side of a driveway that led from the sidewalk to a five-room boarding house. FrancEyE remembers it was 'half a court' because there was no facing row of bungalows, just a vacant lot, as if the builders had run out of money.

Francis Crotty was a short, pugnacious mid-Westerner with sparkling eyes, slightly bulbous nose and a moustache, a busy and resourceful landlord who was adept at fixing things. His wife, Grace, was a thick-set woman with red hair. Because they owned the court outright, and didn't have to worry about every cent, the Crottys charged reasonable rents and made sure their tenants got enough to eat by going on 'dent runs' to stores which sold damaged cans of food and day-old bread at a discount. 'They would buy a whole bunch of it and give it to people who were poorer than they were,' remembers former neighbor, Sina Taylor. There were also communal dinners at Thanksgiving and the Crottys would host 'drinking days' when they handed around whiskey and Eastside beer until everybody in the court was pleasantly smashed. The Crottys were tolerant of eccentricity in others and didn't care that Bukowski and FrancEyE weren't married, even though many landlords wouldn't have rented to them. Bukowski decided they were the best landlords he'd ever had.

He and FrancEyE moved into the one-bedroom end bungalow, next to the sidewalk. The lounge had an old couch, a rickety coffee table and book shelves constructed from building blocks. At the back of the room was a desk and over the desk Bukowski kept what he called his 'cheeseboard', a set of post office pigeon holes which he used for scheme test practice because, although he was a regular mail clerk, he still had to pass tests to hold his post office job. The rest of the time he used it to file papers. The typewriter and typing table his parents had given him were by the window so he could watch people while he wrote, as he described in 'the new place':

as I type people go by
mostly women
and I sit in my shorts
(without top)
and going by they
can't be sure I am not entirely
naked. so
I get these faces
which pretend they don't see
anything
but I think they do:
they see me as I
sweat the poem like beating an
ugly hog to death
as the sun begins to fail over
Sunset Blvd.
over the motel sign
where hot sweaty people from
Arkansas and Iowa
pay too much to sleep while
dreaming of movie stars.

Although Bukowski and FrancEyE liked the new place, they were not suited to living together. She involved herself in causes and with groups which Bukowski, the outsider, considered a waste of time. He wrote to the Webbs that FrancEyE was fighting 'to save and understand all mankind' and it was not a battle he thought she had much chance of winning. He was also contemptuous of her poetry workshop friends, people like Stanley Kurnik who sometimes came over to talk about literature. 'Hank did not like my workshop friends,' she says. 'My workshop friends were cardboard. They were an intrusion on him. They were Hollywood People. They were phonies. But they were my only friends!'

The fact he was about to become a father didn't make him at all happy and, when Jory Sherman visited, Bukowski suggested the baby might not even be his. 'I was furious,' says FrancEyE. 'But at the same time I knew he was drunk, so I didn't make a thing out of it. He was doing that as part of his posturing in front of Jory.'

Bukowski moaned about FrancEyE in letters to friends, making fun of the books she read, even complaining that she was getting fat. His dissatisfaction also came out in poems, like 'the new place', where the poet is interrupted in his work by 'the woman' calling him to dinner:

> the food is getting cold and
> I've got to go
> (she doesn't understand that
> I've got to finish this thing)

'The new place' was published later that year in *The Wormwood Review*, a small literary magazine edited in Connecticut by Marvin Malone, who became a great supporter of Bukowski. Another poem in the issue, 'poetess', which Bukowski dedicated to FrancEyE, showed a more affectionate side to their relationship. Bukowski describes how she looks after him when he has been drinking, and praises her own poetry by saying 'she wrote like a man'. FrancEyE was not entirely comfortable with the idea that writing like a man should be a compliment, but she knew he meant well.

Jon and Gypsy Lou Webb arrived in LA in August, 1964, to talk to Bukowski about a second book, because the first had been such a success. Bukowski met them at the Crown Hill Hotel, introducing FrancEyE, pompously, as 'my woman'. Jon Webb told him that no man owned a woman, he just borrowed her. After a few drinks they went back to the bungalow on De Longpre where Gypsy Lou noticed the Outsider of the Year plaque they had sent from New Orleans was hanging prominently on the wall, next to a pyramid of empty beer cans. Bukowski sat staring at the plaque when he was drinking. 'He would look at it and almost cry and say he didn't understand how anybody could ever have done anything so beautiful for him,' says FrancEyE. 'He didn't think he would live to have such a wonderful thing happen.'

Jon Webb made Bukowski promise he would write new material for their next book, because they'd already used the best of his old stuff, and they spent four days working out the details. When Bukowski took the Webbs to Union Station to catch their train back to New Orleans, the bond of friendship had been strongly forged. From the Webbs' point of view, Bukowski had shown himself to be worthy of their hard work, a man who 'said it like it was', also some one rather different from the image he presented in his writing. He was not tough at all, decided Gypsy Lou. 'He was a gentle giant, really a sweetheart.'

Bukowski had grown so fond of the couple he told Gypsy Lou they would name their baby after her, if it was a girl, and when they had gone he wrote them a letter saying they were the sort of people he always hoped to meet but rarely had and, if they could work the miracle of *It Catches My Heart in Its Hands* again, his life would be complete.

As the expected date of the birth approached, Bukowski remembered Barbara's miscarriage and became anxious that his years of drinking might cause the baby to be born damaged. He also worried the pregnancy might be rough on FrancEyE, who was now forty-two, becoming quite angry that she had allowed herself to get into this condition, as if it were nothing to do with him. But on 7 September, 1964, she gave birth to a perfectly healthy baby girl. She chose Marina as the first name, after a courtesan she had been reading about, and Bukowski chose Louise as the middle name in honor of Gypsy Lou.

Marina would be Bukowski's only child and he was a devoted father from the beginning. 'He would change her, take care of her. He loved to watch her when she was finding her toes and fingers,' says FrancEyE. 'I was so grateful for having her when I saw what a wonderful father he was.'

He began to include news of the baby's progress in letters to friends, praising her beauty, good nature and intelligence. In a letter to Corrington, he wrote: 'The girl-child is Marina Louise Bukowski and I am a sucker for it. Very large mouth and eyes and when that mouth opens and spreads into the big grin laugh, all sunflowers and sun, and I break in half, she has me.' Now, when the suicide complex came upon him, there was one good reason to resist.

The arrival of the baby did not make his relationship with FrancEyE any happier, however. Bukowski's night work made it almost impossible to organize a domestic routine that gave them all enough sleep. FrancEyE mostly stayed up until Bukowski came home from the post office, in the early hours, before going to bed. Then they were woken by Marina at dawn, and again at 8 a.m. by construction work on the vacant lot next door. Bukowski liked to sleep until noon, so FrancEyE tried to take Marina out in the mornings, but when she came back he wanted to write. He wouldn't say she had to be quiet because he was working, but if something bothered him he would come and yell, so she crept around with Marina, frightened even to turn the radio on.

Jon Webb was concerned Bukowski was not writing the poems they needed for the completion of the new book, the early pages of which he and Gypsy Lou were already in the process of printing, so in March, 1965, he invited Bukowski to New Orleans for a break.

The Webbs were renting a bug-infested room on the ground floor of a building on Royal Street, in the French Quarter. It was more workshop than home with a printing press taking up most of the floor space, art materials on the shelves, and reams of paper everywhere, paper the manufacturers guaranteed would last eight hundred years. Webb had built the bed on stilts so they could store paper underneath, and Bukowski was amazed to see pages of his book stacked on wooden slats over the bath tub. 'It was a terrible place,' says Gypsy Lou, who was becoming increasingly irked with the conditions. 'There wasn't room for anything.' Bukowski drew a cartoon in which she tosses the pages in the air, yelling: 'Bukowski! Bukowski! I can't stand it anymore!'

The Webbs were utterly dedicated to the book and regularly worked twelve-hour days, leaving Bukowski to his own devices. He drank with the artist, Noel Rockmore, whose etchings would be used on the cover, and spent evenings flirting with Minnie Segate, a friend of the Webbs who was putting him up during his two-week stay. He was having such a high old time that Jon Webb told him sharply to stop larking about and get down to writing the poems they needed.

'Got any poems, Bukowski?' he would ask, when he saw the poet at his door. If he had none, Webb told him to go away and write.

Bukowski feared working under pressure would turn his writing 'into journalism'. He was also uneasy about the book's proposed title, *Crucifix in a Deathhand*, which Webb chose from a line in one of the new poems, even though Bukowski thought there were many better titles. He had begun to outlive his welcome at Minnie's, coming home drunk at all hours and generally making a fool of himself, and wrote to his friend, Al Purdy, that he felt he was just getting in the way.

Towards the end of the vacation, John William Corrington drove over from Baton Rouge to meet Bukowski. Corrington was flushed with success having recently returned from England where he had taken a doctorate at the University of Sussex. He had also recently had his first novel published. Neither achievement impressed Bukowski who made his feelings clear in letters. When they began corresponding, in 1961, Bukowski addressed him with the utmost courtesy as 'Mr Corrington', impressed that an academic was interested in his work, but the relationship had degenerated to the extent that he had started a recent letter, 'fucker'. Despite this, Corrington was excited about meeting Bukowski. 'He believed they would immediately become fast friends,' says the poet Miller Williams, who came along for the ride.

Bukowski was sitting on the loft bed drinking beer when they came in the room. Also present were Jon Webb and two of his young friends, Ed Blair and Ben C. Toledano. There was an uneasy atmosphere from the start. According to Blair, Corrington was very gregarious, very confident in himself, and thought everybody loved him, 'the kind of person Bukowski wasn't going to go for'. Corrington and Williams talked about literature and university life, and Toledano chipped in about being a lawyer. Bukowski felt at a disadvantage in such company and said nothing.

When Corrington started telling Bukowski what his English Dean had said on the subject of James Joyce, he couldn't stand any more. 'Fuck your Dean,' he said.

Corrington was deeply offended, but Bukowski was not about to apologize and began sneering at everything Corrington said, especially when he tried to talk about Republican politician Barry Goldwater, saying he was a good man. They were at loggerheads now, too stubborn to back off and decided to pout at each other throughout the rest of the evening. Miller Williams believes Bukowski was chiefly at fault. 'It was the kind of self-destructive defensiveness that an early adolescent will engage in,' he says. 'Corrington was very hurt that he had been rejected by someone whose work was important to him and whose approval he very much wanted.' It was the end of their friendship.

With a relatively large print run and New York publisher, Lyle Stuart, handling distribution, *Crucifix in a Deathhand* was the biggest book of Bukowski's career to date, and the Webbs did another beautiful design job. Printed in a large format, and illustrated with nightmarish etchings by Noel Rockmore, it looked like an album of Gothic fairy tales. But with the benefit of hindsight, Bukowski was correct to fear his poetry would be compromised by writing under pressure.

In his more honest moments, he admitted he had slipped. He knew Webb wanted better, but he could not produce poems to match the standard of the first book. Jon Webb reported that Henry Miller was enthusiastic, but when Bukowski wrote to Miller, whom he admired and whose book *Tropic of Cancer* has much in common with his own later novels, suggesting they get together, Miller declined and scolded Bukowski for drinking too much. He said it was a sure way to kill inspiration.

There were notable poems in the book, however, few better than 'something for the touts, the nuns, the grocery clerks and you . . . '. This was virtually a polemic against capitalism, although Bukowski maintained he was not a political writer. 'I am not a man who looks for solutions in God or politics,' he said. He did not align himself with the Left – although FrancEyE remembers him expressing admiration for Communist Dorothy Healey – any more than his college flirtation with Nazism had matured into a sympathy with the Right. At the same time some of the poems in *Crucifix in a Deathhand*, and later work like *Factotum*, show an interest in the problems of the urban under class. 'What I've tried to do, if you'll pardon me, is bring in the factory-workers aspect of life,' he said. 'The screaming wife when he comes home from work. The basic realities of the everyman existence . . . something seldom mentioned in the poetry of the centuries. Just put me down as saying that the poetry of the centuries is shit. It's shameful.' He achieved his goal in 'something for the touts, the nuns, the grocery clerks and you . . .' without political posturing.

> . . . the days of
> the bosses, yellow men
> with bad breath and big feet, men
> who look like frogs, hyenas, men who walk
> as if melody had never been invented, men
> who think it is intelligent to hire and fire and
> profit, men with expensive wives they possess
> like 60 acres of ground to be drilled
> or shown-off or to be walled away from
> the incompetent, men who'd kill you
> because they're crazy and justify it because
> it's the law, men who stand in front of
> windows 30 feet wide and see nothing,
> men with luxury yachts who can sail around
> the world and yet never get out of their vest
> pockets, men like snails, men like eels, men
> like slugs, and not as good . . .
>
> and nothing. getting your last paycheck
> at a harbor, at a factory, at a hospital, at an
> aircraft plant, at a penny arcade, at a
> barbershop, at a job you didn't want
> anyway.
> income tax, sickness, servility, broken
> arms, broken heads – all the stuffing
> come out like an old pillow.

By this stage in his career, his work was familiar to the readers of practically every small literary magazine in America, and a good many in Europe. Well-produced if obscure books like those made by the Webbs enhanced his reputation and many young poets began to look to him as a leader. One of these was Douglas Blazek, a Chicago poet and foundry worker who produced his own little magazine, *Ole*, on a $100 Sears & Roebuck mimeograph machine.

This sort of primitive technology was responsible for the sloppy appearance of most little magazines, but in Blazek's case it was in keeping with the gritty nature of the work.

When Blazek discovered Bukowski had written short stories, back in the '40s, he asked for some prose for *Ole* and Bukowski responded with a breakthrough piece, *A Rambling Essay On Poetics And The Bleeding Life Written While Drinking A Six Pack (Tall)*. It was meant as an essay, more than a short story, a statement of his literary beliefs, but what came across most strongly was that he was writing about himself.

He wrote that his father was a 'monster who bastardized me upon this sad earth', thus fostering the abiding myth he was illegitimate; and he invited his readers to call him 'uncultured, drunken, whatever' as if he were a Philistine. The message was that Bukowski had 'crawled drunken in alleys from coast to coast' and the poetry that came from these experiences was all the more powerful for it.

'Being the age that I was, I had my mouth wide open and I was swallowing it all,' says Blazek. Many of those who read the essay in *Ole* also took it as a true account of Bukowski's life and wanted to know more about the poet who said he had shouldered carcasses in a slaughter house (in fact, he worked half a day in a slaughter house on one occasion during his supposed ten-year drunk).

When he got back to De Longpre, after visiting the Webbs, Bukowski found he had fan mail and wrote Blazek on 17 April, 1965: 'I get these letters on the essay I wrote for *Ole* 2 and they seem to think I said something; I am a fucking oracle (oriol?) for the LOST or something, is what they tell me. that's nice. but I AM THE LOST.'

Blazek went on to publish a Bukowski chapbook of a single prose piece, *Confessions of a Man Insane Enough to Live with Beasts*, a portmanteau of nine short stories based on his childhood, adolescence and youth. It further promoted Bukowski as the hero of his own work, even though he used the device of a fictional first-person narrator. The name, Henry Chinaski, was noticeably similar to his own.

'*Confessions* became a dry run for his first novel, *Post Office*, and from then on I think he duplicated himself,' says Blazek. '*Ham *on Rye*, all of that, was regurgitated. All his previous stuff was just a dry run for the more substantial works that John Martin published at Black Sparrow Press.'

It is true that many of the stories that later became significant parts of his novels first appeared in these short stories. For example, Bukowski first wrote about Jane Cooney Baker in *Confessions of a Man Insane Enough to Live with Beasts*. He introduced her as K:

> K. was an ex-showgirl and she used to show me the clippings and photos. She'd almost won a Miss America contest. I met her in an Alvarado St. bar, which is about as close to getting to Skid Row as you can get. She had put on weight and age but there was still some sign of a figure, some class, but just a hint and little more. We'd both had it. Neither of us worked and how we made it I'll never know . . .

Ten years later he wrote about her in his novel, *Factotum*, but it was essentially the same thing:

> I found myself on Alvarado Street. I walked along until I came to an inviting bar and went in. It was crowded. There was only one seat left at the bar. I sat in it. I ordered a scotch and water. To my right sat a rather dark blonde, gone a bit to fat, neck and cheeks now flabby, obviously a drunk; but there was a certain lingering beauty to her features, and her body still looked firm and young and well-shaped. In fact, her legs were long and lovely.

Both versions show how much he manipulated the facts of Jane's life to make a story.

Even though FrancEyE wanted him to do things with her and Marina, Bukowski's weekends were still mostly taken up with drinking. He stumbled around the bars, getting into fights and sometimes getting himself locked up. When he stayed home, he emptied beer bottles by the half dozen, clanging empties into the garbage until neighbors yelled for him to shut up, or singing songs from *Oklahoma!* with Francis and Grace Crotty at the back of the court. Alcohol was so much a part of daily life that the first word Marina learned to read was 'liquor' and she came to know Ned's liquor store as 'Hank's Store' because her father spent so much time there.

One night around Thanksgiving, 1965, Bukowski came home from the post office, got a beer from the refrigerator, and told FrancEyE it wasn't working.

'You have to get out of here,' he said.

He promised to help her find a place where she could live with Marina, and said he would continue to support them. 'He hated having an unhappy woman around, and he knew how unhappy I was,' says FrancEyE, who had been thinking of moving out anyway.

Marina believes she is lucky the split came before she knew any other life. 'I didn't have any unhappy memories of that and, obviously, if it had been a year or two later I would have been at least initially miserable,' she says. 'How my father raised me and how my mother raised me was pretty unconventional, just the fact that they weren't together was one piece of the puzzle, but I always felt a really strong connection to him. He let me know both by his actions and his words that he loved me more than anything, so I always took that for granted as a child. It is something that is so basic and so important and it just made everything in the world OK.'

Despite his many problems, and his drinking, FrancEyE found she could rely on Bukowski even after they split. 'I could never handle money,' she says. 'My money would run out and we would be out of food. Whenever I called Hank, and said, "Can we come over and eat?" Or, we need this or that, he was always right there.'

But when she had time to reflect on their relationship as a couple, FrancEyE did not come to an entirely positive conclusion. She was especially hurt when some of Bukowski's letters were published in the early 1990s, revealing how little he had understood her, and how he often belittled her in correspondence with his friends.

In response, FrancEyE wrote the poem, 'Christ I feel shitty':

At least it's clear now
He hated me
for being somebody I never was.
Maybe I loved him
for the same reason.
I thought he would want to hear amazing stories
when all he wanted was somebody to clean up the kitchen,
just like he said all along.

BLACK SPARROW, AND THE SIXTIES

It is one of the ironies of Bukowski's career that his eventual success was largely due to the hard work of a Christian Scientist who drinks nothing stronger than iced tea. John Martin was the manager of an office supply company when he first read Bukowski's poetry, and it literally changed his life. He decided Bukowski was a great genius, 'the Walt Whitman of our day', and set out to become his publisher.

First he read all the books that were available. He bought *It Catches my Heart in Its Hands* and, through Jon Webb, got an inscribed copy of *Crucifix in a Deathhand*. Then, in October, 1965, he wrote to Bukowski asking to buy signed copies of the early chapbooks, adding that he thought Bukowski was 'a most important and marvellous poet'. Bukowski sent him a copy of *Confessions of a Man Insane Enough to Live with Beasts*, and Martin wrote again ten days later, saying he wanted to invite him to lunch, adding: 'I've never had the pleasure of talking to a really fine poet.' Bukowski postponed the meeting while he found a place for FrancEyE and Marina to live, but invited Martin over to De Longpre after he wrote again in January saying he'd been given bottles of liquor for Christmas, but didn't drink, and wondered if Bukowski wanted them.

Bukowski was drinking beer when he looked up and saw a smartly dressed gentleman on his porch. His visitor had wisps of reddish hair around a mostly bald head, although he was still young, and was grinning broadly.

'I've always been a great admirer of your work,' said John Martin, introducing himself. 'I'd like to come in.'

'Oh well, come on in. Want a beer?'

Martin declined, reminding Bukowski that he didn't drink. 'That kind of put me off right there: this guy's inhuman, he doesn't drink beer!' said Bukowski, recalling the meeting.

For his part, Martin was taken aback by Bukowski's scruffy appearance and the filthy conditions he was living in, now FrancEyE had left. 'He had this absolutely destroyed room,' he says. There were rusty razor blades round the sink, the toilet didn't flush properly and the work surfaces were covered dust and bits of food.

Martin asked if he had any writing he could look at, and Bukowski told him to look in the closet.

'What's this?' asked Martin, looking at a stack of paper that reached up almost to his waist.

'Writing,' replied Bukowski.

'No kidding?'

'Yeah.'

'How long it take you to write this?'

'Oh, I don't know, three or four months.'

'Oh, this is astonishing. You mind if I read it?'

'Go ahead.'

Bukowski cracked open another beer while his visitor began wading through the mass of paper. There were countless poems and short stories, and most of it had never been published. It was such a treasure trove Martin could barely contain his excitement.

'Oh this is very good!' he exclaimed. 'This is great!' Another gem revealed itself. 'This is an immortal poem!'

'Oh yeah?' drawled Bukowski.

After what seemed a long time, Martin stopped reading and said he was thinking of starting a small press. He would like to take three or four of the poems with him, look them over at home, and maybe print them up as broadsides. 'There'll probably be some money in it for you. I don't know how much.

We'll have to see,' he said. Bukowski shrugged and said he could go ahead. Hell, he'd put his hand in his own pocket to help editors publish his work. The Webbs had paid him in kind with copies of the books. To get paid money would be something new.

Apart from being a successful businessman, John Martin was a serious book collector who had an impressive library of first editions. It was his interest in D.H.Lawrence that led him to read about the career of B.W.Huebsch, founder of Viking and Lawrence's American publisher. He discovered Huebsch had started out by publishing writers who were not yet established, and Viking grew as they became more successful. It dawned on Martin that many of his favorite writers, including Bukowski, had been ignored by the New York publishers. He also wanted to work with his wife, Barbara, in the way Harry and Caresse Crosby had worked together on the Black Sun Press. Inspired by the example of Huebsch, the Crosbys, and by a William Carlos Williams poem about a sparrow, he decided to launch Black Sparrow Press. 'I liked the combination of the élite black and very common sparrow,' he says, explaining the name.

He selected five of the poems from the bundle he had taken from Bukowski's closet and decided to print thirty copies of each, twenty-seven numbered and three lettered: A, B, and C, for author, publisher and the press operator at work who had agreed to print them up.

The first poem was 'True Story', which concerns a man who has castrated himself. Martin says he chose it because 'it's a pretty grim poem and it just struck me as being very existential.'

> they found him walking along the freeway
> all red in
> front
> he had taken a rusty tin can
> and cut off his sexual
> machinery
> as if to say—

see what you've done to
me? you might as well have the
rest.

In March, 1966, Bukowski went into hospital to have his haemorrhoids removed. He took time off work afterwards and wrote a hilarious account of the operation, *All the Assholes in the World and Mine*, which was published by Douglas Blazek. He was still off work in April when John Martin brought the first Black Sparrow broadsides over to be signed. He also gave Bukowski a check for $25. It was money he badly needed because his post office sick pay had run out, his medical insurance didn't cover the hospital bills, and the child support was due.

Bukowski and Martin were very different personalities, but their differences worked to their advantage, forming the basis of a long and happy association. Once Bukowski came to terms with dealing with a teetotaller, although he never wholly understood it (what did Martin do if he didn't drink?) he trusted him more than a fellow drinker. 'He knew I'd never make a drunken stupid move, make a deal I shouldn't make,' says Martin. And although Martin is an astute businessman, Bukowski realized he was far from being conventional, and that he really did appreciate the work. Mutual friend and poet, Gerard Malanga, describes Martin as a paradox: 'He is kind of a straight guy in a funny way, but he is very hip. You can be straight and hip.'

Both men were pleased with the way the broadsides turned out and almost right away Martin decided to try and publish books. He sold his collection of first editions to the University of California at Santa Barbara and used the $50,000 he raised to build Black Sparrow into a company that could publish Bukowski and other new or neglected writers. He was soon bringing out broadsides and chapbooks as striking in the simplicity of their design as the Loujon books were ornate.

Barbara Martin was responsible for the distinctive Black Sparrow artwork. Her use of classic typography, with plain rules, turned out to be the perfect complement to Bukowski's pared-down poems, work like 'a little atomic bomb' which they published in a chapbook called, simply, *2 Poems*:

o, just give me a little atomic bomb
not too much
just a little
enough to kill a horse in the street
but there aren't any horses in the street

well, enough to knock the flowers from a bowl
but I don't see any
flowers in a
bowl
enough then
to frighten my love
but I don't have any
love

well
give me an atomic bomb then
to scrub in my bathtub
like a dirty and lovable child

(I've got a bathtub)

just a little bomb, general,
with pugnose
pink ears
smelling like underclothes in
July

The best of Bukowski's mature poetry was written in this minimalist style, although it is not to everyone's taste. 'Bukowski's poetry was essentially stories, just like his prose,' says Lawrence Ferlinghetti. 'It just happened some days that he didn't get the carriage of the typewriter to the end of the line. Depends how badly hungover he was when he started to type.' But Bukowski was achieving the trick he'd been trying to pull off since his twenties. Inspired by the direct prose style of John Fante and Ernest Hemingway, and more recently by the poetry of Pablo Neruda, Robinson Jeffers and others, he was 'writing down one simple line after another' and bringing humor in as well, because he believed 'creation cannot be all that serious, or you fall asleep.' John Martin loved the work and saw Bukowski as a totally original voice.

'When I started Black Sparrow, I was publishing guys who thought they were French symbolists. I was publishing guys who thought they were surrealists, and you had to sit and work with the poems to get the meaning,' he says. 'Then here comes this voice out of nowhere and you have no doubt what he means, and what he is trying to say.'

Bukowski liked to mock the counter-culture, having little time for drugs, pop, music or radical politics. But many of the young writers and publishers who liked his work were deeply involved in these things and Bukowski was inevitably drawn into what was happening in the late 1960s.

Another of his new admirers was a student called Steve Richmond whose wealthy family had set him up in a cottage by the ocean at Santa Monica. He studied law at the University of California, but spent most of his time getting laid, dropping LSD with his buddy Jim Morrison, and writing poetry about the amazing things going on in his head. What really freaked Richmond out was reading Bukowski's poems in *Ole* magazine. Like John Martin, but in a spacier way, he decided Bukowski was 'a genius of the world' and made a pilgrimage to De Longpre Avenue to meet his hero. Bukowski made such an impression on him that he abandoned his plans to become a lawyer and opened a poetry book shop where he sold Bukowski chapbooks.

Flattered by the attention, Bukowski began hanging out at Earth Books, where he cut a very different figure from Richmond and his hippy friends. Bukowski's hair was very short and slicked back. His nose was red with broken veins. He wore short-sleeve button-down shirts, the neck open to reveal a triangle of white T-shirt. On his feet were brown or black lace-up shoes, 'post office shoes' as Richmond called them, and he wore a shapeless sports jacket if it were cold.

He was usually toting a brown paper bag containing two six-packs of beer. Everybody else was smoking dope and dropping acid, which didn't impress Bukowski at all. 'Bukowski thought it was so phony,' says Richmond. 'Timothy Leary and the hippies. He was right in a way.'

In a letter to Richmond, Bukowski wrote: 'LSD, yeah, the big parade – everybody's doin' it now. Take LSD, then you are a poet, an intellectual. What a sick mob. I am building a machine gun in my closet now to take out as many of them as I can before they get me.'

The hippies who drifted into the store, off Ocean Park Boulevard, generally liked Bukowski's work. But if they had read his latest chapbook, *The Genius of The Crowd*, they would have seen that, although he was against many of the conventions of society, he was not for the counter-culture either:

> . . . The Best At Murder Are Those
> Who Preach Against It
> AND The Best At Hate Are Those
> Who Preach LOVE
> AND THE BEST AT WAR
> FINALLY ARE THOSE WHO PREACH
> PEACE

Richmond was inspired to publish a selection of poems by Bukowski, and himself, in a radical new magazine which he called *The Earth Rose*. The page one headline read:

> **FUCK**
> **HATE**

This was followed by a sub-heading:

> **Whereby, on this day we able minded creators do hereby tell you, the Establishment: FUCK YOU IN THE MOUTH. WE'VE HEARD ENOUGH OF YOUR BULLSHIT.**

The cops arrested Richmond for obscenity, and seized his stock, including many of Bukowski's books.

After taking his first acid trip in 1962, John Bryan quit his job with the Hearst Corporation in San Francisco and moved to LA to spread the good news about LSD. 'We were into acid evangelism. We thought we could save the world by getting everybody high on psychedelics,' he says. 'For a while we almost did it.' He rented a house in Hollywood and started printing a magazine called *Notes from Underground* which provided formulas for making LSD.

Bukowski contributed poems to Bryan's magazine and, through this association, met other poets and publishers who were deeply into drugs, like the writer John Thomas. Bukowski got into the habit of dropping by Thomas' house after finishing his graveyard shift and would sit up half the night talking about his problems at the post office, and his hassles with FrancEyE, while Thomas guzzled amphetamines which he was addicted to.

Bukowski said FrancEyE had become swept up in the idealism of the hippies and was dragging Marina along to peace marches and other protest events which he believed she was far too young for. He worried Marina might get hurt. He was also exasperated by FrancEyE's inability to manage her money, finding her so irritating he could no longer bring himself to use her name, referring to her laconically as 'the mother of my child'. He also complained at length about not getting laid.

In interviews he gave later in life, Bukowski denounced drugs in general, and marijuana in particular, but John Thomas and Steve Richmond remember Bukowski taking a variety of drugs in the late 1960s, including a lot of marijuana. John Thomas gave Bukowski handfuls of uppers and downers from the bowl of pills he kept on his coffee table, when Bukowski came over after work. He also gave Bukowski yage and his only LSD trip.

'What is this stuff?' asked Bukowski after taking the acid.

'What's the matter?' asked Thomas.

'I've got a lump of ice in my stomach the size of a bowling ball, and it's sort of jiggling around down there,' Bukowski replied. 'But the man who can rule his stomach can rule the world!'

John Bryan's magazine, *Notes from Underground*, was short-lived and, after working for a while as managing editor of the *LA Free Press*, he decided to launch a newspaper. *Open City* would feature radical writing and politics in the tradition of the little magazines, but by selling through vending machines and news

stands he hoped to reach many more readers. He asked Bukowski
to write a weekly column.

'Let's call it "Notes of a Dirty Old Man",' he said. 'You are a
dirty old man, aren't you?'

Bukowski liked to ridicule Bryan and the other journalists who
worked on the paper as a bunch of 'scummy Commie hippy shits',
but the column ran for almost two years and made him more
famous than anything he had done so far, even if many of his
friends felt the moniker 'dirty old man' did him an injustice. *Open
City* contributor Jack Micheline wrote in his prose poem, 'Long
After Midnight': 'He is not a DIRTY OLD MAN; he has never
been a DIRTY OLD MAN. He is an American postage stamp.'

The newspaper was a quintessential hippy production, actually
sold by hippies on Sunset Strip, and featured articles about new
music and psychedelic drugs. Bukowski attended staff meetings
where the editorial content and agitprop were earnestly discussed,
but he was unimpressed by what he heard. 'The crew did not seem
very fiery. Strangely calm and dead and well-fed for their ages.
Sitting around making little flip anti-war jokes, or jokes about pot.
Everybody understood the jokes but me. Run a pig for president.
What the fuck was that? It excited them. It bored me.' His world
view was shaped by the problems of everyday life, as a postal clerk
trying to make the rent; he was not at all interested in Vietnam, or
pop music, or tie-dyed T-shirts, or the Civil Rights movement. If
he said anything about politics, likely as not it was a provocative
remark about what a fine fellow Adolf Hitler had been. 'If he
had any politics, he was a fucking fascist,' says Bryan, who took
the bait.

Bukowski wrote his column using slap-dash syntax and irregu-
lar spelling. He rarely bothered to capitalize letters or use conventional punctuation. But the apparent sloppiness was a stylistic
experiment and, despite appearances, he was fairly serious about
what he was doing. He wrote in the first person using his real
name and, initially, he used his past life as subject matter: the
death and funeral of his father, the Philadelphia barfly years,
starving for his art in the shack in Atlanta, and marriage to 'the
Texan heiress'. By the summer of 1967, he'd exhausted his stock
of anecdotes and began inventing sex stories, which he delighted in

Bukowski's maternal grandparents Nanatte and Wilhelm Fett (seated) celebrate their golden wedding anniversary with family and friends in Andernach, Germany, in 1943. *(courtesy of Karl Fett)*

Charles Bukowski's paternal grandparents Emilie and Leonard Bukowski at their home in Pasadena, California.
(courtesy of Katherine Wood)

Bukowski's parents lived in an apartment in this building in Andernach, Germany, when they were first married and Bukowski was born here on 16 Aug, 1920. The window on the second floor under the cross is the room in which he was born.
(picture taken by Howard Sounes)

COMING TO AMERICA

This is the postcard Bukowski's mother sent to her parents from the docks at Bremerhaven, Germany, on 18 April, 1923, just before she and Henry Bukowski and their son sailed for America.
It shows the SS President Fillmore, the ship which took them to Baltimore. *(courtesy of Karl Fett)*

In 1924 Bukowski's mother sent this photograph of herself, her husband and their son from her mother-in law's house in Pasadena, California, to her parents in Andernach, writing that Henry had won an argument about who should hold their son for the picture.
(courtesy of Karl Fett)

The infant Bukowski looks thoroughly glum on a day out with his parents at Santa Monica beach, California. Kate Bukowski wrote to her parents in Germany that Henry wanted her to send photographs of them at the beach to prove he was showing them a good time in America. *(courtesy of Karl Fett)*

Henry and Kate's *goldschatz,* their golden boy, in his new home town of Los Angeles in the mid-1920s. *(courtesy of Karl Fett)*

The bungalow at 2122 Longwood Avenue, Los Angeles, as it was when the Bukowski family lived there in the 1930s. Bukowski was made to manicure the front lawn every Saturday and beaten if he missed a single blade. *(courtesy of Karl Fett)*

Bukowski and his father pose in the family model-T Ford in which they took trips out of Los Angeles into the orange groves of the surrounding countryside. *(courtesy of Karl Fett)*

When he was 16, suffering from terrible acne and attending Mount Vernon Junior High School, Bukowski posed for a class photograph. He is in the front row, fifth from the left with his arms crossed. The first boy in the front row, wearing an open-neck white shirt and grey trousers, is Bukowski's friend William 'Baldy' Mullinax. *(courtesy of Mount Vernon Junior High School)*

Bukowski (centre) looks older than 18 in his Los Angeles High School year book photograph for the graduating class of summer, 1939. *(courtesy of Los Angeles High School)*

Sgt Henry Charles Bukowski Jnr in his ROTC uniform along with school friends; *from left to right;* Bloomer, Cavanaugh and Corbeil *(courtesy of Los Angeles High School)*

Jane Cooney Baker, the great love of Bukowski's life who inspired so much of his best work. This is the first photograph of Jane ever published. It was taken for her High School year book in Roswell, New Mexico, in 1927 when she was 17 years old. *(courtesy of Roswell High School)*

Taken at his parents' Longwood Avenue home in July, 1947, this photograph shows a remarkably well-groomed Charles Bukowski, aged 27, at a time in his life when he later claimed to have been living as a bum. *(courtesy of Karl Fett)*

A rare glimpse of Bukowski, relaxing with his 'magic dog', taken in the early 1950s when he was living with Jane Cooney Baker. On the back of the picture Bukowski wrote this caption: '... long ago on a deserted beach with a fine and beautiful dog.' Note: the marks on the picture are from the pressure of Bukowski's handwriting on the back. *(courtesy of Special Collections, The University of Arizona Library)*

This building at 603 N. 17th Street, Philadelphia, was a rooming house where Bukowski lived when he was in the city during his ten year drunk. *(picture taken by Brenda Galloway for Howard Sounes)*

Bukowski lived with Jane at this apartment court at 268 S. Coronado Street in downtown Los Angeles. *(picture taken by Howard Sounes)*

Barbara Frye's physical deformity is clear in this photograph taken at the Frye Ranch in Wheeler, Texas, in 1954 - the year before she met and married Bukowski. She was born with two vertebra missing from her neck giving the impression she was permanently hunching her shoulders. *(courtesy of Leah Belle Wilson)*

Bukowski and his first wife, Barbara Frye, pose together in December, 1956, just over a year after they married. This is the first picture of the couple ever to be published. *(courtesy of Leah Belle Wilson)*

The former premises of The Phillips Hotel in Hollywood. Jane Cooney Baker lived in one of the rooms facing onto Vermont Avenue and died a couple of days after suffering a hemorrhage here in 1962.
(picture taken by Howard Sounes)

Bukowski at the N. Mariposa rooming house in the early 1960s. Note the acne scars on his face and the way the wallpaper behind his left elbow is held together with sticky tape.
(courtesy of Special Collections, The University of Arizona Library)

The rooming house at 1623 N. Mariposa Avenue, Los Angeles, where Bukowski moved in 1958 after he split with his first wife and where he wrote some of his best early work. *(picture taken by Howard Sounes)*

Working in his room at N. Mariposa on the typing table his parents bought for him when he was a teenager. Copies of the Webbs' *Outsider* magazine are on the table beside the typewriter. *(courtesy of 'Gypsy Lou' Webb)*

The bungalow on De Longpre Avenue in East Hollywood where Bukowski moved in 1964 with FrancEyE, 'the mother of my child'. *(picture taken by Howard Sounes)*

Bukowski's landlords at De Longpre Avenue: Francis Crotty (left with hat) and Grace Crotty (middle with cat). On the right holding the pumpkin is neighbor and friend, Sina Taylor. *(courtesy of Sina Taylor)*

Bukowski in his crummy bungalow on De Longpre Avenue, East Hollywood. *(courtesy of Liza Williams)*

FrancEyE and Bukowski were man and wife in all but name and she was the mother of his only child. Here FrancEyE is seen with their daughter, Marina, who was born in 1964. They all lived together at De Longpre Avenue. *(courtesy of FrancEyE)*

The Terminal Annex building in downtown LA where Bukowski worked for many years as a mail clerk and which he described so vividly in his seminal novel, *Post Office. (picture taken by Howard Sounes)*

Writer and small press publisher Douglas Blazek who published early breakthrough prose work by Bukowski in *Ole* magazine. *(courtesy of Douglas Blazek)*

Writer Jory Sherman, a friend of Bukowski's when he lived at N. Mariposa Avenue. *(courtesy of Jory Sherman/photo credit: J. Jones)*

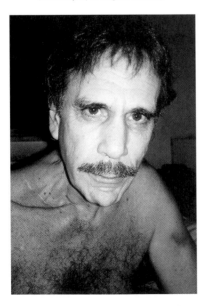

Poet Steve Richmond, a close friend for many years who thought Bukowski's attitude to drugs hypocritical. *(picture taken by Howard Sounes)*

John Bennett, small press publisher and friend of Bukowski's. *(courtesy of John Bennett/photo credit: Jane Orleman)*

The writer and academic John William Corrington (far right) who had a long and warm correspondence with Bukowski until they met at the home of Jon and 'Gypsy Lou' Webb in New Orleans and fell out. On the left is Miller Williams who was also at the meeting. *(courtesy of Joyce Corrington)*

Beat poet and gay writer Harold Norse who controversially claims Bukowski flashed his penis at him and asked to see Norse's penis in return. *(picture taken by Howard Sounes)*

German-born photographer Michael Montfort who accompanied Linda Lee and Bukowski on their first trip to Europe in 1978. *(picture taken by Howard Sounes)*

Bukowski with his publisher and friend Jon Webb.
(courtesy of 'Gypsy Lou' Webb)

Bukowski and 'Gypsy Lou' Webb at Bukowski's
bungalow in Hollywood in August, 1964, when
the Webbs came to check him out.
(courtesy of 'Gypsy Lou' Webb)

Bukowski wanted to be photographed in a tough guy pose for his 1969 book, *The Days Run Away Like
Wild Horses Over the Hills*, so photographer friend Sam Cherry took this picture of Bukowski clinging onto
a boxcar in downtown LA. Bukowski was so fat and lacking in agility he almost fell off.
(courtesy of Sam Cherry)

reading to an elderly woman who lived next door before handing in his copy.

It was exciting seeing his stuff in print every week. 'Think of it yourself: absolute freedom to write anything you please,' he wrote of the experience, 'sit down with a beer and hit the typer on a Friday or a Saturday or a Sunday and by Wednesday the thing is all over the city.'

There was a constant need for new story ideas, and Bukowski wasn't choosy about where he got his material from, even when it meant upsetting friends. That summer he went to visit Jon and Gypsy Lou Webb at their new home in Tucson, Arizona, with a vague idea they would record some of his poems. The Webbs had arranged for Bukowski to stay rent-free in a cottage on the nearby university campus, but he was in a cantankerous mood and bitched about the searing desert heat, reluctant to leave the cottage at all during the day. The real reason for his bad humor was probably jealousy. The Webbs were engrossed in printing a Henry Miller book, *Order and Chaos Chez Hans Reichel*, rather than another Bukowski project. When Jon Webb suggested Bukowski write a piece for the next issue of *The Outsider*, attacking the drug culture, he whimsically decided to defend the hippies and refused. The recording project came to nothing and, when he got back to LA, Bukowski wrote a spiteful column about his friends, referring to Jon Webb sarcastically as 'the great editor'. Mischievously, he mailed a copy to a reporter at the *Tucson Daily Citizen*.

At one time or another, Bukowski managed to upset almost everybody who was close to him. Another victim was Douglas Blazek, whom he had been corresponding with since 1964. Blazek worshipped Bukowski and was not shy of expressing his devotion. 'I looked up to Bukowski as something of a god,' he says. Passing through LA in the fall of 1967, he telephoned asking if it would be convenient to visit, and Bukowski called in sick to the post office so they would have plenty of time together.

But when they met, it seemed to Blazek that the friendship built up over the years was being sloughed off by Bukowski. 'He saw me as, I would think, an ordinary person, nothing special, nothing distinguished,' says Blazek, 'nobody who was going to do anything great in this world, or help make him great.'

Blazek formulated a theory about why Bukowski the correspondent was so different from Bukowski in the flesh. When he wrote his wonderful letters with the jokes, poems and funny drawings he often included, so intimate and revealing, he could allow himself to be vulnerable because he was at a safe distance. His antagonism and aggression came to the fore when he met people face to face. 'As much as he wanted a camaraderie, he wanted to be friends, he wanted to be open, he wanted to share love, he couldn't allow himself that luxury having been hurt so much in the past,' says Blazek. 'This made him rather mean-spirited as an individual.'

John Martin managed to stay friends with Bukowski, when so many failed, partly because he didn't drink with him and therefore wasn't around when Bukowski became boorish, but mostly because he was constantly thinking of new ways to earn money for Bukowski on what were essentially marginal publications.

He knew Bukowski liked to draw and was shrewd enough to realize original artwork could make their little books more valuable so he bought Bukowski art materials and got him to make simple abstract illustrations – he could do one every ten minutes – which were pasted into limited editions of the chapbooks, or sold separately. They proved popular with collectors and Martin kept Bukowski happy by paying a ten per cent royalty in advance for everything they did. Bukowski had nothing but praise for his new publisher. He even bragged that Martin let him pinch his beautiful wife, Barbara.

In fact, Barbara Martin remembers how reticent the dirty old man was when she met him. 'When we would talk on the phone he would be flirtatious, in a very nice way, but when we first met he didn't really talk to me much.'

The first Bukowski book published by Black Sparrow Press was *At Terror Street and Agony Way*. Although little more than a glorified chapbook, it included good new work like 'traffic ticket' which describes Bukowski's hatred of his job. In this, and other work, he subverts the popular perception of Los Angeles as a place of endless sunshine, just as he subverted the image of Hollywood as being glamorous, choosing to describe wintry days when LA is dull and cold:

I walked off the job again
and the police stopped me
for running a red light at Serrano Ave.
my mind was rather gone
and I stood in a patch of leaves
ankle deep
and kept my head turned
so they couldn't smell the liquor
too much
and I took the ticket and went to my room
and got a good symphony on the radio,
one of the Russians or Germans,
one of the dark tough boys
but still I felt lonely and cold
and kept lighting cigarettes
and I turned on the heater
and then down on the floor
I saw a magazine with my photo
on the cover*
and I walked over and picked it up
but it wasn't me
because yesterday is gone
and today is only catsup.

The little Black Sparrow books and the *Open City* column were turning him into a minor local celebrity and there were people at the post office who resented this. They misunderstood Bukowski's cool as meaning he didn't care about the job, because he was getting to be such a big shot. Even friends like Johnny Moore were confused. 'I thought he had plenty of money,' he says. 'It was the way he used to carry himself, the way he used to talk.'

Bukowski was confronted on the steps of the building one day by a mail clerk who angrily exclaimed he was full of shit.

'What do you mean?'

'I saw that magazine.'

* The third issue of *The Outsider* magazine, published in the spring of 1963, had Bukowski's face in the cover.

'What magazine?'

'I dunno the name of it, but I saw it, about you being a poet. What a bunch of bullshit! And your photo, with the little beard.' Bukowski said he didn't know what he was talking about.

'You knows, you knows what I talking about. Don't bullshit me.'

It turned out the clerk had been in a barber shop and picked up a copy of *Dare*, a magazine which had paid Bukowski $50 for one of his poems. He'd only agreed to have his picture published because he needed to pay the child support.

Somebody tipped off the post office that Bukowski was writing 'dirty stories' for a 'hippy paper', and that he was not married to the mother of his child. It was a situation management thought might bring the post office into disrepute and a spy was sent to De Longpre Avenue to snoop round for information about FrancEyE, and about Bukowski's political interests. Francis Crotty told the spy to stop hassling ordinary people, and sent him away saying Bukowski 'wasn't no Commie'.

Bukowski was called in to see the assistant director of personnel and another manager. Spread in front of them were copies of *Open City*, which was all the evidence they had against him. They were concerned about a story about sodomy* and a not altogether complimentary column about the post office.

'Have you ever had any books published?' he was asked.

'Yes.'

'How many?'

'I don't know, four, five, six, seven . . . I don't know.'

'How much did you *pay* these people to publish your work?' It was clear they thought he had got above himself. They said they were considering charging him with Conduct Unbecoming a Postal Employee. Bukowski reminded them of his constitutional rights and they commented, wearily, that they hadn't had a case like this in years, asking if he was planning to write about the post office again. He said he didn't think so and that brought them to stalemate.

---

* The incident in the 1950s when Bukowski had anal sex with a male friend by mistake.

When he emerged from the interrogation, Bukowski bumped into his union rep, David Berger, who had come down to see what the problem was.

'Hey, Bukowski, what's up?' asked Berger.

'Nothing. They wanted me to resign, but I'd be damned if I would.'

It was because of the *Open City* column that Bukowski got to meet Neal Cassady, one of the few beat figures he admired. Cassady was the former drifter and railroad worker who had been the lover of Allen Ginsberg and, more famously, the basis of the character Dean Moriarty in Jack Kerouac's *On The Road*. In recent years he had served time in San Quentin for a drugs conviction and, upon his release, became a member of Ken Kesey's Merry Pranksters, driving the Pranksters' psychedelic bus. Bukowski admired Cassady because, apart from his ambivalent sexuality, he was a man after his own heart – someone who had worked factory jobs, been in jail and liked to drink beer and bet on the horses. So when Cassady passed through LA just after Christmas, 1967, Bukowski was pleased to meet him.

Cassady was on his way to Mexico to see friends when John Bryan offered to put him up at his house in Hollywood. As a joke, he appointed him circulation manager of *Open City*. Cassady was famous for his skill at the wheel of an automobile – it was one of the themes of *On The Road* – and he and Bryan spent two weeks dropping speed and smoking dope as they drove round LA in a black Plymouth sedan checking the vending machines were stocked with copies of the paper. One overcast winter's day they spun round to De Longpre Avenue to see Bukowski.

Cassady was forty-one, several years younger than Bukowski himself, and yet he was clearly in a bad way; hollow-eyed, thin and jittery. Bukowski later wrote a column about the meeting – 'a simpatico account of Neal' as Ginsberg notes – describing him as 'a little punchy with the action, the eternal light, but there wasn't any hatred in him'. He offered him a beer and was impressed by the way he slugged it down as if it were water.

'Have another,' said Bukowski, deciding Cassady was even crazier than he was.

When they went out to the Plymouth, Bukowski was alarmed to discover that, despite the beer, pills and dope, Cassady was still going to drive.

It was raining and he started showing off what Ginsberg describes as his 'driving genius . . . accuracy and boldness'. This consisted of driving as fast as possible on the wrong side of the road. They slid around the greasy East Hollywood streets as a storm broiled, skidding from vending machine to news stand, heading in a zig-zag across town to Bryan's Carlton Way house where they were due to have dinner. In his column, Bukowski described how they almost had a fatal collision as they approached Carlton Way. He wrote that he would always remember the coupé that came towards them as Cassady swerved through traffic, imagining it hitting them 'like a rolling steel brick thing', but decided it didn't matter as one had to die sometime.

Bryan's recollection is that Bukowski was not quite so calm. 'Bukowski had a fit,' he says. 'He started screaming, "Stop the car! Let me out!"'

'Fuck you!' shouted the pranksters from the front and, when they finally pulled to a stop, Bryan claims Bukowski had shit his pants.

Before they parted company, Bukowski told Cassady that Kerouac has written the main chapters of his life, but that maybe he would write his last one. It was sadly prophetic. A couple of weeks later they heard Cassady had died in Mexico.

Bukowski had John Bryan to thank for the book of *Notes of a Dirty Old Man*. Bryan negotiated a $1,000 advance from Essex House, 'the very finest in adult reading by the most provocative modern writers', or 'porny' publishers as Bukowski called them, and he was grateful enough to promise Bryan ten per cent of the money. Despite the book deal, all was not well between Bukowski and 'the beaded and the bearded', as he called the staff of *Open City*, partly because there was such a cultural and generation gap between them.

'It was a period of great agitation and experimentation and Bukowski didn't really fit in very well, coming from an earlier period,' says Bryan.

The association came unstuck after Bryan asked Bukowski to edit a literary supplement. Bukowski chose to use an explicit short story by Jack Micheline about the sexual antics of an underage girl. The story, *Skinny Dynamite*, appeared in the seventieth issue of *Open City*, in September, 1968, and because of it Bryan was arrested on obscenity charges. Micheline protested that his story was simply about a girl who likes to fuck and got letters of support from Bukowski, Allen Ginsberg, Hubert Selby Jnr and Norman Mailer. The case dragged on into 1969 and, although the charges were eventually dropped, it was the beginning of the end for *Open City* which folded shortly before its second anniversary.

To add insult to injury, Bukowski wrote a satirical short story, *The Birth, Life and Death of an Underground Newspaper,* about a paper he called *Open Pussy*, and the pretensions of its editor. There were particularly crude comments about the editors's wife. The story had obvious parallels with *Open City* and, when it was published in *Evergreen* magazine, it helped trash another friendship.

'Bukowski was very talented,' says Bryan, 'but he was really an asshole.' He had a new nickname for his former friend: Bullshitski.

One of Bukowski's main objections to the beat writers was that so many were homosexual. 'He would say, you go from one coffee shop to another and there are poets hiding out in the bathroom sucking on each other's ass,' says Jack Micheline. 'He didn't like Ginsberg. He didn't like fags.' But he overcame his prejudice in the case of the poet Harold Norse, author of *Beat Hotel* and other books. Norse was introduced to Bukowski's work while living in Paris. 'I thought it was marvelous,' he says. 'I sent him something of mine and, from then on, it was a very close correspondence, very warm indeed. He called me Prince Hal, Prince of Poets.'

By 1967, Norse had moved to London where he knew Nikos Stangos, poetry editor with Penguin books. Stangos edited the Penguin Modern Poets series, which had already published poets as diverse as Kinglsey Amis, Allen Ginsberg and Stevie Smith, and was on the look-out for new writers. 'My editorial brief, which was my own decision, was that the series should be very eclectic and should not ignore any strong, interesting, avant-garde or experimental work,' he says. He decided Norse should be the central figure in the thirteenth book in the series, each of which featured three writers, and Norse suggested that the other poets should be American surrealist Philip Lamantia and his new pen friend Bukowski. Stangos wrote to Bukowski from London asking if he was interested, and Bukowski replied that it would be an honor to be included with Harold Norse whom he went so far as to describe as a 'Godhead'.

When Norse returned to the United States in 1968, Bukowski called him regularly on the telephone to ask when the book was coming out and to talk about how unhappy he was at work.

'It's super triple hell, baby,' he'd say. 'The post office is nailing me to the cross.'

Norse suggested they meet for a drink at his place in Venice Beach and, one night during a rain storm, Bukowski drove over.

Norse's first impression was of, 'a big hunchback with ravaged, pockmarked face, decayed nicotine-stained teeth, and pain-filled green eyes,' as he wrote in *Memoirs of a Bastard Angel*. 'Flat brown hair seemed pasted to an oversized skull – hips broader than shoulders, hands grotesquely small and soft. A beer gut sagged over his belt. He wore a white shirt, baggy pants, an ill-fitting suit, the kind convicts receive when released from prison. He looked like one, down and out.'

Bukowski was charming, at first, calling his friend 'Prince Hal' and extravagantly praised his poetry until Norse told him to knock it off. After a few drinks they decided to record their conversation on Norse's reel-to-reel, thinking maybe they could sell the tape to a book dealer. Bukowski spoke first.

'I'm sitting here with Hal Norse,' he said, 'a damn good writer . . . But I'm Charles Bukowski! . . . Number one!'

'What are you doing?' asked Norse, switching off the machine.

'I'm only having a bit of fun, Hal,' Bukowski laughed. 'You know I think you're the best. Turn it on.'

They tried again.

'This is Charles Bukowski. I'm at Hal Norse's pad. He thinks he's a writer, but don't they all? I'm the king!'

That was the end of the tape-recording idea.

They drank until 3.00 a.m. when Norse went to bed leaving Bukowski on the sofa. A couple of hours later, when Norse went to the toilet, he saw Bukowski sitting up, flashes of lightning illuminating his face as the rain lashed the windows. He was talking and chuckling to himself, and yelled out, as if demented: 'Who are you anyway, you blond kid, you?'

It was companionable having someone of his own age to talk to, when most of his friends were so much younger, and Bukowski began to spend a lot of time hanging out with Norse. After one day together, he wrote: 'You know, as you walked along the beach with me back to my car, well, I don't wanna sound like a god-damn romantic, but I got a real feeling of human warmth for a change.'

There was another side to Bukowski's character, as Norse was to discover. The good Bukowski was 'sort of sad and not very aggressive or arrogant', quick to praise the work of others and polite and courteous to strangers. But when he was drinking, a more troublesome Bukowski emerged: an egocentric braggart who picked fights and was not above antagonizing Norse with talk of 'faaaaags', a word he'd drag out in a sneering way, saying at least Norse was not one of those 'swishy faaaaags'. Why, he was almost manly, like Bukowski himself. The homophobia irritated Norse and he believes it may have been a cover for Bukowski being bisexual.

Norse claims that when Bukowski was drunk he sometimes got his cock out and asked to see Norse's cock. This did not appear to be meant as a joke. 'He was fascinated to see other men's cocks. It's a sexual thing,' says Norse. 'You can't get away from that.' There was no physical contact, no move by Bukowski to have contact, or sign from Norse he would welcome it. In fact, Norse says he was revolted by the notion of sex with his friend. 'I was having sex with the most beautiful youths in California and here's this horrible-looking man with a purple pitted face, like the Phantom of the Opera, and his belly falling like blubber over his belt. If he sat down, his paunch went halfway down to his knees,' he says. 'I would blow my brains out if I ever had to touch Bukowski sexually.'

There is little doubt Bukowski would have been horrified to be considered anything other than entirely heterosexual. 'He would have punched you about that,' says Norse, 'which proves he was trying to keep something down.' Friends like Jack Micheline are outraged by the suggestion Bukowski might have been bisexual, saying Norse's recollections are tinged by jealousy and bitterness. It is true Norse later fell out with Bukowski, and was already slightly cross he had plagiarized one of his letters for use in *Notes of a Dirty Old Man*, but his is not the only evidence Bukowski might have been bisexual.

There was the incident at his apartment in the early 1950s when he had anal sex with a male friend, apparently by some extraordinary mistake. And Sam Cherry's son, Neeli Cherkovski, recalls an occasion when Bukowski was drunk and asked if he wanted to get into bed with him. Nothing happened and in the morning Bukowski made a joke of it.

'Remember I came up to you and I asked, "You wanna go to bed with me?"'

'Yeah,' said Cherkovski.

'I thought you were some woman I knew whose name was Nelly,' said Bukowski, laughing.

'Did Nelly have a moustache?'

It is also true that Bukowski enjoyed saying and doing out-rageous things to shock and it is entirely possible he was teasing Cherkovski and Norse, both of whom are homosexual. Further-more, there is ample evidence Bukowski was enthusiastically heterosexual when he had the opportunity, and was sober enough to perform.

As the '60s came to an end, even the Beatles picked up on Bukowski. Paul McCartney had become interested in new writing and asked his friend Barry Miles to suggest poets whom The Beatles could record. Miles came up with a list that included Bukowski and, although McCartney had never read his work, he approved the suggestion. 'He was just very interested in the avant-garde, very open-minded about these things and prepared to take my word for it if I said this guy was OK,' says Miles who was appointed manager of Zapple, the spoken word section of Apple Corporation, and flew out to LA to make the recordings.

The Zapple deal was set up via John Martin, who was assuming the additional responsibilities of being Bukowski's agent, but when it came to cutting the record Bukowski was too shy to go into the studio at Capitol Records in Hollywood. 'He didn't want anybody to watch him because he hadn't done any reading,' says Miles. So he took a reel-to-reel tape machine over to De Longpre where he found Bukowski with what looked like an old-time hooker, slowly putting her stockings back on.

He gave Bukowski the tape machine and a box of twelve blank tapes, and a couple of days later Bukowski settled down on his sofa, opened a beer and started recording. He read more than fifty poems, pausing to give a commentary on the state of his life, and to gripe about Francis Crotty who was noisily working on a car outside the window. All the tapes were full by the time Miles returned a week later. In fact, Bukowski had enjoyed himself so much he had tried to record on both sides, not realizing professional tape only goes one way, and had erased half his work. The highlight was an eight-minute rendition of 'fire station' which, in Miles' opinion, showed a natural talent for dramatic reading. 'He builds it and reads it just brilliantly.'

At the end of the decade, Bukowski had the Zapple record to look forward to*, the Penguin Modern Poets book coming out in Britain and *Notes of a Dirty Old Man* out in paperback in the United States. A visitor from Germany, Carl Weissner, was even talking about translating his stories for publication in Europe. A small press in Berkeley had brought out a new chapbook, *Poems Written Before Jumping Out of an 8 Storey Window*, and John Martin was compiling another poetry anthology. Bukowski still found time to launch his own little magazine, an alternative to what he saw as the self-conscious cleverness of the Black Mountain School. He loathed the Black Mountain poets, even though John Martin was an admirer and published some of their work.

'He would get a little jealous of somebody like Robert Creeley, who he didn't understand, and he had some sharp things to say (about him),' says Martin. 'He was threatened by them. He didn't

---

* Due to the subsequent break-up of the Beatles, and the folding of Zapple, the recording was not released until 1997 when it appeared on CD.

understand what they were doing and maybe what they were doing was the right way and what he was doing was silly. Bukowski didn't realize that there were different types of poetry.'

He wanted to call his magazine *Laugh Literary and Man the Fucking Guns*, but co-editor Neeli Cherkovski persuaded him to change 'fucking' to 'humping'. The cover carried a manifesto written by Bukowski: 'In disgust with poetry Chicago, with the dull dumpling pattycake safe Creeleys, Olsons, Dickeys, Merwins, Nemerovs and Merediths – this is issue one volume one of *Laugh Literary and Man the Humping Guns*.'

Bukowski was no better dealing with submissions than he had been back in the 1950s, when he co-edited *Harlequin* with Barbara Frye. Most of the stuff sent in was very bad and Bukowski began defacing manuscripts, scrawling insults like 'These won't do, baby' or 'Shove it, man.' He poured beer over poems he didn't like, or dipped them in egg, before mailing the rejected work back to the authors.

The new book John Martin had been working on was *The Days Run Away Like Wild Horses Over the Hills*. It was a retrospective of poems that had first appeared in chapbooks and little magazines, with an emphasis on the grief poems written after Jane died, and was one of the milestone books of Bukowski's career. It came out in a beautiful edition with a simple but striking jacket devised by Barbara Martin. There was no blurb on the back, no quotes from other writers saying what a brilliant fellow Bukowski was, just the ten words of the title running down the cover, like a poem.

'Bukowski's titles are wonderful,' Barbara says. 'They make the cover. I always look at his title and I don't have to do any more.'

Inside was a photograph of Bukowski as a grim-faced hobo, riding a box car. It looked authentic, but had been carefully posed because he wanted to appear as someone who had lived the hard times he wrote about. Sam Cherry, who really had been a hobo, took Bukowski down to the railroad yard behind Union Station and told him to climb up into a derelict wagon so he could get the shot. The ladder was several feet above the ground and Bukowski made a great performance of trying to get onto the car, even though he'd told Cherry he'd ridden box cars many times. Cherry noticed the awkward way Bukowski grasped the bars, and decided he had never ridden a boxcar in his life. 'It was not the professional way to get on a train,' he says. 'He didn't know what he was doing.' Bukowski finally managed to pull himself up, with Cherry and his son pushing from below, and stayed there just long enough for the photograph.

'Hold me up, guys, for Christ's sake!' he cried. 'It's been a long time since I rode the freights.'

He had promised Harold Norse that he would dedicate the book to him, as thanks for getting him involved in the Penguin deal, but changed his mind at the last minute.

'It's dedicated to the woman that died that I loved,' he said when he gave Norse a first edition. Indeed Norse saw it was dedicated to Jane. 'I was going to dedicate it to you, as I promised . . .' Bukowski went on, watching Norse's reaction.

'Oh, why didn't you?'

'Well, you know, my publisher John Martin, he looked at it and said, "What do you want to dedicate it to Harold Norse for? People might think you are *friends*."'

'Well aren't we?' he asked.

'Of course we are, Hal, you know that.' It was some time before the coin dropped and, when it did, Norse was furious. They continued to see each other occasionally, and talked on the telephone now and then, but he never really forgave the insult and Bukowski had managed to upset yet another friend who had been good to him, and who had helped his career in a significant way.

With so much going on, Bukowski desperately wanted to leave the post office so he could devote himself to his writing. He was forty-nine and the job was also grinding him down physically. Sticking mail for almost twelve years had given him chronic back and shoulder pains. But when he tried taking time off to attend to his literary work, the post office let him know he couldn't have any leeway. They warned him for absenteeism in the April and May of 1969. In June, Bukowski wrote to his friend, John Bennett, that the stress of trying to juggle his writing and his job was making him mentally and physically sick. In August he was briefly suspended without pay for absenteeism, and he was absent without leave on various dates through September, October and November.

It was the end of the line, and he knew it, as he told Harold

Norse. 'He was moaning and whining most of the time in a very sad and lugubrious way, not for sympathy, just feeling, "This is the end, what can I do?"' says Norse. 'The post office would have killed him if he hadn't taken the plunge.'

POST OFFICE

One of the most famous stories about Bukowski's career is that he became a successful writer after bravely quitting the post office, at the age of forty-nine, with only the promise of a small monthly pay check from John Martin to keep him from Skid Row.

The truth, as revealed in his post office file, was rather different. Bukowski did not leave the post office voluntarily; he was forced into quitting after they wrote to him, in the late fall of 1969, saying he was about to be dismissed for absenteeism. He could try and appeal, but the result was a foregone conclusion. He had taken too much time off work to do his writing, and they were sick of him. Bukowski did not tell John Martin about this letter, however, when he went to him with a proposition.

'If you get me out of the post office, I'll write more books than you can publish,' he said.

John Martin began to consider whether he could afford to pay Bukowski a small salary, against royalties, to cover his living expenses so he could write. They worked out that he needed $35 for his rent, $20 for groceries, $5 for gas, $15 for beer and cigarettes, $10 to pay the telephone bill and $15 for Marina's child support. It came to exactly $100 a month. That was a quarter of John Martin's monthly income, and he had a wife and child to support, so it was a serious undertaking. Bukowski might simply have got drunk with the money, and not produced anything worthwhile. But he had faith in him.

'OK, I'll take a chance – I'll give you $100 a month, for life, guaranteed no matter what happens,' he said, 'if you quit the post office to write full time.'

There was no written contract, just a gentleman's agreement. It was enough for Bukowski to go to the post office and resign his job before they fired him.

The deal with Martin was not the only money Bukowski had to cushion his freelance writing career. A thrifty man, he had built up a savings account of several thousand dollars, the basis of which was money left by his father. He had more money coming to him from the sale of his papers to the University of California at Santa Barbara, a deal set up by John Martin. He also had $3000 in his pension fund, which he could draw out if he was in trouble. He had no outstanding debts, and spent very little on himself. In fact, Bukowski had a reputation among his friends as being tight with a buck. 'He was like a fucking conservative German, like a conservative banker,' says Steve Richmond. 'He paid every bill on time and dreaded debt. It scared the shit out of him.'

He had always refused requests to give public readings in the past, simply because the idea terrified him, but now every dollar counted. When his friend Peter Edler invited him to read at The Bridge, a book store off Hollywood Boulevard, Bukowski said yes. The date was set as Friday 19 December, 1969, and in the hours before his appearance, Bukowski worked himself into in a terrible state of nerves.

'What am I going to do? I just don't know how to do this,' he told friends.

Far from the handful of people they expected, a couple of hundred fans showed up on the night. The place was packed. Bukowski was lit by a spotlight, sitting in an easy chair on stage with the galley proofs of *The Days Run Away Like Wild Horses Over the Hills*. 'He is sitting there like a grandfather,' remembers Steve Richmond, one of many friends who came to watch. 'Nice scene – everybody so close to him. It was a magic thing.'

Although extremely nervous, he read fluently, choosing his best work, and the audience stayed with him. As his confidence grew he smiled, drank beer from a bottle and even extemporized a poem, 'Carter to resign?', from an article in a daily newspaper.

Richmond notes how different the evening was compared with the rambunctious readings Bukowski gave later in his career, when poet and audience traded insults. 'It was so perfect, so right, everybody believed in him and was feeling for him, not in a pitying way, and feeling his pain when there was pain.'

The evening was such a success, Peter Edler invited Bukowski back the next night to do it all over again.

At the end of his final graveyard shift, a few days later, Bukowski wished everyone at the post office such a casual goodbye the clerks thought he was just going for the night. That was fine by Bukowski, who didn't want a fuss. He drove home via Ned's, where he bought beer, and got royally drunk. He stayed that way for several days, completely disorientated by the sudden rush of freedom. 'After living in the cage I had taken the opening and flown out – like a shot into the heavens,' he wrote.

Now, as he rolled free of his terrible job, there was nothing to do at 6.30 p.m. each day but call up friends to come and get drunk with him, and he had a party at the bungalow through the end of December, 1969, until New Year's Eve when he finally threw his guests out, locked the door, and pulled down the shades so he could sleep.

Two days later, on the afternoon of 2 January, 1970, Bukowski sat down at his Royal typewriter and started his first novel: 'It all began as a mistake.'

He stopped, struck out the word 'all' and returned the carriage.

It began as a mistake.
    It was Christmas season and I learned from the drunk up the hill, who did the trick every Christmas, that they would hire damned near anybody, and so there I went and the next thing you knew I had this leather sack on my back and was hiking around at my leisure. What a job, I thought. Soft!

That was 1950, when he was shacked with Jane and working downtown as a temporary mail carrier. He remembered the lonely women he delivered to, the ones whose husbands were at work, others whose husbands had not come back from the war. Crazy bitches some of them, but what bodies they had. He would put some sex in this book, for laughs. Writing *Notes of a Dirty Old Man* had taught him sex sold.

> I think it was my second day as a Christmas temp that this big woman came out and walked around with me as I delivered letters. What I mean by big was that her ass was big and her tits were big and that she was big in all the right places.

He worked at the novel day and night over the next three weeks, hardly leaving the bungalow as he reviewed his past life through the foil of Henry Chinaski: the death of Jane, changing her name to Betty; his marriage to Barbara Frye and their trip to Texas; buying the '57 Plymouth new, the same '57 Plymouth that sat outside now, rust spots around the door sills, dead leaves on the windscreen. He described the tyrannical supervisor when he was a substitute carrier; the day he tried to deliver mail during a deluge; the endless scheme tests he had to take to keep his job; and the events of the past few months, culminating in his quitting to write a novel.

When it was finished, he went back with a biro crossing out repetitions and tightening sentences. Then he took a fresh sheet of paper and worked on a title. His first thought was to call it *Six Pack No Scheme*. He wrote out more than twenty other names, ticking those he liked best: *12 Years Gone*, *Death of Betty* and *Postal News* were favorites, but still none was exactly right. Finally he had it, and he dialed John Martin's number in West LA.

Before he left the post office, Martin had told him that he should try and write a novel, if he thought he had one in him, because it was their best hope of making money. Bukowski hadn't said he would be starting right away.

'Come and get it,' he said when Martin answered.

'What?'

'The novel.'

'You wrote a novel?' he asked, astonished.

'Yep, all done.'

'What's the name of it?'

'*Post Office*.'

Post Office is the seminal prose work of Bukowski's career just as *The Days Run Away Like Wild Horses Over the Hills* is his seminal poetry book. It is the first, and arguably the best, of a series of five novels charting the life and times of Henry Chinaski in an innovative but accessible prose style that, in its simplicity, is remarkably similar to the poetry. The novels have proved popular with readers all around the world and, in the years following its publication, *Post Office* has been translated into fifteen languages.

It is not a perfect novel. Bukowski included material relevant to his life as autobiography, but which does not make for a cohesive work of fiction; the section about his marriage to Barbara seems out of place; and the last quarter of the book is weak. But *Post Office* is highly original and accomplished for several reasons.

It is the spare style of the prose that is most striking. From reading Fante and Hemingway, he had learned to write in a straight-forward way with lots of dialogue. From Fante, in particular, he took the idea of dividing the novel into very short chapters, or numbered sub-sections of chapters, some only half a page long. 'I was concerned with "pace",' Bukowski explained, 'a briskness of style which would not lie and which would still keep the reader awake while I was getting at what I wanted to say.'

An even greater achievement is the totally convincing way in which he writes about work. He succeeds in making the drudgery of carrying and sorting mail real and relevant to every reader who has had a job they disliked. Sorting letters is not a sexy subject for fiction, but he makes it interesting and that is a significant accomplishment because repetitive work is the stuff of so many lives. In his critical study of Bukowski, *Against the American Dream*, Russell Harrison writes: 'No contemporary American novelist has treated work as extensively or intensively as Bukowski . . . Indeed Bukowski's outstanding achievement is his depiction of work, most notably in *Post Office*.'

Finally, *Post Office* is very funny, a humor which leavens all the other ingredients. As Bukowski was fond of saying, Hemingway was a great writer but his books aren't a barrel of laughs. He made sure that Henry Chinaski's misadventures, as lover and postal worker, were recounted with a sardonic humor that saves the novel from becoming pretentious. This would be true of the best of his subsequent novels, and is undoubtedly one the main reasons for their enduring popularity.

Although he finished *Post Office* remarkably quickly, Bukowski did not reward himself with a break. Quite the contrary, he felt compelled to write almost constantly now that he was free of his job, partly because he was terrified of not earning enough to support himself. He wrote masses of poetry in the first few months, so many poems that he ran out of small magazines to send them to. And within weeks of finishing his first novel, he began planning a second which at this early stage he called *The Horseplayer*.

John Martin came by now and then to check on Bukowski and talk about their books, and sometimes they went out to eat at a local restaurant, but they spent relatively little time together and this distance helped preserve their friendship. The fact that Martin was now his primary source of income was also a strong reason for Bukowski to stay on good terms with him.

In April, a collection of Bukowski first editions came up for sale at a literary auction in New York, alongside collections of Faulkner and Hemingway. Although the Bukowski books raised only a fraction of the prices commanded by the more famous writers, they sold easily and it became apparent there was a lucrative market in collecting his books, magazine appearances, letters and manuscripts, even his child-like paintings. But Bukowski had only a limited understanding of the value of his artwork, as Martin discovered when he telephoned to arrange the collection of forty new paintings he had buyers for. When he asked what would be a good time to pick them up, Bukowski said he didn't have the paintings anymore. He didn't think they were very good so he'd put them in the bath and pissed all over them. He wasn't quite sure why, perhaps he was crazy. And he couldn't get them back, because he'd dumped the whole mess in the garbage. Martin was aghast at this, and asked if he had any idea how much money they could have made.

The success of The Bridge reading encouraged Bukowski to accept other offers to read in public, although he never overcame his nerves or his inherent distaste at clowning for an audience. Neither would he read for free, like some of his acquaintances whom he felt liked to hear the sound of their own voices. This was work and his minimum fee was $25, plus expenses.

In May, he caught a train to New Mexico for a university reading, and afterwards went to bed with a woman who had been in the audience, managing only a 'drunken half-fuck'. The next morning he flew up to Seattle, Washington, for an engagement at Bellevue Community College. It was the first plane ride of his life and he celebrated by getting wrecked.

He was woken with a hangover at 8.30 the following morning at the home of one of the academics who had invited him, and whom he had insulted the previous evening. He was so sick with nerves he threw up in the parking lot before going into the college.

They showed him into a small room where a handful of fashionably dressed students had gathered to hear him read. He noticed the girls in front crossed their legs so he couldn't see up their skirts.

'This is my fourth reading,' he told them bashfully. 'I'm pretty raw.'

He read with little expression, stumbling over his words. The funnier poems, like 'Soup', Cosmos and Tears', barely raised a chuckle and there was no applause when he concluded a poem. He tried 'Another Academy', a poem about being down and out, not an experience these kids seemed in danger of having, but something he feared he might be again:

> how can they go on, you see them
> sitting in old doorways
> with dirty stained caps and thick clothes and
> no place to go;
> heads bent down, arms on
> knees they
> wait.
> or they stand in front of the Mission
> 700 of them
> quiet as oxen
> waiting to be let into the chapel
> where they will sleep upright on hard benches

leaning against each other
snoring and
dreaming;
men
without.

. . . I heard one guy say to
another:
'John Wayne won it.'
'Won what?' said the other guy
tossing the last of his rolled cigarette into the
street.

I thought that was
rather good.

Pouring a drink of vodka and orange from his Thermos flask, he gave the students a little half-time speech that played up to his image.

'I have a friend who keeps taking me down to Skid Row,' he said. 'Since I spent the early part of my life there, I don't learn too much by going back.'

He drank himself stupid at the airport as he waited for his flight home to LA. The whole experience had been a nightmare, but with the bank account sagging he had no choice.

When he got home, his pen friend Ann Menebroker called to say she was in San Bernadino at a poetry conference and suggested they meet. They had been corresponding for years in such an affectionate way that their letters constituted a platonic love affair. 'I have grown to love that part of you that comes over the phone or through the mails,' she wrote. Now Bukowski was intrigued to find out what she was like.

When he arrived at Ann's hotel, she introduced him to a group of poets who Bukowski roundly insulted, inviting one to go outside and have a fist fight with him. Then they drove back into Los Angeles, Bukowski rapping about the characters they passed on the sidewalk, making his world come alive for Ann.

'He was exactly the way I pictured him,' she says. 'I thought he was very interesting. I fell in love with the man. I loved him for years.' Even though she did not find him physically attractive, she decided his personality transcended his looks and they went to bed that night and the following night, although Ann didn't let him have full intercourse because she was married.

Bukowski found Ann very attractive and said he knew she was married with children, up in Sacramento, but he wanted her to come and live with him in LA. He needed her; she was the first woman for a long time he had felt comfortable with. But she turned him down.

'There was a very strong pull, but I couldn't do that,' she says. 'I had a normal sane life where I was.'

With Ann gone, and hardly any money to play the horses, he found himself stuck at home all day with his poems, and his paper, and his crayons, like a child. He became increasingly frustrated and irritable. When new tenants began blocking his Plymouth with their cars, he convinced himself it would end in a fight and sent away for a $3 switchblade.

He saw the knife advertised in the classified section of one of the pornographic magazines he was buying having decided he could make extra money writing 'dirty stories'. The editor of *Fling* magazine, which specialized in photo-spreads of women with huge breasts, replied with an encouraging letter saying he would welcome submissions with a lot of kinky sex. Bukowski began churning out short stories that, while being set in his regular low-life milieu, contained scenes of bizarre and often violent sex including sado-masochism, rape, even bestiality.

He put his problems aside in August for his fiftieth birthday, which he celebrated by getting drunk for a week. Then he sobered up to the bleak realization that he was fifty, unemployed and broke.

When Carl Weissner finished translating *Notes of a Dirty Old Man* into German, he and Bukowski decided to invent a review quote by Henry Miller in a desperate attempt to boost sales. As Bukowski wrote to Weissner, rather guiltily, things were so bad they had little choice but to pull such a stunt:

I'm not too happy with the fake H(enry) M(iller) quote, and I would not tell (John) Martin about it or he'd flip – maybe.

> But if you think it will make the difference in selling 2000 or 5000, go ahead. It's best that we survive.

Because the book was published in an expensive hard cover edition, it still sold only twelve hundred copies and earned Bukowski next to nothing. He grew ever gloomier about his freelance writing career. *Post Office* had not been published yet. He was having trouble collecting money from the sex magazines, which had printed some of his dirty stories. And he had been pinning his hopes on getting a grant from The National Endowment for the Arts, working on the theory that most writers they gave money to didn't deserve it. Then they sent a letter saying he'd been turned down. It was one disappointment after another and all the time his bank balance was diminishing. At his lowest point, which came in September 1970, he considered using the $3 switchblade to cut his throat.

'I thought the life of a writer would really be the thing,' he wrote in a letter to Neeli Cherkovski, 'it's simply hell. I'm just a cheap twittering slave.'

LOVE LOVE LOVE

8

After Jane Cooney Baker, probably the greatest love of Bukowski's life was the sculptress Linda King whom he met in 1970.

Linda's first impression of Bukowski was that he was too old, too fat and too drunk to be of interest to her. She didn't even want to tell him her real name.

'It's Morona,' she said, when Peter Edler introduced her to Bukowski at De Longpre Avenue.

'OK, Morona, sit down,' said Bukowski. 'So you write poetry?'

'Yes, I like to SCREAM mine.'

She got up on the coffee table and declaimed a poem about a nervous breakdown she'd suffered. Yes, she was a looker, thought Bukowski, but wouldn't you know she'd be crazy, too? He turned up the radio so he wouldn't have to listen, and Peter Edler was so embarrassed he tried to put his hand over her mouth.

When Edler said he had to go, Linda said she'd go with him.

'Oh no, you're staying here with Hank,' he said, and left them together.

There not being much else to do, they kissed, just lightly, almost without interest.

'You're a tease,' said Bukowski.

'Yes, I'm a tease.'

He tried to kiss her again, but Linda got up to go, pausing in the doorway for one more touch before skipping out the door and along the avenue to her car. As she drove away, she told herself she was definitely not going to get involved with 'that old troll'.

Linda was a thirty-year-old brunette, raised as a Mormon on a ranch near Bryce Canyon, Utah. Shortly after getting married, she had a severe mental breakdown, receiving electro-convulsive therapy, and afterwards came to Los Angeles to try and become an actress. After her marriage ended, she settled with her two children in the suburb of Burbank, renting a place on Riverside Drive, and, when her acting ambitions came to nothing, she began concentrating on her sculpting and poetry, both of which she was good at. Hanging out at The Bridge, she met Peter Edler and got to hear about Bukowski. He sounded like an interesting man whom she'd like to meet.

After that first visit to De Longpre, Linda read more of Bukowski's work and was surprised to discover he rarely wrote about women, and what he did write betrayed some ignorance. So she sent him a poem of her own:

> come out of that hole, you old Troll
> come and frolic
> with the liberated Billies
> we'll put some flowers in your hair

Also enclosed was a letter asking if he would sit for a sculpture of his head. He replied that he would, and she was welcome to come over when she liked.

It was around 11 a.m. when Linda came back to De Longpre. She found Bukowski coughing up blood.

'You want me to come back later?' she asked.

Bukowski said it was alright, he went through this every morning.

'When I first met him he really was pretty ugly,' says Linda. 'He was 240 lbs and his hair was really short, like an old Will Rogers haircut.' But the more she saw of him, as she worked at modelling the head, the more attractive he seemed. 'He was very funny. He had a way of living, making each moment real. Sometimes he would be real stubborn and not talk at all, but for the most part, if you were around him, you felt this aliveness.' Their conversation and body language became increasingly flirtatious as the weeks went by, and Bukowski wrote her romantic letters. Linda's friends warned her not to get involved with a man so much older, a drunk with no money who didn't even have a proper job, but she found herself casting coquettish looks at him as they worked on the head, which began to mimic his slightly suggestive smile. 'I fell in love with him,' she says. 'We kind of fell in love over the clay.'

'Bukowski, you're a good writer,' she said one day, when she was working. 'But you don't know anything about women.' He admitted he hadn't had much experience. The last time he had had sex was after the reading in New Mexico and, other than a couple of one night stands, he had basically only had three lovers in his whole life: Jane Cooney Baker, Barbara Frye and FrancEyE. Linda said she thought as much.

She was in the kitchen when he came and pressed himself against her. He got a quick kiss. Then Linda pushed him away, saying if they ever became lovers, which he should know was highly unlikely, he would have to go down on her.

'I'll never get mixed up with a man again who doesn't like to eat pussy,' she said. Bukowski was forced to admit he had never done such a thing. 'Oh well, you know, ha ha, too bad for you,' said Linda, who often spoke with a peculiar chuckling laugh. 'Forget it.'

Bukowski couldn't stand the teasing any longer. He scooped her up in his arms, carried her to the bed and proceeded to 'eat her cunt like a peach', as he wrote in an unpublished love poem.

After a difficult first year as a freelance writer, 1971 started well for him. *Post Office* was published in February, in a beautiful edition designed by Barbara Martin, the cover made to look like a letter. Bukowski's friend Gerald Locklin gave it a rave review in the *Long Beach Press Telegram*, saying he doubted a better novel would be published in America that year. February was also the month Bukowski started sleeping with Linda.

They got off to a shaky start. He was using the tranquilizer drug Valium, to help him sleep at nights, and the cocktail of booze and pills rendered him impotent. Linda gathered it had happened before, because he didn't seem at all surprised or worried. Instead he had a good time letting her squeeze the blackheads that covered his back and chest. He said it felt almost as good as sex, but she wanted more than that out of a relationship.

She made him cut back on his drinking, told him to stop taking Valium and put him on a diet and exercise régime. He slimmed down to 160 lbs, losing so much weight cheekbones appeared on his face for the first time in thirty years. Linda found she had to scrape some clay from the head. He grew his hair and beard long, in keeping with the fashion, and she encouraged him to buy bell-bottom trousers and floral-print shirts. When the make-over was complete, she said they could try again.

Bukowski assured her there was no need to use a rubber because, even if he got an erection, and held it, he would withdraw in time.

'You came inside!' she yelled in a rage, jumping up and down on the bed. 'Jesus Christ, man!'

'I was too hot. It just happened. What do I do?'

'Do? You're fifty years old. You're supposed to know things.'

They were soon having sex every day, like young lovers, and Bukowski became infatuated with her. He told Linda he loved everything about her, even the way she walked. She made him feel so strong he believed he could knock down walls with his hands. One morning, when he was cooking eggs for breakfast, he was so befuddled by love he put the pan of water in the refrigerator, rather than on the stove. Linda was taken aback by the intensity of his feelings. 'I didn't want a man loving me that hard; it was like it was obsessive instead of natural.'

With obsessive love came jealousy. Bukowski invited Linda to parties at his place, but couldn't cope with the way she danced and flirted with his friends. There was a New Year's party and a party for the third and final issue of his magazine, *Laugh Literary and Man the Humping Guns.*

'It's a collating party,' he said, when he asked if she would come.

'A copulating party? No, really, what did you say?'

'Putting the magazine together, that's collating.'

'Oh, sure. Who's going to be there?'

'A bunch of half-assed poets, myself.'

'Now if it was a copulating party . . .'

'It will be. You and me after.'

She danced like she was having sex. Her favorite step was the White Dog Hunch, named after a dog in her home town of Boulder, Utah, that tried to mount every human being it met. Bukowski was driven half-mad with jealousy as he watched her gyrating and rubbing up against his guests, a jealousy fueled by alcohol. He wanted to kill the sons of bitches she was dancing with. He wanted to kill Linda, too.

When everybody had gone home, he told her she was a slut, one of the whores of the centuries, just like Jane. And being a fiery young woman, a feminist who believed she was within her rights to dance with whoever she liked, however she wanted, Linda told him to fuck off. They were finished. To hell with Bukowski!

Linda would leave Bukowski and come back to him countless times during their relationship and when they were apart, they continued their battles by mail. After this first break-up, she wrote that her name was not spelt J – A – N – E, but L – I – N – D – A, and that he should get her out of his 'smelly Jane bag' because she couldn't 'live with dead bones and dead memories'.

She wrote that he was denying the genuine love she had to offer, 'to protect yourself from pain . . . or maybe you're just glommed (*sic*) onto the word pain to excuse your self-indulgence of drinking. The pain is false. It's a drama. It's the show . . . You sometimes talk like you're the only man with feeling in the whole world. It probably comes from only caring how Charles Bukowski feels. You have intense interest in the pain of yourself. I don't think that you can care that much for anyone else including me . . .'

Referring to the way he wrote about women, she added: 'your women are all weak and floppy and untrue. My heart is a wild sensuous white bird and it's always wanting to fly. Fly Bukowski. you're afraid to fly.'

They soon got back together and went to another party where Linda flirted and Bukowski became jealous again. He drove her home in a fury afterwards, accusing her of having affairs behind his back. A day or so later she received a bizarre letter from Bukowski, saying he wanted to have fun as well so he'd picked up a man on the way home. At the time, Linda thought he was trying to rile her, but she later wondered whether he meant he'd had sex with a man.

'I think that if he (did) it was like this drunken thing. When he got real drunk he would do anything.'

She typed out her reply on a length of Lady Scott toilet paper, writing that she hoped he'd had a good time, whoever he was with. She wanted him to know she had not been unfaithful, and that whichever woman Bukowski ended up with – she listed women she was jealous of, including Ann Menebroker – she hoped they had a good screw. They could thank Linda for teaching him how. She ended the toilet paper letter by telling him to blow his nose with it.

Although enraged by Linda's flirtatious behaviour, Bukowski had no compunction about trying to screw any woman who looked at him twice and, now he was getting better known as a writer, more women were interested in him. 'He had double standards, typical of the chauvinist world. He pissed me off regularly,' says Linda. 'He needed to be fought!'

She accused him of stirring up trouble to get material for his writing, which turned out to be true, and in a letter, in May, 1971, described a cruel streak in her lover: 'It runs down the middle of you and pretty wide, too . . . even if you had an easy woman with twelve soft pillows to sleep on you'd still find some reason it wasn't enough . . . I hope you can write your novel now with one more shitass woman for material.'

But she forgave him in the end. In a note addressed to her 'darling insane lover', a few days later, she said she simply had to write and tell him how much she loved his 'crazy ass'.

Each summer Linda went home to Utah for 4 July. After doing the White Dog Hunch in town, with the local cowboys, she and her sisters went camping on land the family owned. Before she left for her holiday, Bukowski gave her a novelty ring with a horse's head on it, as a token of his love. A couple of hours later he found himself staring at the remains of their last breakfast. Her egg shells seemed special somehow. He tried to work at his typing table, but every woman that passed by reminded him of Linda, so he stopped work and got drunk for six days.

When he sobered up, he began to bombard Linda with love letters and long-distance telephone calls. If she was out when he called, he wouldn't leave the bungalow until she phoned back.

Then he stopped going out at all in case he missed her. Having better things to do with her time than make endless long-distance calls, days went by without any word from Linda and Bukowski imagined the worst. Even Marina, a devoted six-year-old with braces on her teeth, could not cheer him up. He apologized for his depression, saying he loved Marina more than the 'hair in his ears' but Linda would be away for two weeks!

One morning he woke from a nightmare that Linda was with another man. He got up and wrote an anxious letter, asking what she was doing. A couple of hours later he wrote a second letter, assuring her that all the women in his life had been like grains of sand compared with her, even Jane. He went out to post the letters and then started drinking. When he was good and drunk, he telephoned Boulder, but Linda's sister said she was out. When he finally reached her, Linda assured him patiently that she loved him. There was nothing to worry about. She would be back soon. He put the phone down and wrote his third love letter of the day, just to let her know he felt better.

Although she placated him on the telephone, the letters Linda sent from Utah seemed designed to make him jealous.

She sent this on 1 July, 1971*:

Dearest Buk . . .
I'm saving my pussy for you. Talking . . . dancing . . . flirting don't count. It's who gets the pussy that counts. You should know that. Now if you don't want the pussy I'm sure there's others who would, but the only thing is that it's got to liking your kind of petting REAL GOOD. There's nobody who can make it purr quite like you . . . When I get back to town I'm going to kiss you about an hour before I do anything else . . . I'm just going to tease that SHIT out of you . . . I'll run my tongue along over the top of your penis and just tickle it. Not really touch it. God damn you . . . I'll tease you so much that you'll have to kiss my pussy like you've never kissed it before . . . Goddamn I love you . . . I want that crooked cock

* Spelling, syntax and grammar have not been changed in Linda's letters, or in Bukowski's.

of you're hard. I want to bite it all the way up and down in a hundred little bites that don't hurt, just feel good. I'm going to kiss that thing so much. And I'm going to kiss you so much, I'm going to tease you until you're a madman and you finally lose all sense of what real and what isn't real and you finally have to rape me or go screaming and pulling the hair from your head. Yah, that's what I'll do. You're going to have to make that rape scene in your head a reality. I'm not going to kiss you. I'M NOT going to kiss you. YOU'RE going to have to MAKE me . . . if you think you can. You Son of a Bitch. If I had you up here right now I'd take you out and rape you right in these Boulder pines. I'd throw you down in the dirty and get on top and ride you until you had sand, pine needles, ants and rocks glued to your ass . . . I tie you to one of these goddamn trees bare-assed with only a dangling set of cock and balls free and then I'd work them over until they were no longer dangling, but looked like part of the branches of the tree. And while you are tied to the tree I'd bring four guys and dance with them all right in front of you . . .
See you in LA
Linda

There were many other letters like it. In one she wrote that, when she danced with men in Utah, she didn't think about him at all. Bukowski almost went mad when he read it. He smashed his hand down and cut himself so deeply he could see bone.

The affair continued after she returned to Los Angeles, and they split many times. Whenever this happened Bukowski got the head she had made, and given to him, and took it back to her, leaving it on the doorstep if she wouldn't let him in. Linda responded by mailing him venomous letters.

'Piss on you Bukowski,' she wrote in September, 'you've been puking on the woman race too long.' She wrote that she would never have sex with him again, and he should know a few home truths, now they were finished: he had never faced up to his drinking for what it was, a weakness. Her mistake was not realizing he was doing exactly what he wanted, 'killing yourself a drink at a time'. She also harangued him for writing for pornographic magazines: 'you men sell the dirty mags. men buy them. write for the men – they'll love you.'

When they made up, as they always did, she brought the head back to De Longpre Avenue. Bukowski's friends got to know that if the head was missing there was trouble with Linda. If it was at his bungalow, everything was OK between them.

'It was exciting,' says John Martin, who watched with amusement. 'She was young and she was probably the first real sexual relationship he'd ever had in his life and he was in his fifties. He had Jane, but that was a drinking relationship. I don't know how sexual it was.'

Although he loved her with all his heart, there was a distinctive admixture of misogyny in Bukowski's relationship with Linda. He was never quite sure whether she was an angel come to save him, or a devil who wanted to humiliate him in front of his friends. He expressed his ambivalent feelings in an extraordinary letter to Steve Richmond, in November, 1971:

> . . . don't wait for the good woman. she doesn't exist. there are women who can make you feel more with their bodies and their souls but these are the exact women who will turn the knife into you right in front of the crowd. of course, I expect this, but the knife still cuts. the female loves to play man against man. and if she is in a position to do it there is not one who will not resist. the male, for all his bravado and exploration, is the loyal one, the one who generally feels love. the female is skilled at betrayal. and torture and damnation. never envy a man his lady. behind it all lays a living hell.

The police were called to Bukowski's bungalow three times in November, 1971, once to the bloody aftermath of another party. Before the guests arrived, Bukowski and Linda had promised each other that, whatever happened, they would stick together during the evening. They were sick and tired of fighting. But he got drunk and insulted her so viciously she had no choice other than to go outside and cool off. When she came back, Bukowski asked everybody to leave. When the room was cleared, he came towards

Linda as if to kiss her, at least that's what she thought he was going to do, to say he was sorry for carrying on. Instead he punched her in the face. He punched her so hard he broke her nose.

In the morning she woke with two black eyes. She remembered Bukowski saying he'd never hit a woman, and despised men who did. That was a laugh. He had probably done it many times, probably hit Jane when he thought she'd stepped out of line.

Linda wrote him a farewell letter:

Well Bukowski, it's really sad that our relationship had to end with so much violence. I hated to see that last display of weakness on your part . . . My nose will heal . . . maybe a little wider and a little crookeder and my black eyes will go away in time, but there's something in you that isn't going to heal . . . You're sick . . . You really wanted to wipe my face out didn't you. That had nothing to do with your feelings for me. It was hatred inside of your coming out. I didn't even raise up my hand to defend myself . . . You'll have to do some tall writing spiced with a lot of lies to get around this one, but you'll do it. You'll glorify Bukowski for whatever he does.
I guess that's it.
Linda

It wasn't the end. Not long afterwards, Linda moved into bungalow number four at the back of Bukowski's court. She began getting more involved in writing poetry herself. She contributed to a chapbook, *An Anthology of LA Poets*, which Bukowski edited, and she and Bukowski collaborated on *Me and Your Sometimes Love Poems*, a chapbook which, as she wrote, documented:

> . . . our kisses and fights
> and fuckings
> Mad and wonderful

By this stage, the fights arrived daily for their sustenance, like breakfast pancakes, sweetened with jealousy. He accused her of having sex with a host of people, even a blind priest he believed she was seeing, and became convinced she was having an affair with her dentist. He said her bad tooth was not the only part of her that got filled when she went to the surgery.

Indignant that this was untrue, and furious that Bukowski was flirting with other women when he got the opportunity, Linda took off for Utah in the spring of 1972, leaving behind a pair of her panties and a note:

> Hank
> I'll be gone by the time you get back. You used to have all of me, but now all you have are my yellow panties to smell when you jerk off.

Yellow, as she knew, was his favorite color. It would give him something to write about until she got back.

WOMEN

9

Buk

Liza Williams was watching Bukowski poke round her office. He was an ugly old buzzard, for sure, but she found him strangely attractive and knew he was on the prowl for a new girlfriend.

Bukowski and Liza had known each other since they wrote for _Open City_ and, when the paper folded, the _LA Free Press_ picked up both their columns. Liza had a day job as well; she was a senior executive with Island Records.

She was not as sexy-looking as Linda King, and she was almost as old as Bukowski himself, but Liza was smart and funny and Bukowski knew Linda was jealous of her. He leaned over the desk and gave her a great big kiss, which shocked Liza because she thought him so ugly.

'You wanna come out?' he muttered.

'Sure!' Liza replied, brightly. She was intrigued by his personality, and thought she might find out more about what made him tick if they dated.

A few days later, Bukowski sent a special delivery letter to Linda in Utah, writing that he was with Liza. He didn't love her, he said, but she had fallen in love with him and he feared she might try and kill herself if he ended it, so he was going to stick with her for a while. He hoped Linda didn't mind.

Linda thanked him by reply:

Dear Bukowski,
. . . I was so happy to hear she is intelligent, kind loving,
warm, but really I don't care for the details. Next thing I
know you'll be letting me know how you ate her cunt and
how she panted in pleasure . . . It does sound like you have
a lot in common . . . at least you both believe in suicide . . .

Just as Linda predicted, Bukowski was soon boasting in his
letters about how good the sex was, although Liza says the
relationship was hardly sexual at all.
Linda replied:

Bastard Bukowski,
Just as I predicted you got me told, more or less, how you
kissed Liza's pussy and how she panted in pleasure. Listen,
you slob, I want you to know once and for all I don't want
to hear how Liza trembled . . .
GO PISS UP A ROPE . . .
Linda

While Linda was enjoying her 4 July holiday, Liza took
Bukowski on vacation, at her expense, because she noticed he
never went anywhere or did anything apart from drink, play
the horses and write. They flew to the resort island of Catalina,
twenty-six miles off the coast of California, and booked into the
Hotel Monterey in the port town of Avalon, the best room in the
house with a view over the bay. Bukowski's habits were unchanged
by being away from home. He bought beer at the corner liquor
store, stripped to his undershirt and shorts, tuned the radio to a
classical station and sat in an easy chair by the window to drink
in his solitary, mournful way.
'Wait 'til I give you my purple turnip,' he muttered, taking a
swig. It was a pet name for his cock, but Liza had heard it all
before.
'The relationship was not really sexual at all, even though he
talked a big sex line, because he was always drunk,' she says. 'He
might have liked to screw if he had been sober enough, but after

drinking two six-packs, which would be his regular evening ration, he couldn't do anything.'

She went out exploring and he stayed in the room to write a poem, 'cooperation', about being taken on holiday by a wealthy woman and not knowing quite how to behave:

> she's going for a walk
> on the island
> or a boatride.
> I believe she's taken a modern novel
> and her reading glasses.
>
> I sit at the window
> with her electric typewriter
> and watch young girls' asses
> which are attached to
> young girls.
>
> the final decadence.

When she got back laden with parcels, Liza told him about all the exciting things she had seen and done, and the fun they could have together.

'Oh Hank, I had such a great day,' she said. 'I ate . . . and went on a boat taxi, and saw . . .'

'The fucking boat taxi,' he said, dropping an empty can in the bin. 'Who wants to go on the fucking boat taxi? You're crazy.'

'Oh, well . . . What did you do, Hank?'

'I wrote another *immortal* poem.'

The vacation continued in this desultory fashion for seven days. They toured the island, ate out and met friends of Liza's, but mostly Bukowski stayed in the room on his own writing poems. He spent so much time in the room, Liza bought a budgerigar to keep him company.

When they got back to LA, Bukowski spent a lot of time at Liza's house up on Tuxedo Terrace, in the Hollywood Hills. He lazed about in her double bed, drank cold beer from her refrigerator and goggled at programs on her color television while she was out at work. 'Hank, who had been bereft his whole life, thought he was living in a palace,' says Liza. 'It goes with a flash, music business lady.' Indeed when he came to write his third novel, *Women*, Bukowski made much of Liza's up-market lifestyle, using her as the basis of the character Dee Dee Bronson.

In the evenings, she took him to rock concerts, and hosted parties at her house where Bukowski met many of the most notable musicians and artists working in California. One of these was R. Crumb, famous for his *Mr Natural* and *Fritz the Cat* drawings.

'You know, your stuff is good, kid,' said Bukowski when Crumb came over to say hello. 'It's the real thing. Just keep away from the cocktail parties.'

The advice stuck with the artist who shared many of Bukowski's negative feelings about society, and later became the most successful illustrator of Bukowski's work, collaborating on books including *Bring Me Your Love* and *The Captain is Out to Lunch and the Sailors Have Taken Over the Ship*. 'The guy just says it right for me,' Crumb explains. 'I do believe that it takes a strong dose of alienation to make a good artist or writer in the modern world. You can't be too well-adjusted and still have anything interesting to say.'

When Liza saw Bukowski and Crumb getting along so well, she decided to introduce Bukowski to another artist, Spain Rodriguez.

'Spain's a cartoonist, too,' she said.

Bukowski took an instant dislike to Rodriguez, possibly because he was handsome and Bukowski tended to feel threatened by handsome men.

'I bet you can't cartoon worth a shit,' he said. Rodriguez slammed his fist down and challenged Bukowski to step outside. 'Oh, I bet you are a great cartoonist really,' Bukowski said, backing down. He later wrote a poem, 'trouble with spain', describing the meeting and how he made a fool of himself in front of Liza's friends:

> met this painter called Spain,
> no, he was a cartoonist,
> well, I met him at a party

and everybody got mad at me
because I didn't know who he was
or what he did.

. . . I said:
hey, Spain, I like that name: Spain.
but I don't like you. why don't we step out
in the garden and I'll kick the shit out of your
ass?
. . . everybody's angry at me.
Bukowski, he can't write, he's had it.
washed up. look at him drink.
he never used to come to parties.
now he comes to parties and drinks everything
up and insults real talent.
I used to admire him when he cut his wrists
and when he tried to kill himself with
gas. look at him now leering at that 19 year old
girl, and you know he
can't get it up.

Bukowski and Liza met Gypsy Lou Webb who came though LA in 1972 after Jon Webb died. Bukowski had written an outrageous column in the *Free Press* based on Jon's death, calling the Webbs 'Clyde and June'. In the story, he wrote about how June was almost demented with grief, snatching Clyde's false teeth as a keepsake and pushing her hand into his vault to touch the body. The narrator of the story tries to seduce her after the funeral, saying Clyde can do nothing for her now, that his body is only fit for medical students to practice upon. The students would chop him up like a frog. This was a particularly unpleasant reference to Gypsy Lou donating Jon's organs to a teaching hospital.

'June, the dead are dead, there's nothing we can do about it. Let's go to bed . . .'
'Go to bed?'
'Yes, let's hit the sack, let's make it . . .'
'Listen, I knew Clyde for 32 years . . .'

'Clyde can't help you now . . .'
'His body's still warm, you bastard . . .'
'Mine's hot . . .'

'Everybody knew it was me even though he disguised my name,' says Gypsy Lou. 'I got mad and told him off: "That's a dirty, lousy trick."'

When she finished telling him off, Gypsy Lou told Bukowski and Liza a story even more bizarre than the one he'd made up. Hanging around her neck was a chain strung with a silver pill box and a pair of red dice, the type used in casinos.

'These are Jon's dice,' she said.

Bukowski said he remembered them.

'And these are Jon's ashes,' she said opening the lid of the box. She took a pinch of ash and tossed it in her mouth. 'Every day I eat a bit of him. I dug up my little baby, too . . . then I mixed his ashes in with Jon's, so now I'm eating both of them. When I die, we will be together, forever.'

Although he and Liza had fun together, Bukowski was still in love with Linda and spoke to her frequently on the telephone. Liza was angry when she found out about the calls.

'Here you are living with me, and when she phones you forget everything!' she said.

'I was with Linda sixteen months. I loved her and things grow between people,' Bukowski said, defending himself. 'I still love her.'

'But you said you loved me. You said if I helped you through it that you'd never leave me. Now you want to leave. Is it because she's younger? Maybe you just like women who treat you mean. You've gotten used to that kind of woman.'

'I didn't say she treated me mean. I want to go see her. I want to find things out.'

'All right, you go on up there. But I can't promise how I'll feel about you when you get back.'

Bukowski and Linda were reunited in San Francisco when he read at Lawrence Ferlinghetti's Poets' Theater and, although they had a terrible fight at the party afterwards, Bukowski decided he couldn't live without her and told Liza it was over. They were in bed at De Longpre Avenue and she reacted by becoming almost hysterical, weeping, beating on his chest and demanding to know why. He said Linda had a special hold over him and he guessed he was a louse.

'I loved him with great enthusiasm and then I was heartbroken with great enthusiasm,' says Liza. 'I could never understand why he was going back to Linda. I always thought of her as being rather trashy. I thought she was some kind of shrew with a magic vagina.' Liza got so upset she threw up in the bed, and out came her false teeth. She knew he would write about it in his column, no matter how much she begged him not to. 'He was so happy,' she says, 'it was my full set.'

Linda took out a mortgage on a detached house in the LA suburb of Silver Lake, and she and Bukowski set up home together as a surprisingly domesticated couple. She forbade him from drinking in the house and he managed to stay sober for weeks at a time. He did his share of the household chores and they started having Marina over to stay at weekends.

Marina and her mother had settled in Santa Monica and Bukowski made a point of attending open days at her school, just like a regular dad. Marina was particularly pleased to look out from the stage at her first school pageant to see him in the audience. 'I remembered at the time that he gave poetry readings and he had to get up on the stage and do that sort of thing,' she says. 'It was nice to have him there.'

When she came over to Silver Lake, Marina played with Linda's two children, Gaetano and Clarissa, baking cookies, playing in the large back yard and painting pictures with Bukowski who kept them amused with stories. 'He did make me laugh a lot,' says Marina. 'But it was more of a feeling of being able to play with him and laugh and also being able to tell him anything, that he really knew who I was. I just always felt happy and safe.'

Marina knew Bukowski was different from most fathers, partly because all the adults treated him as if he was special, and partly because he was so different from the traditional fathers she saw on television and in story books. 'I remember reading some story with a very traditional father in it that wore slippers and a robe and smoked a pipe and behaved in a very clichéd kind of way, a very appealing story to a child and thinking: that's sort of your regular kind of father. If you could choose your father, would I trade my father for a regular father?' She decided there was no question. 'I thought, no, I'm really lucky to have the father I have because he may have been really unusual, but he always talked to me just as another person. He didn't talk down the way a lot of adults do to their children and, as a result, I felt much closer to him.'

Linda's daughter, Clarissa, was not such a big Bukowski fan, and often told him off. 'I hate you!' she would say, emphatically. 'You are ugly! You've got a big red nose!'

'I love that kid,' Bukowski told Linda. 'She's the only honest person around.'

Bukowski took Linda to the races, driving across the city using the boulevards never the freeways, and usually sitting in the less popular sections of the grandstand, arriving early and leaving before the last race – everything calculated to avoid the crowds which he couldn't stand. He said he didn't even like it when people brushed up against him. 'If we won, we would go out and have a great dinner afterwards. If we lost, we would say, what the hell, let's have a good dinner anyway,' says Linda. He liked chain restaurants which weren't too expensive, particularly The Sizzler on Hollywood Boulevard where he ordered medium rare T-bone steak with baked potato and side salad. When he craved a drink, Linda took him to Baskin-Robbins' ice cream parlor, hoping he'd be content with a sticky dessert. It worked for a while, as he wrote in 'the icecream people':

the lady has me temporarily off the bottle
and now the pecker stands up
better, and there is much use for the
pecker . . .
however, it changes the nights –
instead of listening to Shostakovitch and
Mozart through the smeared haze of smoke and
scotch and beer,
these nights change
complexities:
we drive down to Baskin-Robbins,
31 flavors

Rocky Road, Bubble Gum, Apricot Ice, Strawberry
Cheesecake, Chocolate Mint . . .
. . .
and later that night
there is use for the pecker, use for
love, and it is a glorious
fuck, long and true,
and afterwards we speak of easy things
our heads by the open window with the moonlight
looking through, we sleep in each other's
arms.

the icecream people make me feel good,
inside and out.
give me 2 quick shots of
vanilla.

'He was nice when he was sober,' says Linda. 'I think his true
self was when he was sober. But when he was drunk it was like a
demon took him over – Bukowski the Bad.'

One weekend they had a big party at the house and, when
Bukowski was drunk, he accused Linda of being a lesbian, which
infuriated her so much she pulled him out of his chair and threw
him in the fireplace. He landed on his backside with his beer in
his hand, not having spilt a drop.

'She gets so . . . angry,' he said, refusing to lose his cool. 'It
fascinates me how . . . angry she gets.'

Linda hurled herself at him and they brawled on the floor until
dragged apart by their guests.

'Get out!' she screamed. 'All of you are getting out.'

Bukowski slowly got himself ready to leave, making remarks
about Linda as he put his jacket on and did his shoes up. He
said she had thick ankles, something she was very sensitive about.
While he was bent over tying his laces, she picked up a bottle of
Jack Daniels and held it over his head. She was shaking.

'You better kill me when you hit me,' he said. 'Because if you
don't, I'm going to kill you.' Then he straightened up and faced her.
'You ain't shit,' he said.

Another night a man came over to the house to talk to Linda about her poetry. She was so flattered to be the center of attention she relaxed the no-drinking rule and they had 'boiler makers' (whiskey washed down with beer). As the evening wore on, it became apparent the visitor was really only interested in talking to Bukowski and Linda pushed them both out of the house.

'OK, you guys, if you want to see each other, leave together,' she said.

The front door was made up of little panes of glass and, when Linda refused to let them back in, Bukowski took off his shoe and began knocking out the glass piece by piece. The visitor joined in, too, thinking it great fun. Linda flung the door open and they fell into the hall, breaking one of her sculptures. 'That's what infuriated me,' she says. 'I came out like a tiger, and drove them back out the door and they fell down the steps.' There was such a racket the neighbors called the police who arrived to find Bukowski back inside the house holding Linda's couch over his head, saying he was going to toss it through the window.

'Don't throw the couch!' said the cops, pulling their guns.

'He's wrecking my place! He's wrecking it!' screamed Linda.

'Put the couch down.'

On the way to the station, Bukowski began to charm the officers, telling them he was a famous writer. He wanted to call his publisher to bail him out. His publisher was an important man, they'd see.

The last thing John Martin wanted was to drive across town at 2 a.m. He told Bukowski he would call Linda, smooth things over between them, and get her to bail him out.

'There's no way I'm going to go and get that son of a bitch,' she said, when he called. 'He was wrecking the place!'

'You know he loves you, Linda. He really loves you. If you go down and get him, you will have his eternal gratitude. He will never do this again.' Martin knew it wasn't true. Their relationship was like the Hundred Years War – an end to hostilities was not in sight. 'And I'll pay for the glass,' he said. 'Don't worry about it.'

Linda wanted Martin to come over and talk about the horrendous things she was going through with Bukowski. 'I thought Martin took this attitude, you are the low-life people. I don't want to get my hands dirty. I publish it, but I don't want to get involved.' But, reluctantly, she agreed to collect Bukowski from the station.

Martin called the police back to let Bukowski know Linda was on her way.

'Oh yes, Mr Martin, just a moment please,' said the desk sergeant, unctuously. 'Charles!' he called. 'Oh Charles, it's for you.'

Martin heard somebody asking Bukowski if he cared for a cup of coffee, and Bukowski replying: 'Yeah, put it down there, thank you.' It seemed to be a very civil evening in the drunk tank. When he came on the line, Bukowski thanked Martin for fixing things and said the superintendent wanted a word.

'Mr Martin,' said the superintendent. 'We are taking good care of your friend here. We are all big admirers of his work.'

It turned out the cops were all avid readers of Bukowski's *Notes of a Dirty Old Man* column, which had a much wider readership now it was appearing in the *LA Free Press*. They hadn't even bothered to lock him up.

Bukowski was starting to get quite a lot of fan mail, some of it from women who were attracted to the honest way he wrote about sex and relationships, now Linda King had taught him a thing or two. 'He had the capacity to love and love deeply and a lot of men don't even have that capacity,' she says. 'He wasn't afraid of that. He let his emotions loose. Bukowski let himself feel all kinds of things.'

One of these women was Joanna Bull, a voluptuous blonde former girlfriend of rock star drummer Levon Helm. She sent samples of her poetry and began visiting Bukowski at the bungalow on De Longpre Avenue, which he had kept as a bolt-hole for when he wanted to get away from Linda.

Joanna was more interested in Bukowski's mind than his body, but she knew he wanted to sleep with her and one night, when she had stayed later than normal, and smoked a lot of dope, she resigned herself to it. But her subconscious was apparently set against the idea. 'When we got to the moment of truth, and we were all wrestling around and doing stuff and preparing ourselves, he realized I hadn't taken off my panties! He was absolutely disgusted.' Afterwards she went into the toilet and threw up. 'It was unbearable to me,' she says.

In July, 1973, Bukowski accompanied Linda on her annual trip to Utah. He was looking ahead to writing his novel, *Women*, and needed to collect material, as he explained in a letter to John Martin: 'I'm making a study on (Linda). If I ever get it down right some day you'll see the female exposed as she has never been exposed.'

On their first night in Boulder, the King sisters threw an uproarious party. 'Every wild character we knew we had there, and I think he was a little taken aback,' says Gerry King. 'He was used to being the wildest person at a party and he had competition at that one.' A couple of days later, Bukowski, Linda and Gerry, together with their children, drove to where the family had a trailer on the side of Boulder Mountain.

Bukowski and Linda slept in a tent the first night, but it rained so hard they had to squeeze into the trailer with Gerry's family. By the third day the cramped conditions were getting on everybody's nerves. What was worse, the beer Bukowski had brought up the mountain was gone. He wanted to go into town for more and, when Linda said he couldn't, he grumpily stomped off into the pines as if he were back in Hollywood, taking a walk along Sunset.

When he had been gone a couple of hours, the King sisters began to wonder what had happened. As Gerry says: 'At first we were annoyed and didn't believe it. Surely he didn't get *lost*.' Of course he had and it made for one of the funniest passages in *Women*, and one of the most comical accounts in modern fiction of a city dweller being lost in the countryside: falling into lakes, being attacked by giant flies, sinking into a bog and all the while hollering for Lydia (as he called Linda in the novel) to rescue him. Finally she did:

. . . 'I tracked you. I found your red notebook. You got lost deliberately because you were pissed.'

'No, I got lost out of ignorance and fear. I am not a complete person – I'm a stunted city person. I am more or less a failed drizzling shit with absolutely nothing to offer.'

'Christ,' she said, 'don't you think I know that?'

When they got back to LA, Linda began to suspect he was seeing other women, partly because he kept disappearing for hours on end, 'to go to the supermarket', he claimed. It seemed a most unlikely excuse.

One afternoon in September, he took her to the Olympic Auditorium to watch the boxing and then rushed her home before going off to do more shopping. Feeling extremely insulted, like she had been party to a double-booking, Linda drove over to a house on Santa Monica Boulevard where she thought one of Bukowski's girlfriends lived and, sure enough, she saw him. He was walking back from the liquor store with a brown paper bag full of bottles, whistling a happy tune.

He heard a familiar sound, like the engine of Linda's car. Bukowski stopped whistling and turned to see that it was Linda's car, the Volkswagen which was so ugly they called it The Thing. She had The Thing up on the sidewalk and was driving at him. The VW was just narrow enough to get between the lamp posts and the buildings. It was on a collision course. 'I backed him up against the wall,' says Linda. 'I wasn't going to kill him. I was mad though.' Bukowski was so frightened he dropped his bag and the bottles smashed on the concrete.

He was bending down to pick up the broken glass when she came round again, stopped the car, got out and marched up to Bukowski. He was holding one solitary bottle of beer he had saved. Linda snatched it and hurled it at the house where Bukowski's lover was peering out at them. It went through her window like a bullet.

Lydia ran off and I walked up the stairway. Nicole was still standing there. 'For God's sake, Chinaski, leave her before she kills everybody!'

I turned and walked back down the stairway. Lydia was sitting in her car at the curbing with the engine running. I opened the door and got in. She drove off. Neither of us spoke a word.

Taylor Hackford's documentary about Bukowski was given a preview screening at the Municipal Art Gallery Theater, in

Hollywood, on 19 October. Bukowski arrived with Linda and Jory Sherman and his wife, taking seats in the front of the auditorium. He had been nervous about the evening and was astounded by how large his face appeared on screen. There were his fights with Linda, the love triangle with Liza Williams, the drunken reading in San Francisco and, finally, Bukowski mulling over his experiences and philosophizing laconically that he 'wouldn't advise women to anybody'. It was a well-made and entertaining film and the reviews were good when it was shown on KCET, a local public television station.

Most of Bukowski's old friends gathered for the party afterwards, but some felt success was beginning to change him. Steve Richmond had been deeply hurt by Bukowski's poem, '300 Poems', published in a new Black Sparrow Press collection, *Mockingbird Wish Me Luck*. Bukowski had insinuated that Richmond's 'gagaku poems', written to the rhythm of Japanese folk music, were lousy and Richmond was so upset by it he almost took an overdose.

Neeli Cherkovski, also at the party, had been taken aback when Bukowski told him, apparently seriously: 'I am getting more well-known with these Hollywood people. I don't know how much time to spend with you guys.' So when Cherkovski met John Martin that evening there was already a degree of estrangement. As Cherkovski recalls the conversation, he suggested Black Sparrow Press might consider publishing other poets like Harold Norse, John Thomas, Jack Micheline, Jack Hirschman and some day maybe himself. The way Bukowski heard it, Cherkovski said: 'You ought to print me and Norse and Micheline and Richmond. Why do you print Bukowski? He's like a worn-out tape machine saying the same things over and over.' The next time he saw Cherkovski, Bukowski cut him dead, saying he wasn't talking to the asshole.

William Wantling was one of several long-standing friends Bukowski had corresponded with for years, but never met. He was a former Marine who had served in Korea, done time in San Quentin for fraud, and had developed a fearsome drink and drug problem – all of which gave him material for writing the sort of gritty poetry Bukowski admired. So when Wantling invited him to read at the Illinois college where he taught English, in the spring of 1974,

Bukowski was happy to accept and arranged to meet Wantling and his wife, Ruth, at Chicago's O'Hare airport.

Despite arriving at O'Hare wearing his dead father's overcoat, which made him look like a bum, Bukowski was beginning to enjoy considerable success. Another volume of short stories, *South of No North*, had recently been published by Black Sparrow Press while the earlier books were being reprinted regularly. City Lights was paying a $10,000 advance for a new edition of *Notes of a Dirty Old Man*, and Bukowski was corresponding with Doubleday about a possible collection of poems. He'd given sold-out readings across the United States and been awarded a $5,000 grant from the National Endowment for the Arts, after years of trying.

Wantling's career, in comparison, had fizzled out. To Bukowski's disappointment, he'd taken a teaching job and stopped writing the type of primal poetry Bukowski so admired. 'He thought it was terrible that Bill was in the university. He thought it was ruining his writing,' says Ruth.

Bukowski gave a bad reading, while members of the audience hissed to each other that the poet was obviously drunk, and afterwards endured a reception in his honor, saying little to Wantling and his wife and being downright rude to every one else. From Bukowski's point of view, he considered he'd done enough for his $500 fee ($300 of which went on the air fare) and didn't want to answer questions as well.

William Wantling felt badly let down. He was having a lot of problems at the time with his marriage falling apart, and hassles with the police because of his drug habit, and had looked forward to meeting Bukowski, whom he idolized. Now it was all spoilt. 'He was extremely disappointed in Bukowski as a person,' says Ruth. 'He said he didn't know why Bukowski came, and that he wished he had never met him.'

When he got back to LA, Bukowski did what he had done so many times before and wrote a nasty, snide column about his trip, totally trashing his friend. He described visiting a provincial poet named Howard Stantling, an obvious variation on the name Wantling, a man who had once been wild and exciting, a former convict and talented poet, but who was now a fucked-up impotent junkie who pedaled round a university campus on a push bike and wrote poetry that was only popular in Australia. It was a vicious, underhand piece of work and was published in the *LA Free Press* in two instalments on 12 April and 19 April, 1974, as his *Notes of a Dirty Old Man* column. Although there is no direct evidence that Wantling read the stories, Ruth believes it is likely he did find out about them. He had a number of friends in LA who would have called to tell him about such an obvious and outrageous character assassination.

Less than two weeks after the second instalment appeared, Wantling was dead.

Always a compulsive and unstable personality, he started drinking heavily after Bukowski left town, and went into a manic phase, telling Ruth he couldn't get his brain to shut off. Letters he wrote to friends show him to have been depressed, questioning his worth as a man and a poet. He told small press publisher, A.D. Winans, that he felt so lousy he wanted to drink himself to death. That's precisely what he did: drinking day and night until he suffered a heart attack and was taken to hospital, screaming in the ambulance that he was old. He was forty-one when he died on 1 May.

Ruth believes that the stories Bukowski wrote about her husband probably had some effect on his behavior in the final weeks of his life, although she does not believe it is the primary cause for what happened because he was already so unstable. Whatever the reason for Wantling's final and fatal bout of drinking, Bukowski felt guilty about his behavior towards an obviously vulnerable friend. He telephoned A.D. Winans and spoke about how he had rejected some poems Wantling submitted to *Laugh Literary and Man the Humping Guns*, writing back that he had seen better from him and his work had never been very good to begin with. He regretted the letter now, and said he hoped Wantling hadn't taken it seriously.

Bukowski also telephoned Steve Richmond to talk about Wantling's death. 'He would usually call at 4 a.m., drunk,' says Richmond. 'But this time he was dead serious and it was like four in the afternoon. He knew: you write something, and the person you write about dies. It's a responsibility.'

Soon after the tragedy, Ruth came through LA on her way to

San Francisco and arranged to spend some time with Bukowski, who was one of the few people she knew in the city. He picked her up in his blue '67 Volkswagen and took her to the races before going back to an apartment he was renting on Carlton Way, having finally left De Longpre Avenue. It was another tatty court, a dark and shabby dump of a place, not far from the corner of Hollywood Boulevard and Western Avenue, one of the seediest junctions in all Los Angeles. Ruth slept on the couch and, in the morning, she and Bukowski went on a trip to Laguna Beach with a young couple, Brad and Tina Darby, who managed the court. Brad also managed a pornographic book store on Hollywood Boulevard, and Tina worked as a go-go dancer.

It was the first time Ruth had seen the Pacific Ocean, which her husband had talked so much about from when he lived in California, and she found herself looking out at the rollers, thinking about her husband, their marriage and the way he'd died. She began weeping, quietly, but this seemed to irritate Bukowski.

'Bill's dead,' he said. 'He can't suck your pussy, but I can.'

As the day wore on, he became more abusive, saying he expected to fuck Ruth and that she was a fucking fool if she didn't give him what he wanted. Her husband couldn't help her now. Brad Darby asked Bukowski to back off, but Bukowski didn't seem to care what he said. When the day came to an end, Ruth found herself cowering beside Bukowski in his bed in the motel room they had taken for the night; there was no couch and she had to sleep somewhere. They didn't have intercourse, but she feels she suffered an *emotional* rape. 'That was the ugliest experience I have ever had in my life,' she says. 'He was unbelievable.'

In the morning, Brad Darby drove them all back to LA, Bukowski refusing to speak to Ruth even though they sat side by side 'this massive, pouting, brooding, hating energy'. She got out at the airport, never to see him again.

A couple of years later, Ruth picked up a copy of his novel *Women* and, flicking through it, realized it was about women Bukowski had known, women like Liza Williams and Linda King and Joanna Bull, and that he had included her as well. He had changed her name to Cecelia Keesing and wrote that she was fat and boring.

We continued drinking. Cecelia had just one more and stopped.

'I want to go out and look at the moon and stars,' she said. 'It's so beautiful out.'

'All right, Cecelia.'

She went outside by the swimming pool and sat in a deck chair.

'No wonder Bill died,' I said. 'He starved. She never gives it away.'

Nasty though this is, the novel did not give an honest account of the events surrounding William Wantling's death. Bukowski did not admit to writing the story that appeared in the *LA Free Press*. He also left out the viler things he said to Ruth at Laguna Beach. But Ruth never forgot what happened. 'That was a horror,' she says. 'That is a rape in my life I haven't got over yet.'

'Does this face bother you?' Bukowski asked the young woman. They were at a party in Santa Cruz after a benefit reading where he had appeared with beat poets Allen Ginsberg, Lawrence Ferlinghetti and Gary Snyder. 'I mean, you find it revolting?' he asked, touching his bulbous nose and oatmeal complexion.

'No,' she answered carefully. 'I think you should judge a man by the inside of him.'

'Well good,' he said. 'Let's go and fuck then.'

Although nervous to the point of sickness earlier in the evening, drinking from a flask of vodka and orange to steady himself on stage, 'one shot for each poem he read' recalls Ginsberg, Bukowski manipulated the crowd of sixteen hundred with consummate skill, asking them disarmingly: 'Isn't this boring?' before giving a captivating reading.

Ginsberg came on afterwards and was chanting a blues litany when he was told there had been a bomb threat. 'So I turned to rhymed improvisation and explained the situation in friendly song, the audience began to understand and began filing out of the theater calmly. All the poets followed, after the audience left, and Bukowski looked at me and said, surprisingly, "Ginsberg, you're a good man." I was a little apprehensive he'd disapprove of me as "academic" or a four-eyed queer, but he was agreeable and friendly.'

When Ginsberg arrived at the party that evening, Bukowski

announced with mock-seriousness: 'Ladies and Gentlemen, we've got Allen Ginsberg as guest of honor tonight. Can you believe it? Allen Ginsberg!' He called for the music to be turned down and, when it wasn't, said to Ginsberg, whom he'd put in an affectionate headlock: 'A man of genius, the first poet to cut through light and consciousness for two thousand years and these bastards don't even appreciate it.'

Ginsberg rubbed Bukowski's back to try and calm him.

'That feels good, Allen, real good,' said Bukowski. 'Have a drink.'

Ginsberg said he'd already had enough.

'Everybody knows that after *Howl* you never wrote anything worth a shit,' said Bukowski, angry his offer of a drink had been rejected. He turned to the people around them, and asked: 'Has Allen written anything worth a shit since *Howl* and *Kay-dish?*'

'*Kaddish,*' Ginsberg corrected him.

'Allen, you're tearing me apart. You're a barracuda, Allen, eating me up with your tongue,' he laughed, contemptuously, and reeled off into a drunken bear-like dance with, as Ginsberg recalls 'his big pants falling down halfway from his behind'.

He was getting quite famous now, although still not as famous as he would become, accepted as an equal by established writers like Ferlinghetti and Ginsberg. He'd even been asked to read at the beats' de facto club, The Naropa Institute, in Colorado, although he declined the invitation. The furthest thing from his mind was joining that gang, no matter how friendly they were towards him. Of the beat writers, only William Burroughs had given him the cold shoulder, snubbing him at a reading, which was ironic because Burroughs was the only one he admired. Bukowski muttered about going outside and fighting him.

'I could push him over with one punch,' he told Harold Norse, who knew them both.

'Yeah, but you'd be dead,' said Norse. 'He'd shoot you.'

It was all starting to happen for Bukowski. His books were selling well; a friend in Los Angeles was working on his biography*; *Rolling Stone* magazine even ran a feature-length profile of

* Ben Pleasants later abandoned the project.

Bukowski, informing its readers that the great French intellectuals, Jean Paul Sartre and Jean Genet, were fans of his work. Sartre and Genet had apparently named Bukowski as the 'greatest American poet alive today'. This plaudit was widely reported in the underground press, becoming one of the most famous remarks about Bukowski, yet it is almost certainly another myth, possibly one created by Bukowski himself.

Leading world experts on the lives and work of both Genet and Sartre have no knowledge of either writer ever having said anything about Bukowski. 'I do not think Bukowski was in the literary tastes of Jean Genet,' says Albert Dichy, director of the Genet archive in Paris. Edmund White, whose biography is the pre-eminent work on Genet, says he is also unaware of any connection between Genet and Bukowski. Sartre experts in Europe and America similarly dismiss the remark and, faced with this evidence, John Martin concludes the quotation is no more than apocryphal. There is certainly no documentary evidence for it in any of the various archives of Bukowski's papers, leading one to wonder whether Bukowski simply made it up, as he had colluded in making up the Henry Miller plaudit, to get publicity.

However the quotation came into circulation, and its origins are still mysterious, the supposed praise of Genet and Sartre added to Bukowski's burgeoning fame.*

It was as much Bukowski's personality as his work that attracted attention, and he became the subject of poems by other writers who found him a fascinating character. Jack Micheline, Harold Norse and Steve Richmond all published work about Bukowski. At Santa Cruz, Linda King kept the audience in gales of laughter with salty poems about their sex life. Writers outside Bukowski's circle wrote about him, too, most notably the short story writer and poet Raymond Carver who met Bukowski at a university reading in California.

'I look around this room and see plenty of typers, but I see no writers for you guys don't know what love is,' Bukowski sneered at the faculty, when he got up on the podium to read. He included

* Further background about this mysterious quotation can be found in the source notes to this chapter.

Carver in the insult, and proceeded to drink him under the table when invited back to his house after the reading.

Carver took the encounter in good spirit, respecting Bukowski's 'raw honesty and living out of extremities' as his widow Tess Gallagher says, and was inspired to write 'You Don't Know What Love is (an evening with Charles Bukowski)' which brilliantly, and affectionately, describes Bukowski in his cups:

> You don't know what love is Bukowski said
> I'm 51 years old look at me
> I'm in love with this young broad
> I got it bad but she's hung up too
> so it's all right man that's the way it should be
> I get in their blood and they can't get me out
> They try everything to get away from me
> but they all come back in the end
> They all came back to me except
> the one I planted
> I cried over that one
> but I cried easy in those days
> Don't let me get onto the hard stuff man
> I get mean then
> I could sit here and drink beer
> with you hippies all night
> I could drink ten quarts of this beer
> and nothing it's like water
> But let me get onto the hard stuff
> and I'll start throwing people out windows
> I'll throw anybody out the window
> I've done it
> But you don't know what love is
> You don't know because you've never
> been in love it's that simple

'Man, that night he wrote about me I was drunk, naturally, and screaming at all these professors and college kids,' Bukowski said. 'Oh boy, I was singing that night and Carver caught that.'

He upped his appearance fee to $1,000, quite a sum compared

to the $25 he asked back in 1970 when he started reading. Bukowski assumed most universities and clubs would be unable to afford him at this price and he would therefore be spared the ordeal of performing so often. But still he got asked and, the more he got paid, the less respect he had for the crowds. They certainly weren't interested in hearing serious work, as he found out when he appeared at Baudelaire's nightclub in Santa Barbara.

'Let's get this god-damned reading over with,' he said, wearily, as he climbed on stage.

John Martin had relocated Black Sparrow Press to Santa Barbara, an hour's drive north of LA, and was in the audience with his wife, Barbara. He rarely attended Bukowski's readings and had requested the poem 'one for the shoeshine man' as a special treat. It was one of Bukowski's greatest works, surprisingly tender and optimistic:

> I am bitter sometimes
> but the taste has often been
> sweet. it's only that I've
> feared to say it. it's like
> when your woman says,
> 'tell me you love me,' and
> you can't.

But subtlety was lost on this crowd. They expected an exhibition of crudity from the dirty old man: sex poems, drinking poems and scatology.

'Cliché! Cliché!' a heckler called out.

The normally mild-mannered John Martin was so offended he pulled the back of the heckler's chair sending him sprawling onto the floor. They squared up for a fight as Bukowski ploughed on:

> the best of you
> I like more than you think.
> the others don't count
> except that they have fingers and heads
> and some of them eyes
> and most of them legs

and all of them
good and bad dreams
and a way to go.

'Charles,' came a cultural female voice, when he'd finished. She obviously didn't know nobody called him that. 'Charles, what do you think of women with big noses?'

'Jesus Christ. I have to sit here and try to answer your dumb shit questions?' He shook his head sadly. Was he a comedian, a clown? There was a muffled thud as the doormen threw the heckler against a parking meter outside. 'What do I think about big-nosed women? I'm not interested in their noses.' There was a ripple of laughter. 'Fuck off!' he said.

It seemed like they wanted him to insult them. 'You disgusting creatures,' he said, obligingly. 'You make me sick.' They laughed like hyenas at that.

He said he knew he was giving a bad reading, but he couldn't care less. If they didn't like it, they could leave. There would be no refund. 'I've already got your money in my pocket,' he said. He appeared slightly demented as he licked the microphone, making a huge slurping sound, and then shuffled his papers into a pile and got up to go.

'Fuck you guys,' he said, as he left the stage.

Claire Rabe, the owner of the club, had watched the performance in astonishment. 'People were absolutely glued,' she says. 'He was the first kind of punk event.' Like many women, she found herself attracted to Bukowski, and although she thought him dreadfully ugly and a 'real slob' (he was so drunk snot was running from his nose) she invited him home and went to bed with him. 'He was wonderfully homely, impressively so,' she says. 'I found him very desirable.'

For all his boozing and womanizing, Bukowski continued to work hard to try and boost his income above the monthly stipend he received from John Martin, recently raised from $100 to $300 in line with the increasing sales of his books. He reviewed a Rolling Stones concert for *Creem* magazine, the closest he came to straight journalism, although much of the article was taken up with meditations on horse racing, and he concluded that Beethoven was much more satisfying to listen to than Mick Jagger. He agreed to *City Lights* releasing an album of the 1972 San Francisco reading. His poems continued to appear in numerous small magazines and as broadsides. And, most importantly, he published a powerful second novel.

Factotum is the story of a young man working at a series of menial jobs, a fictionalized version of Bukowski's own experiences in the 1940s and early 1950s, before he joined the United States Postal Service. It was inspired by *Down and Out in Paris and London*, George Orwell's autobiographical account of being destitute in England and France between the wars. Orwell seems to have suffered greater hardship than Bukowski, if for a shorter period (he certainly didn't have money to waste in bars) yet Bukowski saw the reverse as being true. 'This guy thinks something has happened to him?' he said. 'Compared to me, he just got scratched. Not that it wasn't a good book, but it made me think that I might have something interesting to say along those same lines.'

The defining scene in *Factotum* comes halfway through the novel when Henry Chinaski is fired from an auto parts warehouse by a boss who has been kind to him and who reproaches Chinaski for his laziness:

'You haven't been busting your ass, Chinaski.'
I stared down at my shoes for some time. I didn't know what to say. Then I looked at him.
'I've given you my *time*. It's all I've got to give – it's all any man has. And for a pitiful buck and a quarter an hour.'
'Remember you begged for this job. You said your job was your second home.'
'. . . my time so that you can live in your big house on the hill and have all the things that go with it. If anybody has lost anything on this deal, on this arrangement . . . I've been the loser. Do you understand?'

The refusal to conform to the convention of honest work for honest pay, to take a subservient position in society because that is the capitalist order, is close to Orwell's socialist ideas. In *Down and Out in Paris and London*, he wrote that the tenet that all work is good had resulted in 'mountains of useless drudgery'. In Bukowski's case, the rejection of society went further and was almost anarchistic, although such terminology would have stuck in his throat. 'My writing has no meaning,' Bukowski said, disingenuously. 'It has no moral aspect, it has no social aspect.'

Reviewing *Factotum* in the *New York Times*, Richard Elman wrote: 'Not since Orwell has the condition of being down and out been so well recorded in the first person.' Elman also noted the novel was in striking contrast to the 'callow journalism' of Bukowski's *Notes of a Dirty Old Man* column for which he had become notorious in Los Angeles.

The short stories Bukowski wrote for the *LA Free Press*, and pornographic magazines like *Adam*, *Screw*, *Fling*, and Larry Flynt's *Hustler*, were far less crafted than the work Black Sparrow Press published. Bukowski commonly used extreme language to shock: women were 'whores' and intercourse was 'rape', pandering to his readers' basest expectations. Not only was the work often poor, he didn't enjoy writing it. On the morning he had to deliver his copy, he frequently telephoned John Martin complaining about not having written a word. 'Why am I doing this?' he asked.

Martin reminded him he did it for money and it was nobody's idea but his own. Personally he didn't think much of the *LA Free Press* or the column. 'All they wanted was sex stuff from him and that's where that reputation came from,' he says. 'He was trying to be a dirty writer, not a literary person at all. He would call me – I think he had a 2 p.m. deadline on Thursday – he would call me moaning and groaning at 10 a.m. Thursday; he hadn't written anything, and then he just whacked something out. I have gone through all that stuff to find stories for my books and a lot of it is poorly written, just piss poor. But if you read *Factotum*, there are no "whores". They are all women he tries to relate to. He admires them from afar and thinks they are way beyond him.'

Occasionally Bukowski wrote a powerful story for the newspaper, or the sex magazines, although the subject matter was often distasteful. None was more shocking, nor more accomplished, than *The Fiend* in which Bukowski describes the rape of a child.

Martin Blanchard, an unemployed solitary drunk, spies on a young girl from the window of his apartment. She is aged between six and nine years and he becomes aroused by glimpses of her underwear. He masturbates, gets drunk and then rapes the girl in a garage while her friends watch. Every detail is graphically described and the rape scene reads like pornography:

> Martin Blanchard got her panties off, but at the same time he couldn't seem to stop kissing that small mouth, and she was in a faint, had stopped hitting his face, but the different lengths of their bodies made it difficult, awkward, very, and being in passion, he couldn't think. But his cock was out – large, purple, ugly, like some stinking insanity run away with itself, and no place to go.
>
> And all the time – under this small light bulb – Martin heard the boys' voices saying, 'Look! Look! He's got that big thing and he's trying to stick that big thing into her slit!'
> 'I hear that's how people have babies.'
> 'Are they going to have a baby right here?'
> 'I guess so.'

The Fiend is the most extreme prose piece Bukowski ever wrote. He deliberately describes the rape to titillate his male readers and further manipulates them to sympathize with Blanchard by having him beaten by police at the end of the story. John Martin refused to publish it, but *Hustler* paid $1,000 to use it and, in an interview with the magazine, Bukowski tried to explain and justify the story.

He said he wrote *The Fiend* after seeing a little girl playing in a neighbor's yard, just as he had written. He admitted masturbating himself and frankly said he had felt like raping her. *Hustler* asked what stopped him.

'I didn't do it, no. I felt like doing it,' he replied. 'I'm a potential rapist, but I know that I can't get away with it. It doesn't pay off. If I raped the kid, where do I end up? I don't get any ass for fifteen years, right?'

He conceded that, by and large, little girls were frightened by the idea of having intercourse with men, but said he would let an eight-year-old suck his cock 'if she wanted to'.

'People tell me that it arouses them when they read it,' he said of the story. 'So there must be some truth in it beyond just myself and my feeling, or the character's feeling towards the child . . . They're very nice, you know. They wear those little short skirts, and when they put on their roller skates, you see their panties.'

Bukowski's justification in writing the story was that he was trying to get inside the mind of a rapist to show men something about themselves they might not care to acknowledge.

Most of the time he was bereft of ideas for his column, stealing or bastardizing stories from any source. His neighbor, Tina Darby, helped by regaling him with her adventures as an exotic dancer and by telling him what went on at the sex parties she and Brad went to. 'We would tell stories to each other and they would be in the *LA Free Press*. He would take a conversation, twist it around a little and that would be his column,' she says. He also got material from the low-life characters who lived in the court, like Sam who worked as doorman at a local massage parlor. He became Sam the Whorehouse Man in several stories.

At night, after he had stopped writing, Bukowski sometimes strolled up to the coffee stand on the corner of Hollywood and Western. He might wander into Le Sex Shoppe, the long-established pornographic book store where Brad Darby was manager. They smoked cigarettes and Brad usually gave him some magazines to take home. Other times Bukowski stood and watched the street prostitutes, some of whom he came to have a nodding acquaintance with.

'I think he felt at home there, and he thought of himself as a tough guy, so he liked sometimes to go up to the corner, stand around, watch the lights change,' says Darby. 'Everybody knew him, so everybody would wave at him and call his name out. He liked that.'

When he was at the coffee stand, Bukowski often met comic book distributor, George Di Caprio, who lived at a court on the opposite corner of Hollywood and Western with his wife, Irmelin, and their baby son who grew up to become the film star, Leonardo Di Caprio.

The Christmas of 1975 was the first the Di Caprio family had spent with their new baby. George decorated the bungalow, bought a tree and invited his mother to dinner. Christmas Eve, when they were washing up, there was a knock at the door and in burst the diabolical figure of Bukowski, his face fiery with drink.

'You know, it's just a few inches that separates a man from paradise,' said Bukowski, enigmatically, when he had taken in the scene: the tree, the cards with snow scenes, and baby Leonardo sleeping peacefully in a bassinet. George Di Caprio pondered this cryptic statement, assuming it had a festive meaning. His mother, who was a little deaf, asked what Bukowski had said.

'Yeah, hmm, it's just a few inches . . .' Bukowski began again, and then he yelled: 'THAT PREVENTS A MAN SUCKING HIS OWN COCK!'

In his relentless search for new material, Bukowski often got together with Brad and Tina the night before he had to write his column. These evenings invariably culminated in some drunken prank: Bukowski once announced that any writer should be willing to eat his own words, so he tore up the LA Free Press and swallowed it. Then he vomited over Tina's carpet. Another night he shot himself in the leg with a pistol. Yet another session ended with Brad discovering Tina and Bukowski in bed together, and Linda King went almost mad with jealousy when she found Polaroid photographs of Tina sitting naked on Bukowski's lap.

He also took inspiration from fans who came to Carlton Way to pay homage to him, people like the folk-singer Bob Lind who had a hit in 1966 with 'Elusive Butterfly'. Lind first contacted Bukowski after watching a television rerun of Taylor Hackford's documentary. He gave Bukowski his number and said he would enjoy meeting him. A few days later, at three in the morning when Bukowski was feeling lonely after another split with Linda, he telephoned Lind and invited him to get some beer and come over.

'The first thing I noticed about him, other than that dramatically ugly mug of his, were his shoulders. As I shook his hand, I put my left hand on his shoulder. It felt like cement. You don't expect muscles like that on a man so clearly dissipated,' says Lind. Bukowski explained it was from years of slinging mail bags around at the post office.

He was drinking whiskey and chasing it with Heineken. Lind

got out some cocaine, arranged two lines on the kitchen table and started rolling a dollar bill, assuming Bukowski did coke regularly.

'What is that, kid? What do I do?' asked Bukowski, who had never snorted before.

'It just makes you sharper,' said Lind. When it was Bukowski's turn, he was so nervous he exhaled when he should have inhaled and blew the powder all over the kitchen.

'Oh no, that shit's expensive, kid.'

It had been a dream come true for Bob Lind to meet Bukowski, even if he did waste his cocaine, so he was mortified to open the *LA Free Press* the following week and see himself parodied in Bukowski's column. 'He called me some hippy-dippy name and reduced me to a flower child cliché. He put stupid dialogue in my mouth along the lines of "Groovy Daddio, I'm on cloud nine."' Bukowski further humiliated Lind in his novel *Women*, turning him into the annoying character of Dinky Summers.

Bukowski also entertained a succession of female fans who telephoned or wrote to him, often sending photographs of themselves in the nude. Many were young mothers who had been through a bad relationship and were looking for an older man to look after them. Others were groupies trying to bed someone famous. They had no trouble reaching Bukowski, as he explained in his poem 'how come you're not unlisted?':

> for a man of 55 who didn't get laid
> until he was 23*
> and not very often until he was 50
> I think I should stay listed
> via Pacific Telephone
> until I get as much as
> the average man has had.

He invariably invited his callers over, whatever their motivation, so long as they could bring a six-pack of beer, and Brad

---

* In fact, he was almost 24 before he lost his virginity – to a Philadelphia prostitute.

and Tina Darby often saw young women following Bukowski up the path to the door of his apartment. 'It would just amaze me sometimes,' says Brad. 'Some of them were gorgeous and he had a constant parade.' Bukowski told these girlfriends he was already seeing someone, but she was not the kind of woman he needed. But if Linda King showed up, he quickly bundled them over to Brad and Tina's place and they had to stay there if Linda didn't leave.

One night around closing time Bukowski received a telephone call from a young woman with a particularly sexy voice. She said she was with a girlfriend at Barney's Beanery, the bar on Santa Monica Boulevard. Her girlfriend was a fan of Bukowski's writing and, as it was her thirtieth birthday, she wondered if they could meet him. 'Sure,' he said. 'Pick up a six-pack and come on over.'

Two women duly showed up, both spaced-out. The birthday girl was Georgia Peckham-Krellner. A match-thin brunette dressed like a hooker, she was the woman later immortalized by a famous photograph in which she poses with Bukowski in front of his refrigerator. The other woman, the one who had telephoned, was Pamela Miller. She was twenty-three years old and built like the girls in *Fling* magazine. She was not tall, but she had a big chest and a very pretty face, not unlike the actress Ann-Margret, with green eyes that glittered merrily (partly because she was stoned) and long glossy reddish-blonde hair. She was a girl to drive a man crazy. 'I guess you could say I was attractive,' she says, coolly, recalling her impression on Bukowski. 'I've never had too many problems attracting the opposite sex.' She told Bukowski her friends called her Cupcakes, because of her chest. It was 38 D. He could call her Cupcakes, if he wanted.

Listening to them talking, Bukowski decided that although Cupcakes was the looker, Georgia was the more likable of the pair. Cupcakes seemed to have the personality of a shark.

He told Georgia: 'I wish I could take your soul and merge it into her body.' He looked at Cupcakes, all that red hair, flaming sex. 'I would have the perfect woman.' Cupcakes giggled thinking she was being paid a compliment.

After they left, Bukowski lay on his filthy mattress, and thought about Cupcakes. He had never known a real redhead before. Her hair was like fire.

Cupcakes was working as a cocktail waitress at The Alpine Inn, a German theme bar in Hollywood, and she began coming by Carlton Way after her shift. The conversation was mostly about her – she had no interest in his poetry, which made a change. He discovered she had been born in San Francisco, in 1952, the daughter of an Italian mother and an Anglo-Irish father, a newspaper journalist who left home when she was two. When she was fifteen, Cupcakes became pregnant by her twenty-two-year-old boyfriend. She dropped out of school, had the baby, lost the husband and went to work for Pussycat Theaters, a chain of cinemas showing sex films. She was Miss Pussycat Theaters, 1973.

Life was an endless party and she didn't care about anything much so long as she was having a good time and could get stoned on diet pills, which she was dependent on. She also liked to date older men. 'I suspect that is the main reason I was attracted to Hank. I'm sure it's that classic textbook looking for the father.'

When Bukowski met her, she was living in a beat-up Hollywood bungalow with her daughter, Stacey, driving around town in a ruined Camaro filled with the detritus of her life: cans, pill bottles, clothes, shoes, magazines and cigarette packets. She was behind on the rent. She didn't always have enough money to buy Stacey clothes and was stoned from morning to night on pills she wheedled out of doctors on prescription.

When Stacey didn't have anything suitable to wear to a friend's birthday party, Bukowski took pity and bought the child a yellow dress. Pamela kissed him thank-you. It was so sweet of him.

He took her to the fights at the Olympic Auditorium and the crowd hooted at Cupcakes almost as loudly as they yelled at the contenders; she was bursting out of that damn dress. Bukowski dreamt of burying his face in her hair, those breasts, slipping the dress over her head and ripping her apart.

Then she disappeared for days on end. She said she went to stay with her mother out in the San Fernando Valley, but Bukowski was convinced she was seeing other men (not that he'd slept with her yet). 'I was a little flighty thing who would go away and come back,' says Cupcakes. 'That is enough to make any man nuts.'

In the poem, 'huge ear rings', Bukowski expressed his ambivalent feelings about her:

each time I see her she looks better
and better

200 years ago they would have burned her
at the stake

When Linda King became pregnant she didn't know if the
father was Bukowski, or whether it was one of two other men she
had been dating to get her own back on Bukowski for cheating on
her. Whoever the father was, she knew Bukowski would not support her or the baby. Fed up with the cycle of splitting and getting
back together, Linda resolved to break from him once and for all.
She quit her job, sold her house and decided to move to Arizona.

After a day shifting furniture and packing boxes, she went into
premature labor and miscarried the baby, almost bleeding to death
in the process.

Linda was at home recovering from the miscarriage when
Bukowski called on the telephone. She told him what had happened, but he didn't care. 'He didn't think it was his, so there was
no reaction.' He had news of his own. Cupcakes had been at his
apartment earlier, he said. She'd finally agreed to sleep with him,
but told him to get a new mattress first because the old one was so
disgusting. A store had delivered a $35 mattress within a couple of
hours and he'd given Cupcakes money to go and get champagne
to celebrate. He wanted to know whether Linda thought Cupcakes
would run off with the money? Linda hung up in disgust.

When Cupcakes returned with the champagne, Bukowski told
her how upset Linda had been and they laughed themselves silly.

The following evening Linda King was drinking a bottle of rosé
wine, which a boyfriend told her was good for replenishing blood,
and the drunker she got the more she brooded on what Bukowski
had said. 'The idea of him celebrating with champagne while I was
upset and suffering from my loss of everything so upset me.' She
decided to go over to his place and do some damage.

There was no answer when she knocked at his door on Carlton
Way, so she wriggled in through the kitchen window, found his
Royal typewriter, carried it out through the window and hid it
behind a bush. She went back and stole his radio, his drawings,

paintings, old photographs and, most precious of all, the first editions of his books. It was everything she thought he loved.

Bukowski came home early from the track and found Linda crouching in the bushes. She was trembling with rage, like a lunatic, and the fight that ensued was extravagant even by their standards. Tina Darby, who came out to see what was going on, says Linda seemed to have gone out of her mind. Bukowski was worried for Tina's safety, after the business with the Polaroids, and told her to go back in the house and close the door.

'I don't deserve this,' he told Linda. 'These are all my books. I wrote them. You need to give me back my books.'

Linda got an armful from The Thing and started flinging books at the windows of his apartment. As the glass shattered, she shrieked at him:

'THIS IS FOR THAT WOMAN! . . . AND THAT WOMAN! . . . AND THAT'S FOR THAT WOMAN!'

I stood there as she screamed and broke glass.

Where are the police? I thought. Where?

Then Lydia ran down the court walk, took a quick left at the trash bin and ran down the driveway of the apartment house next door. Behind a small bush was my typewriter, my radio and my toaster.

(From: *Women*)

'She is screaming bloody murder and she's got his typewriter,' recalls Tina, who watched from her window. Linda swung it round her head and brought it down so it hit a parked car and bounced onto the road.

. . . The platen and several other parts flew off. She picked the typer up again, raised it over her head and screamed, 'DON'T TELL ME ABOUT YOUR WOMEN!' and smashed it into the street again.

'I actually did Bukowski a favor,' says Linda. 'John Martin had to buy him a new typewriter. He needed one.'

She was so out of control that Bukowski felt he had no choice but to call the police, and Linda was dragged off to the station sobbing her heart out about how she'd lost their baby. Bukowski said he wouldn't press charges, because she might lose custody of her children, but she had to realize she couldn't behave like that any more. It was over, positively the end of their relationship and they both knew it. If things got any crazier, they would end up killing each other.

Linda went home and made plans to move to Arizona, slightly regretful about what they had lost. 'We really did have a love relationship which he diminished by adding other women with it, acting like it was nothing,' she says. 'We had a very great love, really, but when he got famous he had to have the fruits of his fame. That's what men get famous for, right? All the women in the world. I didn't want to be part of a hundred women.'

RED DEATH SUNSET BLOOD GLORY GALS

11

Within weeks of meeting Cupcakes, Bukowski was besotted with her, hopelessly in love with a woman less than half his age who was quite indifferent to him. She laughed at his depressions, flirted with other men, vanished for days on end and then popped up again as though nothing had happened to find him in a funk of depression with a face like the Siege of Stalingrad.

'Cups, I can't do this any more,' he would say, miserably. 'It's tearing me apart.'

> this time has finished me.
>
> I feel like the German troops
> whipped by snow and the communists
> walking bent
> with newspapers stuffed into
> worn boots.
>
> my plight is just as terrible.
> maybe more so.
>
> victory was so close
> victory was there.
>
> as she stood before my mirror
> younger and more beautiful than
> any woman I had ever known

combing yards and yards of red hair

('the retreat')

Cupcakes was unimpressed by his love poems. They were doggerel, in her opinion, and she enjoyed tormenting Bukowski by parodying his work in a bored, sing-song voice:

> So I woke up in the morning
> and I puked in the toilet
> and then I shaved . . .

'You see,' she said. 'I can write what you write, but better.'

'That's funny, Cups,' he said with a hollow laugh. 'Very funny, yeah. But we really have to end this.'

'Why?'

'Because it's killing me.'

'What are you *talking* about?' she asked, speaking as if he were a stupid child. 'You've watched too many soap operas.' She grabbed his hand and pulled him up from the sofa. 'Come on, let's go. Let's go to the track.' She had a way of jerking him out of his depressions. Some redhead magic.

They got in Bukowski's Volkswagen – which now had a hole in the windscreen where Cupcakes had put her foot through it – and drove to Hollywood Park to catch the first race. Cupcakes said to keep an eye on her because she sometimes wandered off when she was on pills and, sure enough, when he came back from placing his bet she was gone. He went to the ladies toilet, the first aid station and finally found her with another man.

The most any poet could do was write something about his beloved, and Bukowski wrote a whole book about Cupcakes, *Scarlet*, published in a limited edition by Black Sparrow Press. The four poems in the book show that lust was a large part of the attraction he felt for her:

> when she walked in I grabbed
> her and pulled her to my lap.
> I lifted my glass and told
> her, 'drink this.'

'oh,' she said, 'you've mixed
wine with Jim Beam, you're gonna
get nasty.'

'you henna your hair, don't
you?'

'you don't *look*,' she said and
stood up and pulled down her
slacks and panties and
the hair down there was the
same as the hair
up there.

('red up and down')

In Cupcakes' own copy he wrote: 'For the girl who made me write these poems, for the girl who made me feel that feeling which comes so seldom in a lifetime.' He presented it to her as a token of his adoration, a book all about her. She barely looked at it. 'I didn't have a tremendous amount of respect for his writing,' she says. 'His poetry was often negative and not complimentary. I thought I was just fodder.' The book was tossed aside to get dusty and dog-eared, something she pulled out now and again to show friends.

Bukowski had to go away for a few days and tried to see Cupcakes to say goodbye, but she was nowhere to be found. He cruised Hollywood looking for her Camaro and, after he had been everywhere he could think of, he unhooked the Maltese military cross Grandfather Bukowski had given him – it hung from the rear view mirror of the Volkswagen – and draped it from the handle of her front door, as a sign that he had been trying to contact her.

I keep searching the streets for that
blood-wine battleship she drives
with a weak battery, and the doors
hanging from broken hinges.

I drive around the streets
an inch away from weeping,
ashamed of my sentimentality and
possible love.

a confused old man driving in the rain
wondering where the good luck
went.

('i made a mistake')

   Each time he heard the clicking of heels on the concrete path
of his court, he stopped typing, hoping the sound would bring
Cupcakes to him, but the women always passed by. Whenever the
telephone rang, it was like the excitement he felt when his horse
was in among the leaders heading for the post, but he was not a
winner. In the middle of the night he drove back to her bungalow
and, seeing that the cross was still there, left a note:

1.30 a.m. Sunday morning
Red death sunset blood glory gal–
   Why is it that you are the one woman I have met who has
not loved me entirely, madly and out of context? It confuses
me. You must be my superior. Well, that's all right. – I mean,
if I can win 8 races out of 9 I can expect to be upset by a
longshot.
Blubberboy Charley.

   In the morning, when there was still no word, he went back
and left a second note:

Pam:
I HATE YOU FOR NOT ADMITTING YOU LOVE ME.
you are acting like a stupid cunt.

   Hangover remorse followed:

Pam–
I didn't mean it. I still love you. It's just that you never show
any feeling toward me, and Jesus Christ that sometimes cuts
in pretty deep.

I don't mean to load myself on you. I'll work it out. It's just going to take me a bit of time to figure out what the hell's happening.
Hank

And when she still didn't call:

Pam–
Thanks a hell of a lot of shit for nothing.

This behavior seemed excessive to Cupcakes, as it had to Linda King when Bukowski first fell for her. He was loving too passionately, considering the very short time they'd been together. However, Cupcakes would come to regret that she hadn't appreciated the depth of his affection. 'I didn't take him seriously. I didn't take myself seriously. I was just carefree and elusive and everything that drives a man crazy,' she says. 'I was just a silly kid.' If Bukowski forced her to confront his feelings, if he tried to make her hear what she meant to him, she laughed it off. 'I would make light of it, change the subject, because I wasn't capable of loving anyone deeply, or getting attached to anyone then.'

They went to New York for a reading, booking into the room at the Chelsea Hotel where Janis Joplin had liked to stay, high above cacophonous West 23rd Street. It was one of the hottest days of the year and Cupcakes sat on the balcony to try and keep cool. Bukowski watched her from the bed, her red hair glowing in the late afternoon sun. He was feeling particularly close to her because she had fallen asleep on the flight over from Los Angeles, resting her head on his shoulder. He thought it was one of the most tender moments they had shared, even though he knew she had passed out because she was stoned. He couldn't even wake her up for landing.

I looked at her enormous breasts. I watched for some sign of breathing. They didn't move. I got up and found a stewardess.
'Please take your seat, sir. We are preparing to land.'

'Look, I'm worried. My girlfriend won't wake up.'
'Do you think she's dead?' she whispered.

(From: *Women*)

'You know, Cups, the nicest thing you have ever done, the moment I will always remember, is when you laid your head on my shoulder during our plane ride,' he said.

Cupcakes looked at him quizzically. 'I remember thinking, "I can't deal with this; what do I do with this?" I was too young.' Instead of talking to him about his feelings, she decided to distract his attention. 'Look!' she shouted. 'NO HANDS!' She flung her arms out so she was balanced on the edge of the iron railing with nothing but the cheeks of her backside to stop herself falling. 'Wheeeeeeee!'

Bukowski saw that her eyes were glittery from pills and booze. 'Come on, Cups, come back in,' he coaxed her, like a dog. 'Get down now.'

'Wheeeeeeeee!'

Then she fell, just catching herself before spinning down into the garbage cans.

> I've lost a lot of women
> in a lot of different ways
> but that would have been
> the first time
> that way.

('liberty')

The reading was at St Mark's Church, on the corner of 2nd Avenue and 10th Street, and it was a sell-out. Bukowski walked to the stage swinging a six-pack of beer with Cupcakes swinging her hips behind him. 'He was just swamped by his fans,' says Gerard Malanga, who was taking photographs. 'These were guys you never see at a poetry reading.' It was a significant improvement on the last time he had been in the city with a cardboard suitcase and $7 in his pocket only to find 'Aftermath of a Lengthy Rejection Slip' relegated to the end pages of *Story* magazine.

He read five or six love poems to Cupcakes during the evening, but she was too stoned to know what was going on. Later that night, back at the hotel, she fell off the bed and didn't even wake up.

Although he was infatuated with Cupcakes, Bukowski continued to see other women and corresponded with a number of female fans, young girls like Jo Jo Planteen, a twenty-two-year-old student from Sacramento who contacted him as a dare. Bukowski wrote that if Jo Jo ever came to Los Angeles she would find he was a champion at oral sex. He flew to Texas to see two women who had been writing to him, one of whom wanted to take him on an all-expenses-paid trip to Europe. In September, he went to San Francisco for an assignation with a girlfriend of A.D. Winans. 'That seemed to be a thing with Hank,' says Winans. 'When it came to friendships he would make it with your best girl, apparently, that was just one of his failings.'

There was no answer one day when John Martin called Bukowski on the telephone, so he drove down to Hollywood to check he was alright. Sitting on the porch were two blonde girls from Holland, aged about eighteen, dressed in jeans and tank-tops. 'They were like little drops of dew on the leaf,' says Martin. 'They looked like they had never used a bad word in their life.'

'Is Hank in?' he asked.

'Yeah, he's sleeping.'

'What are you guys doing here?'

'We came from Amsterdam to fuck him,' they answered, like they were waiting to get into Disneyland.

Another time the mail man came by and found three women waiting on Bukowski's porch. 'Hank, how do you do it, how do you get it?' he asked. Bukowski replied that the problem was how to get rid of them.

Then there were the groupies who came up to him at poetry readings, giving him their telephone number and saying how much they loved his work. Bukowski once said this was the worst way to meet women, yet it is how he met Linda Lee Beighle who became his second wife.

Linda Lee was born in 1943 into a well-off Pennsylvania family. She ran away from home when she was a teenager and, in the

1960s, followed the hippy trail to India. Returning to the United States, she became a devotee of Meher Baba, the Indian guru who coined the phrase 'don't worry, be happy', and worked for a television station in Miami, Florida, before moving to California where she opened a health food restaurant at Redondo Beach. When she discovered Bukowski was reading at The Troubadour in West LA, in the September of 1976, Linda Lee decided to try and meet him.

Before the show, Bukowski and Cupcakes were drinking in the bar with Joan Smith and her boyfriend. Joan was a former go-go dancer turned poet, and her boyfriend, who was buying champagne, was a magazine publisher. He wanted to get Bukowski to write for him, but Bukowski was unimpressed. 'He was rich and Bukowski didn't like rich people,' says Joan. 'He didn't like being patronized.' Bukowski drained his glass, told Joan she was getting fat, picked up a six-pack of beer, which had become a stage prop for him, and went out to face the crowd.

He read some of the new poems about Cupcakes, poems like 'a stethoscope case' which were later collected in the popular anthology, *Love is a Dog from Hell*.

> my doctor has just come into his office
> from the surgery.
> he meets me in the men's john.
> 'God damn,' he says to me,
> 'where did you find her? oh, I just like
> to *look* at girls like that!'
> I tell him: 'it's my specialty: cement
> hearts and beautiful bodies. If you can find
> a heart-beat, let me know.'

'That's me!' yelled Cupcakes. She was stumbling around in the audience, banging into tables. People laughed. She was totally out of it. 'Hey, that's me!'

'Yeah, baby, that was you,' said Bukowski, reading another about how much he loved her. He didn't notice that she had already left, wandering out onto Santa Monica Boulevard to cadge a lift home.

When the crowd thinned out, Bukowski was left with Joan and her boyfriend, but he was no longer interested in drinking, upset that Cupcakes had left like that. He was making his way out of The Troubadour when Linda Lee Beighle introduced herself, saying she loved his work and had been reading it for years. He looked her over. She was younger than him, but not very young. She was small and thin with a mop of blonde hair. Not bad looking. He wrote his telephone number on a scrap of paper, drawing a picture of a man with a bottle, and she wrote down hers. Then he went home.

Things were still rough with Cupcakes so, a couple of days later, Bukowski drove over to Linda Lee's restaurant, the Dew Drop Inn. She fixed him a health food sandwich and he sat down to eat and take in the ambience of the place. It was decorated with painted rainbows and posters of Linda Lee's guru, a curious-looking fellow with a fixed grin.

There was a bookcase. Three or four of my books were in it. I found some Lorca and sat down and pretended to read. That way I wouldn't have to see the guys in their walking shorts. They looked as if nothing had ever touched them – all well-mothered, protected, with a soft sheen of contentment. None of them had ever been in jail, or worked hard with their hands, or even gotten a traffic ticket. Skimmed-milk jollies, the whole bunch.

(From: *Women*)

Bukowski was in the middle of writing *Women* under the working title *Love Tale of the Hyena*. It was a thinly veiled account of his tangled love life since he quit the post office, inspired by Giovanni Boccaccio's *The Decameron*. Linda Lee, whom he began to date soon after visiting the Dew Drop Inn, became the basis of the character, Sara. 'I was basically one of his guinea pigs,' she says, 'one of those he researched like a curiosity.' But there was a fundamental difference between her and most of the other women Bukowski knew, and included in his book – Linda Lee wouldn't let him have sex with her. At least not at first. Apparently one of Meher Baba's teachings was that

unmarried people should remain chaste, and she had been celibate
for several years. Bukowski gently suggested Meher Baba might be
mistaken, but all he could get from Linda Lee were kisses.

> We kissed in the dark. I was a kiss freak anyway, and
> Sara was one of the best kissers I had ever met. I'd have to
> go all the way back to Lydia to find anyone comparable. Yet
> each woman was different, each kissed in her own way. Lydia
> was probably kissing some son of a bitch right now, or worse,
> kissing his parts.

(From: *Women*)

Reminded of Linda King, Bukowski flew to Phoenix to pay her
a visit for old time's sake and they spent a weekend together. He
said she should come back to Los Angeles with him and battle it out
with Cupcakes and his other girlfriends. Life was boring without
her. 'But I think we both knew it was over,' says Linda. 'He knew
I wasn't coming back.'

Their final farewell inspired the poem, 'I am a reasonable man'.
From reading it in isolation one would never know this was a
woman Bukowski had been in love with:

> we'd had the night together
> and now it was breakfast
> in this Arizona cafe,
> nice quiet place
> the sun coming in
> on the red and white checkered
> tablecloth.
>
> she said,
> 'I can't eat . . .'
>
> the tears were running down
> her face
>
> 'I'll finish your breakfast,'
> I told her,
> 'no use wasting it . . .'

she straightened her back
inhaled and
screamed.

'That was the kind of poem he wrote that I hated,' she says. 'The tone of the poem, like he was above and beyond any feelings, but he might stick around another night for a blow job, if I begged him. He could be quite cruel and spare himself beautifully.' They never saw each other again.

Back in LA, the new Linda was waiting for him. 'He was doing all this stuff with all these women and we became good friends,' says Linda Lee. 'We drank together and we would talk on the phone all the time.' Intercourse was still out of the question, just kissing and some rubbing up against each other in bed, if he was lucky. But Linda Lee was becoming emotionally involved. She sent Bukowski sentimental poems decorated with pictures of hearts broken in two, and wrote letters about how everything she saw, everything she did in her daily life, reminded her of him. She was falling in love with him.

Cupcakes would have been a formidable rival for his affections, but she'd started dating a dental student and woke up in his bed one morning knowing she was finished with Bukowski. She didn't even bother saying good-bye. He was inconsolable, of course, and the unhappiness was evident when the German film maker, Thomas Schmitt, asked him to read a poem for a documentary he was making. He read 'the shower', a poem he had written about Linda King, but it was applicable to all the lost loves, and he broke down when he came to the last stanza:

> . . . you brought it to me,
> when you take it away
> do it slowly and easily
> make it as if I were dying in my sleep . . .

'This is Hank Bukowski,' he said when Amber O'Neil answered the telephone. Amber was another of his fans. She had written from the San Francisco bay area saying how much she loved his stuff and would like to meet him. He told her he'd split with his girlfriend who, he added, had a perfect body. He wondered if Amber wanted to come to LA.

'I'm not the type of woman you are used to down there,' she replied, a little intimidated by the description of Cupcakes. 'I'm very short and not all tits and ass.'

'Well, that doesn't matter,' said Bukowski, who had noticed that she had a very high voice, like Betty Boop. 'Maybe you could come down and we could just talk.'

'Hey! I'm not *that* short.'

'Well, whatever,' he laughed.

'Are you inviting me down?'

'Yeah, sure, I do this all the time.'

It was a Friday evening at Los Angeles airport and Bukowski watched the women coming off the Oakland flight, haughty creatures looking like they had come to conquer LA. He looked slyly at their legs and breasts. Linda Lee said he never looked directly at women and it was true; beautiful women scared him. He wondered which one was Amber. Then he heard that squeaky voice.

'Hello, Mr Bukowski.'

He looked down at what he took to be a young girl: five feet nothing, 94 lbs, wearing jeans, wedges and a red cotton blouse with a low neck and puffed sleeves. He wrote about the meeting in *Women*, calling her Tanya:

> . . . I turned and behind me was this very small child. She looked about 18, thin long neck, a bit round-shouldered, long nose . . .

'Come along, granddaughter,' he said to Amber, who was actually in her thirties, and led her out to where his car was parked.

Amber liked Bukowski's 'shit-brown' apartment, a glorious dump of a place with old coffee cans full of grease in the kitchen, for frying steak and eggs, and a refrigerator loaded with white wine which he had started to drink because Linda Lee thought it better for him than beer and whiskey. Everything in the apartment appeared dark, because it was old and because there was only one forty watt bulb. But the bathroom had the unmistakable look that a woman had been in and cleaned and Bukowski confirmed that Linda Lee had scrubbed it. Amber also discovered Linda Lee had made the wooden bed frame upon which rested the Cupcakes Memorial Mattress, actually constructed the frame out of pieces of lumber. This was the same bed, presumably, they were going to sleep on. If that wasn't weird enough, Linda Lee telephoned to check Bukowski was all right.

Not knowing quite how to proceed with her hero, Amber unzipped his pants, took off her jeans and mounted the penis she had read so much about, working out her nervousness in a sweaty fuck. Bukowski wrote in *Women* that it felt like being raped by a child:

> She worked at it like a monkey on a string. Tanya was a faithful reader of my works. She bore down. That child knew something. She could sense my anguish. She worked away furiously, playing with her clit with one finger, her head thrown back. We were caught up together in the oldest and most exciting game of all. We came together and it lasted and lasted until I thought my heart would stop. She fell against me, tiny and frail. I touched her hair. She was sweating. Then she pulled herself off me and went into the bathroom.

'Mr Bukowski,' she said afterwards. 'I can barely hold my head up. Do you mind if I go and lay down in that homemade bed made by your beautiful friend?'

The following evening he decided to splash out and take her to his favorite restaurant, The Musso & Frank Grill, a landmark on Hollywood Boulevard since before he was born. Amber wanted to look special for their big date and had with her what she describes as a 'Chinese hooker' dress, but it needed ironing and there was neither iron nor ironing board in the apartment. So she heated up the steak pan.

'That's certainly a first,' said Bukowski as he watched her burn a hole.

An easy peace and quiet pervaded the dining rooms at Musso's, air-conditioned cool like a cave after the heat and tourist bustle of Hollywood Boulevard. He told Amber he took so many women here that the barman probably thought he was a pimp. Ruben Rueda certainly knew Bukowski, and knew to watch out if he started drinking whiskey. 'He was a little wild,' he says. 'I had to kick him out a couple of times. I could tell when he was drunk. The first thing I can see is the eyes. I talk and the eyes is gone some place.'

They sat at the bar and ordered drinks. It was a liquor night and Rueda watched Bukowski warily as he ordered whiskey and ordered the same again, but Bukowski was in a mellow mood. Looking at his reflection in the mirror behind the bar, he said: 'You know, I don't look so bad.' Amber realized how important his looks were to him. All his life he had thought of himself as ugly and now, in middle age, with his beard growing grey, he was starting to look good, like he ought to somehow.

'You look very handsome,' she said.

'And you are one hell of a woman,' he replied, tenderly. 'And your eyes are beautiful, too.'

Back at the apartment, Amber found herself sitting in darkness on the couch with Bukowski opposite, the only light coming from the lamps outside in the court. He told her about Linda King teaching him to go down on her. He liked it and said he would like to do it with Amber, if she didn't mind. She replied that she wouldn't mind at all, thinking no man had ever asked so formally to have sex with her, and by the light of the moon, on Linda Lee's homemade bed, he buried his old face between her legs.

Amber was not the only lover Bukowski took to the bed Linda Lee made. He also had an affair with Jane Manhattan, a well-spoken twenty-nine-year-old restaurant manager he met at a reading in Vancouver in November, 1976. They slept together then and later that month she flew to Los Angeles to spend a nine-day vacation at Carlton Way. 'I think I was probably the most lady-like of all Bukowski's friends,' says Jane. 'That was what was so funny. It was that contrast that made the relationship so hilarious.'

He took her to Musso & Frank and they went to watch the horses at Hollywood Park. Jane noticed the tellers and the barmen at the track all knew Bukowski, even if they didn't know he was a writer. 'He was one of the guys. That was the life that he loved. That was when he was happy.'

Shopping with Tina Darby in Hollywood, Jane bought a pair of black high heels. Bukowski was delighted when she showed him. He put his cock inside one shoe and began prancing round the bedroom, pretending to fuck it.

'You don't love me, bitch!' he said and threw the shoe down, sending Jane into gales of laughter. 'He was funny all day every day. A great love of life, and an enjoyment – always to be seeing the funny thing, and making a comment. He was a comedian.'

She saw a different side to him one afternoon when they passed a bar and she suggested a drink.

'I can't go in there,' he said, starting to cry. 'So many years were so terrible and all those hours and days and years that I spent in bars drunk out of my mind. I just feel sick to my stomach when I even look into a bar like that.'

Linda Lee began spending three days a week at the apartment, driving up from Redondo Beach on Saturday afternoon and staying until Tuesday, if Bukowski didn't have any other women visiting. He realized she was falling in love with him. He liked her, too, although he sometimes felt she was becoming too possessive. She had begun to resent women telephoning, and he broke it off a couple of times because of this, but she reacted badly to being rejected. In a letter to Jo Jo Planteen in May, 1977, he wrote that Linda Lee went almost mad whenever they split. Still, he was skilled at deception. When he discovered that one of the leaders of the Meher Baba sect was coming to Redondo Beach in the first week in July, Bukowski suggested to Jo Jo that this would be an excellent opportunity for them to see each other. Linda Lee would be occupied playing host to her religious friend.

Despite his gripes about Linda Lee, they grew ever closer and Bukowski stopped trying to cheat on her. He liked the way Linda Lee looked after him, worrying about how much he drank and what cigarettes he smoked. After all, he was in his late fifties and starting to feel his age. She was attractive and bright and they had fun together, most of the time. Essentially they had become friends and he felt it was time he treated her better, as he wrote to Carl Weissner in August, 1977:

Went down to Del Mar with Linda Lee and we got stinko in our motel room and went swimming and diving in the rough surf at 1.30 a.m. A real gasser and not a bad way to die but I came on out and we got back to the motel, poured some more, and got along that night. She's a good girl and has lived through many of my drunken, mad, unkind nights and has forgiven me . . . so far.

It was still not exactly torrid. Linda Lee likens that side of their relationship to the lifestyle of a monk. 'There was indeed a great importance about celibacy,' she says. 'And that wasn't because he was starving and not able to get sex – I think it was because he had had, off and on, amazing, obscene, absurd experiences with crazy women.' The experiences had been distilled into *Women*, and the companion book of poems, *Love Is a Dog from Hell*. With the completion of these two works, he was satiated with his old ways and ready for a new life.

EUROPEAN SON

12

In May, 1978, Bukowski caught a Lufthansa flight to Germany to give a reading and visit the town of his birth. Linda Lee was travelling with him along with their photographer friend, Michael Montfort, who was hoping to put together a journal of the trip.

The complimentary drinks trolley came down the aisle and they started on the white wine and then they drank all the rosé before moving on to the red. 'Michael, you have a deal,' said Bukowski, when he was pleasantly drunk. 'I'm going to write the book.'*

With business concluded, he set about drinking all the complimentary beer as they sped onward over the ocean he had last crossed as a child on the SS *President Fillmore*.

The first Bukowski book published in translation in Germany was *Notes of a Dirty Old Man*, in 1970, with the bogus Henry Miller quote on the cover. Undeterred by its poor sales, Carl Weissner and publisher Benno Käsmyr put together *Poems Written Before Jumping Out of an 8 Storey Window*, borrowing the title from one of Bukowski's early chapbooks. It quickly sold fifty thousand copies by word of mouth. Three books of short stories followed, all taken from *Erections, Ejaculations, Exhibitions and General Tales of Ordinary Madness*, the most outré work collected in *The Fuck Machine*. Each sold in the region of eighty thousand copies.

* The travelogue, *Shakespeare Never Did This*.

After this success, Weissner and a Frankfurt publisher collaborated on the book which really established Bukowski in Germany, a sampler of the novels *Post Office* and *Factotum* together with short stories. Published as *Stories and Novels*, it was better known as *The Blue Book* and sold almost a hundred thousand.

To Bukowski's astonishment, he was soon more widely read in Germany than in America where his books were printed in small editions of only four thousand copies or so. Even though Black Sparrow Press reprinted most titles every year, sales did not approach his remarkable success in Europe.

John Martin believes Bukowski's vulgarity appeals to German readers. 'You see *Stern* magazine, they love nothing better than bathroom jokes and farting jokes. That's their national humor, so he caught on right away,' he says.

Carl Weissner sees his popularity in terms of a reaction to post-war German literature which was politically correct in an extremely self-conscious way. There was even a school of thought that, after the Holocaust, Germans couldn't write poetry. 'So everything was politicized on the left and all writers were interested in was interviewing workers and housewives. Since Bukowski didn't have a political program, and didn't bother with refined literary highfalutin language, that obviously was an attraction for a lot of people. It was his attitude: not wanting to belong, and largely writing about himself and things he had gone through. He was not considered, except by the right, as a porn writer or anything like that. In fact, a lot of people thought he was a proletarian writer.'

It was also Bukowski's good fortune to have in Carl Weissner someone who took infinite care translating his unusual style of poetry and prose into readable and entertaining German. It was not always a straight-forward job. 'He is easy to translate when he is colorful and uses a lot of adjectives,' explains Weissner. 'But he is difficult when his language becomes very bare, short sentences and stuff.'

Freelance photographer Michael Montfort, a German living in Hollywood, was hired to take the pictures for magazine articles about Bukowski, and made a good first impression by arriving at Carlton Way with a case of wine on his shoulder. 'I felt that he was kind of awkward in posing for a camera,' he says. 'He was a pretty tough guy, but he didn't like it from the beginning.'

Montfort became a fan of Bukowski's work and began advising John Martin which German magazines it was worth giving interviews to. He also sat in on interviews, ending them when Bukowski got too drunk so he didn't look like a complete idiot.

Bukowski had mixed feelings about dealing with journalists. 'Basically I believe that he really rather wanted to be alone,' says Montfort. 'On the other hand, I'm sure that he loved the attention, although he never would have admitted it. It was also having something to do apart from the daily routine. At that time, if somebody paid for a case of wine, it made a difference in his life. If it was arranged and OK-ed, and was on his terms, his time, his date, he would more or less reluctantly play the wild man. He would try and live up to his image.'

One German interviewer was so overwhelmed by meeting Bukowski that he was unable to ask any questions. 'It was like he was frozen, a frozen man!' recalls Linda Lee. 'He was catatonic.' Bukowski was not at all pleased, having interrupted his day, and tried to get the interviewer to relax. 'Hey man,' he said. 'Are you having a little problem. Are you OK?'

He offered him a drink, but still the interviewer couldn't speak. 'Hey, what's your fucking problem?' asked Bukowski, his patience running thin. 'You stupid fucking son of a bitch, don't you even know what the fuck to ask me?'

Apparently not.

'Fuck it! I'll ask you. I'll interview you,' he said. 'So how's it going, my man? What's going on? So what's your name?'

The German began crying, and held out his hand for mercy. Bukowski spat in it and pushed it back.

There had been a spate of terrorist bombings in Germany and the customs men at Frankfurt airport demanded to know what was in the parcels Bukowski had brought with him from Los Angeles. They were simply gifts for Carl Weissner and his son, Mikey, but Bukowski was not used to being questioned in this way and was still a little drunk from the flight. 'It's none of your fucking business,' he snarled.

After ten days of drinking and sight-seeing, Bukowski arrived in Hamburg for the reading feeling very nervous, partly because he didn't know if the crowd would understand enough English to follow what he was saying. The venue was The Marktahalle, a covered market building by the docks, and Bukowski was astonished to see hundreds of fans lining up for tickets when he went over for a sound-check. 'We had no idea so many people would turn up,' says Carl Weissner. 'Because it was at very short notice. There were only a few posters in the town announcing the reading. Nobody was sure he would come, that's why there was practically nothing in the papers. But it was all word of mouth which explains the fact that people from Sweden and Denmark and Holland and Austria came.'

It was a sell-out with a capacity crowd of twelve hundred, paying ten Deutschmarks a head, and another three hundred turned away at the door, five times the number who had come to see novelist Günter Grass. People were standing in the aisles, reaching out to touch Bukowski as he pushed his way to the stage. They offered bottles of wine and chanted his name like they were at a football match.

> There was that audience, all those bodies were in there to see me, to hear me. They expected the magic action, the miracle. I felt weak. I wished I were at a race track or sitting at home drinking and listening to the radio or feeding my cat, doing anything, sleeping, filling my car with gas, even seeing my dentist. I held Linda Lee's hand, about frightened. The chips were down.

(From: *Shakespeare Never Did This*)

'Hello,' said Bukowski, adjusting the microphone, 'it's good to be back.'

He started with 'Free', a poem about airplane passengers drinking complimentary champagne and getting sick. The crowd seemed to enjoy it. The second and third poems were more serious, but the audience stayed with him, not like when he tried to read serious stuff to American crowds. There was laughter when he read a line he meant to be funny, but the rest of the time they listened quietly, applauding when he came to the end. Apparently they understood English perfectly.

My poems were not intellectual but some of them were serious and mad. It was really the first time, for me, that the crowd had understood them. It sobered me so I had to drink more.

(From: *Shakespeare Never Did This*)

There was a rowdy element in the crowd: some bikers, a group of feminists and a young man who screamed abuse as if he were demented. Bukowski dealt skillfully with the hecklers.

'Haven't you gone home to your mother yet?' he asked the young man. 'She's got a little bottle of milk for you, warmed up.'

The crowd applauded his wit and style, and he rewarded them with 'Looking for a Job'. It was meant to be funny and they laughed in the right places:

> it was Philly and the bartender said
> what and I said, gimme a draft, Jim,
> got to get the nerves straight, I'm
> going to look for a job. you, he said,
> a job?
> yeah, Jim, I saw something in the paper,
> no experience necessary.
> and he said, hell, you don't want a job,
> and I said, hell no, but I need money . . .

Encouraged by the reception, he told stories about his life in Hollywood. 'Where I live I drink a certain brand of wine, two or three bottles a night, and the liquor stores run out so I have two liquor stores stocking my wine. If one doesn't have it, I run to the other. The liquor men love me. I'm making those bastards rich and I'm killing myself!' There was more clapping. 'You mustn't applaud when I'm killing myself,' he laughed.

Afterwards he signed books until his hand was sore and drank champagne as the promoter counted out his money in crisp one hundred-Deutschmark notes.

Montfort hired a white BMW and drove them to Andernach to see Heinrich Fett, Bukowski's mother's brother, whom he had been corresponding with on and off since was a child. Uncle Heinrich was ninety but he came bounding down the stairs with gusto, smartly dressed in jacket and tie, and exclaimed in English: 'Henry! Henry! My God, I can't believe it.' Bukowski was close to tears as the old man embraced him. 'It's Henry. After all these years!'

They went to the house of Heinrich's son, Karl, and his daughter-in-law Josephine. She served wine and cake, like Bukowski remembered his German-born grandmother doing in Pasadena.

> It was when one sat and talked gently of things; it was the pause in the battle of life; it was necessary and good. Uncle began talking about his life, of the past . . .

(From: *Shakespeare Never Did This*)

Uncle Heinrich needed no translator as he regaled Bukowski with the family history, stopping occasionally to urge more cake on Linda Lee and to replenish his nephew's glass. 'Your father was a sergeant and he spoke perfect German,' he said. '"That handsome Sergeant Bukowski," your mother used to say, "I'll bet he tries to fool all the girls." A couple of nights later Sergeant Bukowski came up the stairway and knocked. He had meat, the good meat, cooked, plus the other things . . . bread, vegetables. We ate it. And after that, late at night, every night he came up with his meat and we ate it. That's how they met and became married.' Bukowski nodded and emptied his glass. 'Your father was a very intelligent man,' said Uncle Heinrich.

They spoke about what Bukowski was doing in Germany and Uncle Heinrich said he had read some of his books. He liked most of them, but not *The Fuck Machine*. 'That's all right, uncle, after I write something I try to forget it,' Bukowski replied. 'It doesn't matter afterwards, even if they say it's good.'

Bukowski was concerned they might be tiring the old fellow, so he said they ought to be getting along, and they drove back across town to the Hotel Zum Anker, by the Rhine which had flooded the foreshore as it often did at that time of year. Bukowski and Linda Lee went to take a nap while Montfort settled in the bar to label his film. Shortly after he started work, Uncle Heinrich walked in and rapped smartly on the floor with his stick.

'I demand to see Charles!' said the old man. The hotelier pointed to Montfort and suggested he speak to him. Uncle Heinrich banged the floor again. 'I forgot something and have to talk to him now.'

'He's taking a nap.'

Uncle Heinrich would not be dissuaded, so Montfort called the room and apologized, saying he didn't know what to do but Bukowski's uncle was there and demanded he see him right away.

The old man took Bukowski to see the house where he had been born and Bukowski was amused to learn that, until recently, it had been the town brothel. Then they went back to Uncle Heinrich's home where the old man produced a case of letters and photographs Bukowski's mother had mailed from America. There were black and white pictures of Bukowski and his parents at Santa Monica beach, a Stars and Stripes flag in the sand; posing with their Model-T Ford; and at Grandma Bukowski's house – yellowing windows into that terrible childhood. Bukowski couldn't help but cry.

That evening at the hotel he drank like he was possessed, filled with emotion and memories of his parents. 'I have never ever seen a man drink so much wine,' said Rolf Degen, a journalism student who had come to Andernach to meet Bukowski. The film maker, Thomas Schmitt, also joined them in the bar where Bukowski drank at least seven bottles of wine.

There was a group of travelling salesmen singing traditional German folk songs and, although Bukowski did not understand the words, he sensed their pomposity and started dancing and singing in mockery, prancing on the tables and clapping his hands.

They went up to Bukowski's room where Degen pretended to interview him using a shower head as a microphone. Bukowski played along with the game for a while and then hurled the shower head into the street, bringing the hotelier pounding up the stairs to see what was going on. Degen was thrown out and Thomas Schmitt was escorted from the building. Bukowski went out on the balcony and bellowed across the frigid Rhine to them. 'Thomas, you marvellous motherfucker, a long life to you!' he yelled. 'A LONG LIFE TO GERMANY!'

It was book sales in Europe rather than success in the United States that earned Bukowski his first substantial royalties, so much money that his accountant advised him to get a mortgage to reduce his tax liability. This led Bukowski to take a closer look at his general finances and, for the first time, he began to question his business arrangement with John Martin.

At the time, Bukowski was being paid around $6,500 a year by Black Sparrow Press, advance royalties for the novels and books of poems and short stories published in America, apart from those published by City Lights Books which brought in extra income. It was not very much to live on. After paying child support and rent, Bukowski complained he was probably eligible for food stamps. He had also begun to resent producing original artwork for special editions of each new book, the habit he and Martin had established years before. He informed Martin in one angry letter that he felt like wet back labor and reminded him there were New York publishers interested in his work. Several friends had advised him to leave Black Sparrow and Linda Lee, in particular, felt he had been loyal enough. In a June, 1978, letter to Weissner, Bukowski wrote that Martin also took twenty per cent of foreign sales:

> He used to get 10. Linda dislikes him, thinks he is fucking me . . . I appreciate her concern but I don't want to end up like Céline . . . bitching and bitching against editors and publishers, the idea is to write about something else.

His concerns came to a head late on the evening of 11 June, 1978, when he telephoned Martin at home. He said he was no longer happy with being sent a monthly check, currently $500. In future he wanted specific information about sales and a reckoning-up twice a year. If it meant he was paid less some months, that was fine. There was another complaint: he was frustrated with the delay in publishing *Women*, which he considered the best work he had done. The manuscript had been with Martin almost a year and still the book was not out.

'It was the only rancorous call, and he didn't even remember it the next day,' says Martin, but although he assured him they had never been more than a few hundred dollars apart, if that, he agreed to send a regular royalty statement twice a year in future. The monthly payments continued as before. 'In the thirty years I published him we had remarkably few tense moments and I always understood that he was basically in charge.'

Reassured his affairs were in order, and encouraged by a check for $9,000 from his publishers in France, Bukowski and Linda Lee began looking at property to buy. They went all over the Los Angeles area, going as far as Santa Monica and up into Topanga Canyon, before finding an old two-storey detached house in San Pedro, the port town at the southern edge of the Los Angeles sprawl.

The house, which had an asking price of a little over $80,000, had been built on the crest of a small hill overlooking the harbor. There was a hedge in front which Bukowski liked (privacy was becoming increasingly important now he was famous). The living room was large, with an open fire, and sliding glass doors led into a garden planted with roses and fruit trees. Upstairs – he had never lived in a house with stairs before – was a master bedroom and a box room with a balcony overlooking the harbor, a perfect place for writing.

It was strange to be buying property after a lifetime of renting. Frightening, too. What if he couldn't make the payments? But he decided to take the risk and was soon pottering happily in his garden with Butch, the stray cat he brought with him from Carlton Way, a suburban home owner at last.

One night the telephone rang and a foreign-sounding fellow introduced himself as Barbet Schroeder, a film director. He wanted to meet to discuss a movie project. Bukowski's number was unlisted, now he had got laid as much as the average man, and he did not take kindly to the intrusion. 'Fuck off, you French frog,' he said.

Schroeder was thirty-seven, born in Iran and raised in France. He had studied philosophy at the Sorbonne before becoming a promoter of jazz concerts, then a journalist, an actor and finally a director of underground movies. He was a charming man, both in person and on the telephone, and managed to persuade Bukowski to meet him, telling him he had read all his books and wanted to make a ninety-minute film from one of his stories, not to exploit the work but to pay homage to it. Bukowski was not sure, wondering whether any of his stories could stretch to such a long adaptation. Schroeder seemed sincere, however, and Bukowski liked him. He said he would think it over but first he had to go to Paris to appear on a TV show.

Apostrophes was a discussion program broadcast on national French television. It was hosted by Bernard Pivot, a well-known personality in France, and had an audience of several millions. The TV company were so eager to have Bukowski on the show that they paid for flights from Los Angeles, for him and Linda Lee, and put them up in a hotel in Paris. Bukowski figured the show would help his European sales, and he and Linda Lee planned a holiday around it, hoping to visit Carl Weissner and Linda Lee's mother who was staying in the South of France.

Bukowski arrived at the Channel 2 building forty-five minutes early. He had stipulated he wanted two bottles of good white wine delivered to him before he went on the show and the first arrived while he was in make-up. He was soon drinking wine from the bottle, and was very drunk indeed when he was led through to meet his fellow guests. These included a distinguished psychiatrist, who had treated Antonin Artaud, and an attractive female author, of what exactly Bukowski was never sure. They were seated round a coffee table on which were arranged several of Bukowski's books.

Bukowski was the star guest, so Pivot began by asking him how it felt to be fêted in Europe, to be on French television.

'I know a great many American writers who would like to be on this program now,' replied Bukowski, speaking even more ponderously than usual. He was puffing on a *sher bidi*, a type of Indian cigarette Linda Lee had introduced him to. It looked like a joint and smelt awful. He was also obviously drunk, slurring his words and nodding his head. 'It doesn't mean so much to me . . .' he said.

Pivot tried to develop a discussion from this unpromising start, but Bukowski seemed to have trouble following the translation so Pivot turned to the lady writer. After a few minutes Bukowski broke into the conversation, saying he would like to see more of the woman's legs. More specifically, he wanted to examine her ankles. That way he felt he might know how good a writer she was.

Pivot gave him a withering look and Bukowski told him he was a 'fucking son of a fucking bitch asshole' which set the translators an interesting problem as the show was going out live. Pivot fully understood what Bukowski had said. He put his hand over the American's foul mouth and told him to shut up.

'Don't you ever say that to me,' Bukowski growled.

He pulled the translation device from his ear, rose unsteadily to his feet and turned to leave. Pivot bid him au revoir with a Gallic shrug. The other guests watched in astonishment. Bukowski stumbled momentarily, steadied himself by touching the head of the man next to him, and then tottered off, as the translators and audience rocked with laughter.

They made their way down to the reception area where they were met by police. 'When Hank saw that, he got this crazy little fiction going in his head, like the enemy is approaching,' says Linda Lee. He pulled out his blade, a small hunting knife he always carried, and brandished it at them. There was a scuffle, but Linda Lee kept her cool and watched where Bukowski's hands went. She grabbed his blade from him and then they both got the hell out of there.

The TV appearance was punk-like at a time when punk music and attitudes were fashionable in Europe. (He had been interviewed the day before by a punk journalist who endeared himself to Bukowski by asking for heroin – Bukowski said he wasn't carrying – and by saying he liked pollution, which Bukowski thought very funny.) Consequently his antics on *Apostrophes* made headlines in France's daily newspapers. Some took the view that it was a scandal. Others were of the opinion Bukowski had been a breath of fresh air on an establishment show.

'You were great, bastard,' said the excitable journalist who rang from *Le Monde*. 'Those others couldn't masturbate.'

'What did I do?' asked Bukowski, his hangover obscuring the events of the previous evening.

'He didn't remember anything, of course, but the whole of France was running to book shops to buy his books,' says Barbet Schroeder. 'In a few hours they were all sold out.'

A couple of days later Bukowski and Linda Lee were in Nice on the French Riviera, visiting Linda Lee's mother, when a waiter in a café recognized Bukowski and asked for his autograph. He signed obligingly and then glanced across at the neighboring café where he saw five more waiters watching him. When they saw that Bukowski had noticed, the waiters bowed solemnly in unison to show their respect, and then went about their business again. It was a remarkable moment for a man who had spent more than half his life as an unknown writer, a humble postal clerk, but then so many things were new and strange now Bukowski was a success.

CHINASKI IN SUBURBIA

13

Most of Bukowski's former girlfriends had no idea he was using them as material for a novel, and he certainly never asked permission to write about their sex lives. So when *Women* was finally published after a long delay, in December 1978, it was the cause of some consternation to those women who had shared his life before he settled down with Linda Lee Beighle. The embarrassment was further compounded by the fact that *Women* sold more than any of his other books.

Linda King was not fooled by the prominent disclaimer:

> This novel is a work of
> fiction and no character
> is intended to portray
> any person or combination
> of persons living or dead.

The fact that he had changed names – Linda to Lydia in her case, hardly an impenetrable disguise – and made this disingenuous claim that it was all fiction was a joke as far as she was concerned. 'Everybody knew everything he wrote was a real thing,' she says. At least Linda had been aware of what Bukowski was up to; he made no secret of it during their time together. But the book came as a rude shock to women like Amber O'Neil whom he had not bothered to warn.

Since spending a weekend with him in February, 1977, Amber had continued to buy each new Bukowski book and was leafing through *Women* when she came across the character of Tanya, a comically diminutive girl Chinaski meets at Los Angeles airport and takes back to his apartment. She realized, to her acute embarrassment, that Tanya was meant to be her. 'I didn't like the way he said, "All these women got off the plane, and then this girl got off with a long nose and round shoulders," and so on and so forth, 'cos actually I'm kinda cute! So I immediately took offence there, and then I didn't like what he said about the blow job.' Bukowski described two occasions when Tanya gave Chinaski oral sex, once so awkwardly Chinaski concludes: '. . . she knew nothing about how it should be done. It was straight and simple bob and suck.'

'I thought, God, why did he write that? There were so many good things we had.' She also thought the book denigrated women generally. 'He said so many things about women in there that were painful, I just don't understand that. Whereas in *Post Office* there was something about humanity. My frank feeling about it is this: most of his life he felt rejected by women and suddenly he was sought after by women and I don't think he trusted that, and he was pretty cynical about it. He somehow got back all the anger he must have felt.' This was unjust because, by and large, as Amber points outs, women had been good to him.

Joanna Bull first read the novel when she ducked into Papa Bach Book Store in West Los Angeles to get out of the rain. She saw a shelf of Bukowski books and flipped through a couple to see if there was anything that reminded her of some of their experiences, and she found one. She had become the basis for the character of Mercedes. Once again, it was not the most flattering description:

> That evening the phone rang. It was Mercedes. I had met her after giving a poetry reading in Venice Beach. She was about 28, fair body, pretty good legs, a blonde about 5-feet-5, a blue-eyed blonde. Her hair was long and slightly wavy and she smoked continuously. Her conversation was dull, and her laugh was loud and false, most of the time.

This was positively not how Joanna remembered their time

together, or how she perceived herself. 'We talked like mad and I had a beautiful body!' she says, indignantly. But she forgave him, realizing he had to ginger things up to get a story. 'What was he going to say, that we had a sane relationship, that we sat like two civilized people having refined conversation?'

Ruth Wantling thought Bukowski's portrayal of her as Cecelia, including the physical description of her as being 'a cow of a woman, cow's breasts, cow's eyes', was so wide of the mark it was risible. And although Bukowski had written about the evening in the motel at Laguna Beach, and her refusal to have sex with him, it was noticeable that he had left out the crucial details of the circumstances surrounding her husband's death.

The most critical portrait was of Cupcakes who Bukowski used as the basis of Tammie, a pill-popping single mother. 'I come across as an air-headed, cock-sucking nothing, which I wasn't at all,' she says, 'a woman without any substance who is just consumed with getting high. I was very disappointed.' The Tammie of *Women* is promiscuous bordering on being a prostitute. When she first meets Chinaski, she offers to have sex with him for $100. In letters to friends, Bukowski wrote that he believed Cupcakes was dating a string of men and implied she did have sex for money. Cupcakes says this is absolutely untrue and that, apart from the dental student whom she was sleeping with towards the end of her relationship with Bukowski, the infidelities were all in his mind. 'I remember reading *Women* and thinking what the hell is he talking about, why in the world is he portraying me in that way? He was so jealous, and so paranoid, and just thought the worst of me.'

But although Bukowski dealt with his female characters in a critical, almost misogynistic way, at times, he did not spare his male characters either. The men in *Women* are almost all weak, dishonest and sexually insecure. None more so than Chinaski himself. As Gay Brewer points out in his critical study, *Charles Bukowski*, the Henry Chinaski of *Women* is far from being a virile he-man figure; he is frequently impotent with drink, made to look foolish, spurned and mocked and cuckolded by young women who are clearly his superiors. Indeed, the very first lines of the novel reveal Chinaski to be a pathetic, inadequate man:

> I was 50 years old and hadn't been to bed with a woman
> for four years. I had no women friends. I looked at them as
> I passed them on the streets or wherever I saw them, but I
> looked at them without yearning and with a sense of futility.
> I masturbated regularly, but the idea of having a relationship
> with a woman – even on non-sexual terms – was beyond my
> imagination.

There is great humor in this. Like *Post Office*, *Women* is
a very funny book, containing some of Bukowski's very best
comic writing, and it was to prove popular with both male and
female readers.

Bukowski name-checked John Fante in *Women* as being Henry
Chinaski's favorite author, and indicated his enduring respect for
Fante's work by hailing *Ask the Dust* as a great book. John Martin
had never heard of Fante, whose books were all long since out of
print, and assumed the name of the writer and the novel were
purely fictional, especially as Bandini (the name of Fante's hero,
whom Bukowski also name-checked) is a well-known supplier of
garden fertilizer in California. 'I thought this was just a metaphor
for shit.' But when they spoke about it, Bukowski assured him
Fante's novels existed, so Martin made a point of seeking them
out and liked the work so much he set out to discover if Fante
was still alive, thinking he might publish him.

John Fante had turned to screen-writing after his early fiction
was published in the late 1930s, and enjoyed a successful career
in Hollywood during the 1940s and 1950s, including the filming
of one of his own novels, *Full of Life*. But in later years he
found it increasingly hard to make a living, partly because of
his uncompromising attitude to his work, and, by the 1970s, he
was unable to finalize any movie deal. He was forgotten as a writer
and, to make matters worse, his health failed. Fante had suffered
from diabetes for many years and became blind in 1978 when he
was sixty-nine. When John Martin tracked him down to his home
in Malibu, north of Los Angeles, he was at the lowest ebb, a sick
and unhappy old man.

They struck a deal to re-print *Ask the Dust*, and Bukowski

wrote a new preface describing how he had discovered the book in the Los Angeles Public Library all those years ago, like finding gold in the city dump. He went on to praise Fante's prose style warmly, writing: 'Each line had its own energy and was followed by another like it. The very substance of each line gave the page a form, a feeling of something *carved* into it. And here, at last, was a man who was not afraid of emotion. The humor and the pain were intermixed with a superb simplicity. The beginning of that book was a wild and enormous miracle to me.'

It was forty years since Bukowski first read *Ask the Dust* and now, thanks to that casual line in *Women*, he was finally about to meet his hero at the Motion Picture and Television Hospital where Fante was recovering after a double amputation of his legs. Bukowski was very nervous about seeing Fante, partly because he felt he had stolen from him the idea of dividing his novels into very short chapters, to give pace, but this hardly mattered as Fante had never read any of his work and, when Fante's wife, Joyce, read to him from *Women*, he was unconcerned by Bukowski's use of his ideas.

Conversation was stilted when the two writers met, but some of Fante's bulldog spirit came through to Bukowski.

'The doctor came in today, told me, "Well, we're going to have to lop off some more of you." I like that, "lop". That's what he said, the bastard,' Fante told him.

'John, whatever happened to Carmen, the lady in your first novel?' asked Bukowski.

'That bitch. She turned out to be a lesbian,' he replied. 'Got a cigarette?'

Fante was blind. His limbs cut from him. He was forgotten as a writer, but Bukowski was impressed to see that he was still undefeated by life. 'The most horrible thing that happens to people is bitterness,' Fante told him. 'They all get so bitter.'

Fante returned home to Malibu, his spirits lifted by the deal with Black Sparrow Press, and felt strong enough to dictate a final instalment of the saga of Arturo Bandini to Joyce. It was one of the happiest times in their marriage.

One evening Bukowski and Linda Lee made the drive up from San Pedro for dinner and found Fante sitting up at the table, having made a special effort on their behalf.

'I know that you're a drinker, Hank, so I'm going to have a glass of wine with you,' he said.

'There was a close bond of friendship,' says Joyce Fante. 'It would have been stronger had the circumstances been different. It was very difficult for John not being able to see and feeling ill, as he did all the time. I think they would have been close friends if they had met in earlier years.'

Because of the interest and patronage of Bukowski and John Martin, several volumes of Fante's work were re-published and, at his readings, Bukowski urged his fans to buy Fante's books, calling him 'my buddy out of nowhere'. The books sold well, particularly in Europe, and left Joyce well-provided for in her old age.*

The Internal Revenue Service presented Bukowski with substantial tax demands now he was making big money from his writing. He hired an accountant who urged him to spend, spend, spend before Uncle Sam took it in taxes. He should buy a new typewriter, a car, office supplies. He even tried to make a case for deducting Bukowski's liquor as a work expense. The accountant also advised him to invest in land deals and other speculative schemes. But Bukowski was essentially conservative when it came to money, other than gambling on the horses, and preferred to use what he had to minimize debt, so he made additional repayments on his mortgage instead. However, when his '67 Volkswagen finally broke down he saw the sense in buying a new car. It would be a fifty-two per cent tax write-off and, as he wrote in the poem, 'notes on a hot streak', he'd been driving 'the worst junk cars/imaginable' for thirty years. He deserved something good.

The salesman at the BMW dealership eyed Bukowski suspiciously, noting his cheap clothes and the pens in his top pocket. He didn't look like the sort who could afford a new BMW. He looked more like a working guy who would buy a second-hand Chevrolet, with a trade-in. The salesman was so reluctant to stir himself to talk to the loser in his show room, that Bukowski had to call him over.

'I think I like this car,' he said, pointing at a black BMW 320i.

* John Fante died on 8 May, 1983.

'With sun roof, radio and air-conditioning, this automobile costs $16,000,' the salesman told him, stiffly.

'OK, I'll take it.'

The salesman asked, rather superciliously, what kind of arrangements sir would be making.

'I'll write a check,' said Bukowski, casually.

It was the punch-line to a routine he had been working on for weeks because, far from being a casual buyer, he had actually read up on BMWs in advance and knew exactly what model and extras he wanted, and how much he was prepared to spend. He was just enjoying the fun of confounding the salesman's preconceptions, and derived huge pleasure from watching his expression change to one of respect after he telephoned the bank and discovered there was enough cash in Bukowski's checking account to more than cover the price of the car.

Bukowski did not attempt to disguise the fact that he had bought a house and a BMW, removing himself from the low-life world he had always written about, but used these symbols of his newfound wealth to comic effect. In the poem, 'the secret of my endurance', he wrote that he still received mail from men with terrible jobs and women trouble, men like he had been. The letters were often written in blunt pencil on lined paper 'in tiny handwriting that slants to the/ left'. He wondered if they knew their letters were delivered to a mail box behind a six-foot hedge at a two-storey house with a long driveway . . .

> . . . a two car garage, rose garden, fruit trees,
> animals, a beautiful woman, mortgage about half
> paid after a year, a new car,
> fireplace and a green rug two-inches thick
> with a young boy to write my stuff now,
> I keep him in a ten-foot cage with a
> typewriter, feed him whiskey and raw whores,
> belt him pretty good three or four times
> a week.
> I'm 59 years old now and the critics say
> my stuff is getting better than ever.

It was wonderful to lay on the lawn under his fruit trees and do nothing while his neighbors worked. Who would have thought he would be living like this after all those nights at the post office, all those years in cockroach-ridden court apartments? Who would have guessed he would be stretching out like a cat in his own garden under his own guava tree, sunlight through the leaves dappling his belly? He would never get tired of the free hours. It was glorious to have nowhere to go and nothing to do, but wait until dinner, wondering what type of wine he would drink.

He turned sixty in August, 1980, and signed a $10,000 contract with Barbet Schroeder to write a screenplay based on his life, with a promise of more money if the film went into production. The screenplay – which had the working title, *The Rats of Thirst*, later changed to *Barfly* – was an amalgam of the years Bukowski lived in Philadelphia, hanging out at the bar on Fairmount Avenue, and also when he lived with Jane in Los Angeles. He finished it in the spring of 1979 and Schroeder flew to Europe to try and raise the money.

Schroeder was not the only filmmaker interested in bringing Bukowski's work to the screen. An Italian consortium, eager to cash in on Bukowski's popularity in Europe, negotiated a $44,000 deal with Lawrence Ferlinghetti for rights to some of the City Lights stories, and yet another consortium was talking about an adaptation of *Factotum*. As the months passed, Bukowski found himself increasingly embroiled in the machinations of the movie business, for which he had intense distrust. Apart from anything else, he believed Hollywood had been the ruination of John Fante.

> people who hang around
> celluloid
> usually
> are.

('the film makers')

There were several long discussions about who would play Henry Chinaski in *Barfly*, the film which remained Bukowski's favorite project and the one he had most to do with. He met James Woods who had recently starred in *The Onion Field*. The singer Tom Waits came over to San Pedro for drinks. Kris Kristofferson was also suggested for the part, but Bukowski was horrified to learn he would sing and play his guitar in the movie. In the end none of them committed to the project and, without a definite star name, one film company and then another flirted with the idea of financing the movie before pulling out.

Months went by without anything being finalized, and Schroeder found himself spending many evenings drinking with Bukowski and Linda Lee at San Pedro, listening to Bukowski's stories about when he was younger. He decided he should make a permanent record of these sessions and so began to film what became *The Charles Bukowski Tapes*, a remarkable four-hour documentary of Bukowski talking about his life and work.

Most of the documentary was filmed with Bukowski speaking directly to the camera at his home in San Pedro, but they also revisited locations from his past life including the house at 2122 Longwood Avenue. Bukowski showed Schroeder the place in the living room where his father tried to force his face into the vomit on the carpet, and they went into the bathroom where his father had beaten him so many times with the razor strop.

'Here we have the torture chamber,' said Bukowski, looking round sadly. 'This is a torture chamber where I learned . . . something . . . This place holds some memories all right. I don't know, it's just a terrible place to stand and talk about it . . . you don't want to talk about it too much . . .'

Schroeder began to ask a question, but Bukowski turned away.

'Let's forget it,' he said.

Linda Lee was a fan of the British rock group, The Who, and that summer she had been attending every one of their concerts in Los Angeles, partly because Pete Townshend was a fellow devotee of Meher Baba and an acquaintance of hers. Bukowski decided he hated The Who. He didn't like their music, but mostly he hated them because he thought Pete Townshend and Linda Lee were having an affair, which was untrue. One evening when Barbet Schroeder was filming at the house in San Pedro, Bukowski decided to confront Linda Lee about coming home late from the concerts.

'I've always been used because I'm a good guy,' he said. He and Schroeder had been drinking and filming all afternoon in the garden, getting through four bottles of wine, and Bukowski was in a volatile mood. 'Women, when they meet me, they say, "I can use this son of a bitch, I can push him around, he's an easy-going guy," so they do it . . . But, you know, finally I get to resent it a bit.'

'What do you resent?' asked Linda Lee, who had also been drinking.

'Just being pushed.'

'Why do you let yourself be pushed by this kind of shit, you idiot?'

'I've told you a thousand times to leave. You won't leave,' said Bukowski. He said he was going to get a Jewish attorney to throw her out. It would happen so fast she would feel her ass was skinned. Linda Lee smirked at that. 'She thinks I don't have the guts,' Bukowski told Schroeder, who was still filming. 'She thinks I can't live without her . . . You think you're the last woman on earth that I can get?'

'I hadn't thought about it.'

'Yeah, well, you better start thinking.' He was ready to turn her over to the next fellow and he wouldn't be the least bit jealous, being sick and tired of her 'Meher Baba bullshit' and her staying out every night.

Linda Lee protested that she did not stay out every night. 'I don't want you to give these people that impression because it's not true.'

'What a fuckin' hunk of phony shit you are,' he said, menacingly. 'I hate liars. You lied right into their faces, you cunt.' She had been out past midnight, several nights running: 5.30 a.m. one night, 3.30 a.m. another. The night before last she came home at 2.01 in the morning.

'Why are you so offended by me doing something else?'

'I don't want a woman out six nights a week after 2 a.m. I don't care what the reasons . . . The month of May you were out fifteen nights past midnight.' She couldn't help but laugh. 'That's true; the calendar is marked,' he said.

'So what?'

'So what? This is why I am going to get an attorney to get you off my ass.'

'Why are you offended by me doing something else?'

'I live with a woman, or she lives with me. She doesn't live with other people.'

'I *do* live with other people, and I'm going to for the rest of my life.'

Something snapped in Bukowski when she said that. Moving slowly, but with deliberate violence, he swung his legs onto the sofa and kicked her.

'You fucking cunt,' he snarled, his face pushed towards hers. 'You think you can walk out on me every fucking night? You fucking whore! You bitch! Who do you think that I am?' he asked. Then he swung at her. 'You fucking shit . . .'

In the morning, Bukowski had no memory of what had happened, and Linda Lee says he was contrite when she told him. 'I remember thinking afterwards, everybody is going to think this is the way we live our life: he beats me and this and that. I swear he never had before and he never did again.' Linda Lee says she thinks Bukowski's outburst was funny, and believes she was made powerful by it. 'I mean, it's humiliating but also, in a way, it's so good, it's so real.'

While Barbet Schroeder was making his documentary, and struggling to get the money together to make *Barfly*, the Italian director Marco Ferreri, best known for making *La Grand Bouffe*, secured the rights to several stories from *Erections, Ejaculations, Exhibitions and General Tales of Ordinary Madness*. He raised the money in Europe and the American actor Ben Gazzara signed on for the lead part as the Bukowski-like poet, Charles Serking.

The film, *Tales of Ordinary Madness*, would be based primarily on Bukowski's *The Most Beautiful Woman in Town*, a short story about a prostitute who mutilates herself and then commits suicide. Ferreri also wanted to use *Animal Crackers in my Soup* which Bukowski had written for the soft porn magazine, *Adam*. The heroine of the story has sex with a tiger and Ferreri and Gazzara met with an actress to discuss the possibility of filming with a real tiger. Ferreri said they could use glass to protect her. 'It was the most amusing dinner I ever had,' says Gazzara. 'She was sitting there taking it very seriously, until Marco said it was too much trouble.'

Bukowski was unhappy that Ferreri began work before paying him his money – remarking in a letter to John Martin that even Hitler hadn't trusted the Italians – but had mellowed by the time the crew came to Los Angeles, and met Ben Gazzara for a drink.

'I'm really disappointed; you have gone up-scale, Buk,' said Gazzara when he saw Bukowski and Linda Lee had brought bottles of good French wine with them to his hotel room.

'Well, I made a little money, Ben,' said Bukowski. 'I thought I'd live well.'

'I think he was proud that we were making a film about him, but low-key proud,' says Gazzara. 'He had this sardonic sense of humor that precluded his gushing about anything. But I think he was excited by it.'

The US première of *Tales of Ordinary Madness* was held at the Encore Theater in Hollywood on a wet evening in 1981. Bukowski sat at the back drinking from a bottle in a brown paper bag as he watched the Gazzara character giving a poetry reading whilst wearing dark glasses – a bad beginning, in Bukowski's opinion – and drinking out of a bottle in a brown paper bag. Serking molests a twelve-year-old girl before having sex with a blonde played by actress Susan Tyrell. (Gazzara says that as he was carrying Tyrell to the bed to be whipped and raped, she whispered in his ear: 'My father's a minister, wait until he sees this picture!') Bizarre scenes follow with the masochistic character of the prostitute harming herself in various ways, including putting a safety pin through her vagina. At one stage, she lies across Gazzara's bed, enticing him to join her, but he carries on writing.

'If that were me, I would have stopped typing long ago,' Bukowski heckled from the back of the theater, adding that he had never seen a rooming house so clean (the interiors were far from authentic having been filmed in a studio outside Rome, Italy).

'Shhh,' hissed a member of the audience.

'Hey, I'm the guy they made the movie about. I can say anything I want!'

'Shut up!'

'You shut up!'

Bukowski thought Ben Gazzara totally wrong for the part, referring to him mockingly as 'Ben Garabaldi' (sic) and later writing that he had 'appealing eyes like a constipated man sitting on the pot straining to crap.' Lawrence Ferlinghetti, who had sold the film rights to Ferreri, agreed. 'The trouble was (Gazzara) was too good-looking. They should have had a really ugly hero and then the film would have really made it. But the producers didn't have the nerve to do that. They had to go for the Hollywood approach. It could have been a great film if they had a real Quasimodo-type playing Bukowski.' Gazzara defends himself by saying he was not trying to play Bukowski, 'not having lived with him to study his mannerisms. I had to invent my own. I didn't go for putting the pock-marks in the skin and doing the make-up to uglify. I thought the important thing was the artist, the interior man.'

The stories used as the basis for *Tales of Ordinary Madness* are not among Bukowski's best work, being the sensationalist stuff he wrote for the underground press and pornographic magazines when he was short of money, and the Italian director also had difficulty with American material. The press unanimously agreed the film was a non-starter. 'By turns repellent, naïve and risible,' reported *Sight and Sound*. 'They just dismissed the picture out of hand,' says Gazzara. 'Nobody came, reviews were bad, and that was it.' The movie did reasonably well in Europe, however, particularly in Paris where it opened in six theaters with queues around the block.

After the première, Bukowski and a small entourage trailed along Melrose Avenue. Drunk and tired of being followed around, he walked out into traffic and shouted: 'Hey, I thought you guys would follow me *wherever* I go!'

They went into a bar where he baited a group of men: 'Look at the faaaags,' drawing the word out to be as insulting as possible. Later, at Dan Tana's restaurant, he told the mâitre d' he had an 'empty face'.

Driving back to San Pedro that night, Bukowski was stopped by the police, ordered to get out of the BMW and lay face-down on the road while they put handcuffs on him. It was raining. His clothes were getting soaked and, when he looked up at the cops, rain splashed into his eyes.

> earlier that night
> I had attended the
> opening
> of a movie
> which portrayed the
> life of a drunken
> poet:
> me.
>
> this then was
> my critical review
> of their
> effort.
>
> ('the star')

The arrest didn't bother him unduly. In Los Angeles, drunk drivers were sent to 'alcohol studies' class and given a diploma if they completed the course. Bukowski already had a diploma, framed and hanging on the wall as a joke.

His behavior after the première, and when he kicked Linda Lee off the sofa, appears to be that of an out-of-control alcoholic, a man in need of help, but Linda Lee completely rejects this perception of Bukowski's drinking. She says he was a 'smart drunk' and adds that he did not think of himself as an alcoholic because, however much he drank, and whatever he did when he was drunk, he always got up the next day and worked, even if he didn't get up until noon. 'I know a lot of alcoholics, but Hank remained prolific. I don't call that alcoholism. I think alcoholism is when you drink and you can't do anything anymore.'

It's certainly true that he remained productive. Apart from the *Barfly* screenplay, Bukowski quickly completed the text for the travelogue, *Shakespeare Never Did This*. He was working on a new novel, and Black Sparrow published a new anthology of his poetry.

Play the Piano Drunk/Like a Percussion Instrument/Until the

Fingers Begin to Bleed a Bit is an off-putting title for a book, but this 1979 anthology includes some of Bukowski's best and most unusual poetry, great work like 'blue moon, oh bleweeww mooooon how I adore you!' which treats the subject of infidelity with typically dark Bukowskian humor:

> I care for you, darling, I love you,
> the only reason I fucked L. is because you fucked
> Z. and then I fucked R. and you fucked N.
> and because you fucked N. I had to fuck
> Y. But I think of you constantly, I feel you
> here in my belly like a baby, love I'd call it, . . .

He never published love poems about Linda Lee equal in passion to those he wrote about Linda King, Cupcakes or Jane Cooney Baker. Indeed the most heartfelt poems in the new Black Sparrow anthology were for Jane, seventeen years after her death. But the book was, at least, dedicated to Linda Lee and contained some work specifically about their relationship, like 'mermaid' in which he describes finding her soaping herself in the tub:

> you looked like a girl of 5, of 8
> you were gently gleeful in the water
> Linda Lee.
> you were not only the essence of that
> moment
> but of all my moments up to then
> you bathing easily in the ivory
> yet there was nothing
> I could tell you.

Compared with calling her a fucking cunt, and kicking her off the sofa, this shows some tenderness towards his girlfriend, but it was not necessarily a truer reflection of their daily life. 'We had a lot of crazy arguments, verbal arguments and stuff like that,' she admits. Bukowski complained to friends that she had been a good woman when he met her, but had changed. He said she wanted 'soul-expansion' and sometimes he feared she was unbalanced.

In the summer of 1981, Bukowski wrote to Joan Smith, the former go-go dancer, that he was finished with Linda Lee and had given up the search for the perfect mate, but hinted it would be nice to see Joan. 'I thought, well, this might be my big chance, you know, to finally be alone with Bukowski,' says Joan, who had always held a torch for the writer.

She telephoned Bukowski and he said she should come over to see the new house. A date was set and, a few days later, Joan called again to confirm. A woman answered and handed the telephone to Bukowski. 'Joan Smmmiiiiiiittthhhh?' he said, giving her two-syllable surname about twenty syllables, as if he couldn't quite remember who she was.

It seemed that Linda Lee was back.

Bukowski's fourth novel, *Ham on Rye*, his thirty-seventh book, was published in the summer of 1982. It addresses his childhood and relationship with his father. The title is a pun on *The Catcher in the Rye*, one of Bukowski's favorite novels, as well as meaning Chinaski was trapped between his parents, like ham in a sandwich. The novel is the most straight-forwardly autobiographical of all his books, taking Chinaski from his earliest memories of living in America, going to grammar school, junior high, high school and delivering him at the beginning of World War Two a frightened and bitter young man. Bukowski was writing with the objectivity of hindsight, rather than having his nose up close to the mirror, as he said of *Women*, and the book is better for it. At the same time it lacks humor, dealing with the one area of his life where he found almost nothing to laugh about.

There was irony in writing a long book about his disgust for his parents and their suburban lifestyle when Bukowski was now living the suburban dream himself – even more so – and the irony was not lost on Linda Lee. One day when Bukowski was cutting the lawn with his new electric mower she decided to test whether he was over the traumas of his past, got down on the grass and pointed to something. Finally Bukowski switched off the mower and asked what the hell she thought she was doing.

'You missed a blade!' she said.

'Oh shit,' he sighed, 'my father has gone but you are here.'

HOLLYWOOD

14

M ost week days, Bukowski drove to wherever the horses were running at that time of year: Hollywood Park in the mainly black district of Inglewood; Del Mar, just north of San Diego; or Santa Anita, near Temple City where his father died. He went to the maiden races and harness racing. He even went to the track when the races were telecast from out of state, feeling that something was missing from life if he didn't get a bet on.

The inside lane was best if he had to take the freeway. He opened the sun roof and tuned the radio to a classical station, driving at a leisurely speed while the other fellows raced to their appointments.

> driving in for a wash and
> wax with nothing to do but light a cigarette and
> stand in the sun . . . no rent, no trouble . . .
> hiding from the whores . . .

(From: *Horsemeat*)

He arrived at the track mid-morning and had the BMW valet-parked, its bodywork glistening after a wash.

'Hey, champ!' the valets greeted him. 'Got any tips?'

Bukowski smiled and took his ticket. He bought the *Daily Racing Form*, a program, a cup of coffee and went and sat in the grandstand, away from the finishing line crush, but within view of the tote board. Then he studied the morning line and handicapped the runners, marking the program with one of the Pentels he carried in his shirt pocket. Bukowski liked long shots, horses not fancied to win, but which paid better odds if they did. A few minutes before the first race he placed a regular win bet, between $10 and $40 depending on how sanguine he was. He never bet heavily so he rarely won more than $300, and there were plenty of times he didn't win. By 1982, after nearly thirty years studying horses, he estimated he was $10,000 in the hole. As he was making more than ten times that every year from writing, it hardly mattered. The track was just a way of passing the time because, prolific though he was, he couldn't write all day and all night.

There was much about the track he didn't like. He hated the thirty minutes between races, time for the crowd to buy hot dogs and beer. It was dead time. He tried writing in a note book, but found himself reading the newspaper instead: Ann Landers, the financial pages, sports and crime stories. 'I am up to date on all the crap in the world,' he wrote in *Horsemeat*, a limited edition book about racing. He disliked his fellow gamblers, 'the lowest of the breed', florid with stress and chewing on cigars. They were always yelling, like his father yelled throughout his life, yelling between races about which horse would win, behaving like maniacs when the animals were running and then cursing the 'salami' when their horses lost, tearing betting slips into confetti, even eating them. They didn't seem to know there was nothing generous about the track. 'It is not a place to go to jump up and down and holler and drink beer and take your girlfriend,' Bukowski wrote in *Horsemeat*. 'It is a life–death game and unless you apply yourself with some expertise, you are going to get killed.'

Above all else, he became irritated when punters spoke to him, either because they were fans, or because they wanted company.

> the pimpled young man with his cap on backwards
> came up to me at the racetrack
> and asked, 'who do you
> like?' and I answered,
> 'don't you know that when you talk about that

the horse never
runs?'
. . .
in a further effort to delete him from
the scene
I stated, 'I don't bet daily doubles,
parlays, quinellas or
trifectas.'
it was useless: 'who do you like
in this race?' he asked
again.

'Your Mother's Ass,'
I informed
him.

as he checked his program
I walked
off.

('horse fly')

If they were really persistent, he put rubber plugs in his ears.

After eating an evening meal with Linda Lee at home in San Pedro, Bukowski usually took a bottle of wine up to his study where he worked late into the night. Sometimes Linda Lee complained, saying she was alone when he went upstairs. He replied that when she was out late with her friends, in the $10,000 sports car he'd bought her, he was alone. In the late summer of 1982 they split again.

With only his cats for company – as he grew older Bukowski became increasingly fond of stray cats – and little more than drinking and horse racing for recreation, he became melancholy about the man–woman conflict which had taken up so much of his time in recent years. He complained to friends that women thought they were doing him a favor by living with him. They made excessive demands, inviting friends over and wanting him to accompany them to parties. In a letter to Linda King he wrote that he knew why men died earlier than women, it was because women killed them.

With little to distract him, he worked harder than ever, writing on a sophisticated IBM Selectric typewriter, which his accountant said was tax deductible, and drinking expensive French wine. If there was Mozart on the radio, or 'The Bee' as he affectionately called Beethoven, he kept going into the early hours of the morning, producing a new book of short stories, *Hot Water Music*, and a large anthology of poems, *War All the Time*, the last Black Sparrow book he did original paintings for.

R. Crumb was commissioned to illustrate two Bukowski short stories which were published in individual editions. *Bring Me Your Love* concerns a man whose wife is in an asylum. *There's No Business* describes the declining fortunes of cocktail lounge comedian Manny Hyman. His old-fashioned routine is failing to entertain the customers at Joe Silver's lounge at the Sunset Hotel:

Joe shook his head: 'Manny, you're going out there like a bitter old man. People *know* the world is shit! They want to forget that.'

Manny took a hit of vodka. 'You're right, Joe. I don't know what's got into me. You know, we got soup lines in this country again. It's just like the 30's . . .'

Although these new stories were written in the third person about characters other than Henry Chinaski, showing a greater sophistication in Bukowski's prose style, there was still a strong element of autobiography underlying the work. John Martin believes that in creating a loser like Manny Hyman, Bukowski was writing about what he feared he might become if people stopped buying his books. He had been down so long it seemed logical hard times might return. And the impression that Manny *is* Bukowski is reinforced by R. Crumb's illustrations, as Crumb explains: 'The character Manny Hyman was such a close variation on Bukowski's own self-portrayals, I ended up making him look Bukowski-like, but maybe a little more Jewish, not quite so heavy-set or seedy-scruffy as Bukowski.'

Bukowski and Linda Lee lived apart for much of 1983, although he saw her regularly and helped with her domestic crises and depressions. He felt she was not coping well without him and decided to alter his will in her favor to give her some long-term security if he dropped dead. In April, 1984, Bukowski informed his attorney that Linda Lee was to receive one third the value of his estate, including royalties and property, upon his death. Marina, who had previously stood to inherit everything, was not informed. In August he amended his will again, increasing Linda Lee's share to half. This was not an inconsiderable sum as Bukowski earned in excess of $110,000 in 1984 alone, and most of his income was saved.*

He was making so much money he was able to write a check to clear his mortgage. Bukowski remembered how his father nagged at him when they lived at Longwood Avenue, saying he had no ambition. 'Son, how are you ever going to make it?' he repeatedly asked. Well, he had made it. The car was paid for. The house was paid for, and there was money in the bank.

When their relationship was really rocky, Linda Lee went on a hunger strike refusing to eat or talk to him. Bukowski wrote to a friend that he feared she might die, so he asked her to marry him. That cheered her up. She was very nice again. A more romantic version of the proposal appeared in the limited edition book, *The Wedding*, where Bukowski wrote that he and Linda Lee were in the garden with their four cats when he suddenly said: 'Let's get married!' as the perfect end to the perfect day.

Linda Lee knew they would never have children together. She was still only forty-one, but Bukowski was sixty-four, 'old enough to be my father', and had absolutely no desire to go through fatherhood again. 'I knew I had to make a very big choice in my life: marry Hank and not have children, or not marry Hank. It was tough.' But she chose to marry and the wedding was arranged for the first Sunday after Bukowski's birthday.

Plants were brought in to prettify the house. A room was specially prepared for Linda Lee's mother. Timber arrived for the construction of a screen to hide the trash cans. A Persian rug was purchased to cover stains where Bukowski had spilt wine. Meanwhile builders were knocking through a wall so there would be easy access to the hot tub being installed in the garden.

---

* Linda Lee eventually inherited the entire estate.

Bukowski became anxious about paying for so much extravagance. The dollar was high against the European currencies, and he feared foreign royalties were declining, so he went back to writing for the porn magazines. Some of the stories were incredibly strange and one, about three men having intercourse with a pig, was rejected as too strong even for *Hustler*.

It was while he was preparing for his second marriage, after almost thirty years as a bachelor, that Bukowski discovered the fate of his first wife, Barbara Frye. For a couple of years after they split she had sent Christmas cards and the occasional note about how well she was getting on with her new husband in Aniak, Alaska. They had two beautiful daughters and were very happy. She was writing children's books and had discovered she was psychic. Then there was a telephone call, but nothing since.

It turned out that one of Barbara's daughters developed a drug problem and burned down the family home. Unable to face rebuilding, Barbara and the daughter travelled to India where they became involved in a weird religious group and where Barbara died in mysterious circumstances. The daughter returned to the US without the body and the family never received a death certificate. The final macabre twist came when the daughter committed suicide.

The wedding was scheduled for 1 p.m. on Sunday 18 August, 1985, at the Church of the People in Los Feliz, east of Hollywood. As the big day approached, with thousands of dollars spent, and guests arriving from out of state to stay with them at the house, Linda Lee took to her bed with the flu, leaving Bukowski to cope with the arrangements on his own. She asked him to pray for her recovery. 'FUCK IT ALL!' Bukowski exploded. 'DON'T YOU REALIZE THAT THERE ISN'T A GOD?'

He smashed a full-length mirror to the floor in exasperation. Linda Lee's mother, Honora, looked at him like he was the devil.

Marina arrived with her boyfriend, Jeffrey Stone. Michael Montfort and his wife arrived. Barbara and John Martin came down from Santa Barbara. They found that Bukowski had undergone an astonishing sartorial transformation. For the first time since anyone could remember he was dressed in a suit. It was cream-colored with a blue pinstripe. He was also wearing a floral tie and snake skin shoes.

John Martin was best man and Bukowski insisted they had a glass of champagne together, even though Martin had never drunk alcohol in his life. He became dizzy after one sip and decided the room was spinning.

'I don't understand it,' growled Bukowski, as if encountering a form of alien life. 'How can you go your whole life without drinking?'

'How can you drink all your life?' asked Martin.

A doctor had been summoned to see Linda Lee and told Bukowski to take her to a clinic because she was not well enough to get married. Meanwhile the house was filling with people, all talking excitedly and looking at their watches. Just when it seemed Bukowski would have to tell them the wedding was called off, Linda Lee appeared on the stairs, in her wedding dress. 'Ladies and gentleman, the bride!' announced Bukowski, mightily relieved.

He led her out to a white Rolls Royce which whisked them along the freeway to the church. Handel's *Water Music* played and sunshine streamed in through the glass.

There was a reception afterwards for eighty friends and family at a Thai restaurant in San Pedro. As he passed through the room greeting his guests, and accepting their congratulations, Bukowski reminded them that he was paying for everything so they better enjoy it. He also treated his friends Steve Richmond and Gerald Locklin to an impromptu speech about the shortcomings of women, perhaps not an entirely appropriate subject for a wedding reception. The bride and groom drank and ate, cut a giant cheesecake and danced to a reggae band. 'He was in a happy mood and laughing.' says Martin. 'People would jostle him and he would spill wine on himself.'

Afterwards Bukowski's closest friends went back to San Pedro for more drinking. When he waved the last of his guests good-bye, he looked more like the Bukowski of old: shirt out, a wine stain down the front and his trousers hanging round his backside.

Sean Penn was a rising Hollywood star having recently appeared in the thriller, *The Falcon and the Snowman*, although he was more famous for being the husband of Madonna. When he saw the *Barfly* screenplay, he was so enthused about the film that he offered to play Henry Chinaski for the nominal fee of one dollar. He loved Bukowski's writing, and began composing poems of his own. His only stipulation was that Barbet Schroeder relinquish the director's chair to *Easy Rider* star Dennis Hopper, a good friend of his. This caused a problem and Bukowski invited Penn, Hopper and Schroeder over to San Pedro to talk it through.

Schroeder was offered a lucrative deal by Penn and Hopper to stay with the project as a producer, but he was less than pleased at being sidelined and reminded them that *Barfly* was his project, his first Hollywood film and he was determined to direct it. Bukowski was loyal to his friend. He didn't like Dennis Hopper anyway, distrusting his newfound sobriety, the look of his clothes, and jewelry and what he thought was the hollow sound of his laugh. 'One time something was said, and it wasn't quite funny, and he just threw his head back and laughed,' said Bukowski. 'The laughter was pretty false, I thought. The chains kept bouncing up and down, and he kept laughing.'

'You hear that fucking laugh, did you see those chains?' asked Schroeder when Hopper and Penn had left.

The meeting made Schroeder so anxious he telephoned his lawyer and dictated an addendum to his will that, whatever happened to him, Dennis Hopper would never be allowed to direct *Barfly*.

By saying no to Dennis Hopper, they also lost the services of Sean Penn which was a shame because he probably would have been good in the part, with his chippy manner and his love of Bukowski's work. It was not the last they saw of him, however.

The actor started visiting Bukowski socially and, despite a forty-year age difference, they became good friends. Penn admired Bukowski's uncompromising attitude to his writing. He saw him as a true artist who lived on his own terms. They also both liked to drink. 'I loved the guy,' he says, simply.

'Sean wasn't such a huge star when we met him, although he was beginning to get there,' says Linda Lee. 'He was just sort of a kid. He used to call us his surrogate parents. He would just come over here and tell us his problems, sit and get drunk and chat and be away from that insane Hollywood. Sean liked Hank, and Hank liked Sean because Sean was willing to be with him in a natural way.'

Sean Penn began bringing his actor buddies over to meet Bukowski, people like Harry Dean Stanton who had recently starred in *Paris, Texas*. 'Harry Dean's a very strange fellow,' Bukowski said. 'He doesn't put on much of a hot-shot front. He just sits around depressed. I say, "Harry, for Chrissakes, it's not so bad." When you're feeling bad and someone says that, you only feel worse.'

M*A*S*H star Elliott Gould turned up one night in Sean Penn's pick-up truck. Penn presented Bukowski with Madonna's new album and they talked about poetry. Gould says Bukowski reacted to meeting celebrities 'like a regular guy, totally normal'.

Bukowski was not overawed by film actors because he had little regard for their work. He could count on the fingers of one hand the films he liked. *Who's Afraid of Virginia Woolf?* and *All Quiet on the Western Front* would be among them. Being more culturally sophisticated than is generally supposed, he also liked Akira Kurosawa's work and his all-time favorite movie was *Eraserhead*. Bukowski demonstrated his dislike for mainstream movies, and their stars, when he met Arnold Schwarzenegger in September, 1985, at a birthday party for Michael Montfort's wife. For no particular reason, other than he felt like picking a fight, Bukowski told Schwarzenegger he was a piece of shit. 'Hank was certainly not overly impressed with any of it,' says Harry Dean Stanton. 'He didn't care much for many movies, as I don't. Anybody who is perceptive is not going to talk about the thousands of great movies. It is relative to any art form. Excellence in any field is always a rarity.'

Sean Penn also brought Madonna over to San Pedro. She was at the height of her fame and her visit amazed neighbors who had thought of Bukowski as little more than the neighborhood drunk.

'Hank, is it really true Madonna came to see you?' asked a little girl who lived in the street. She was impressed, but a little suspicious it might be a put-on.

'Sure.'

'But why would Madonna come to see you, Hank?'

Although he had affection for Sean Penn, Bukowski didn't like Madonna at all. Linda Lee says the singer reminded him of some of the crazy women he had known, but he held back from saying so in case he hurt his friend's feelings. 'Hank couldn't stand her,' says Linda Lee. 'He did not like her because he didn't believe in her. He was sort of looking and going, "Oh fuck, you have got a good one here, man."' Still they went out together to eat and Bukowski and Linda Lee were invited to a party at their home.

'Everybody was excited at the notion that Charles Bukowski was coming to the party that they were coming to,' says Penn, recalling the evening when the poet lumbered into his lounge. 'He comes and spends about two minutes on his drink before he decides he is just going to prowl around (the) room and steal everybody else's drinks . . . This was always the mode whenever you did go out with him somewhere, some circumstance when he wasn't just at home. The wine was no more to drink. Now it was mix everything and die.'

Penn's mother, actress Eileen Ryan, decided she wanted to dance with Bukowski and endeared herself to him by saying he was a big phony. 'The pants are coming off,' says Penn. 'He is trying to take my mother's clothes off. My mother, at this point, is in her late sixties, and everybody is sitting back and saying, "This is what he is supposed to do." It was the first time they had seen a legend actually behave like a legend.'

Sean Penn and Harry Dean Stanton were eating dinner at San Pedro one day when Bukowski forgot his self-imposed rule and came out with a crack about Madonna. It was so insulting that Sean Penn started getting up as if to fight him. 'Hey, Sean, sit down,' said Bukowski in his best tough-guy voice. 'You know I can take you.'

After years of hard work and disappointment, Barbet Schroeder finally found a company willing to back *Barfly*. Cannon Pictures was owned and run by Menahem Golan and Yoram Globus, Israeli-born cousins with a reputation in Hollywood for being mavericks. They were also financing another literary project – Norman Mailer's *Tough Guys Don't Dance*, which the Pulitzer

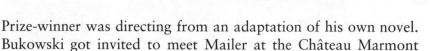

Prize-winner was directing from an adaptation of his own novel. Bukowski got invited to meet Mailer at the Château Marmont hotel on Sunset Strip.

Standing on the penthouse terrace, Bukowski saw an entirely new view of the city he had known since childhood – the view the rich enjoyed. He could see the sweep of the shimmering city from Los Angeles airport to where the San Diego freeway emptied a stream of tiny lights into the San Fernando Valley. Helicopters fluttered back and forth, and way out there somewhere was the ocean. It was pretty impressive, certainly a better view than he used to have from his window at De Longpre Avenue.

They swapped stories – Mailer told him a good one about meeting Charlie Chaplin – and then they took the elevator down to the garage to get Bukowski's car. They were going to a birthday party for one of the executives at Cannon and Bukowski was driving. He was amused when Mailer told him he also drove a black BMW. 'Tough guys drive black BMWs, Norman,' he said.

As Bukowski described in his novel, *Hollywood*, he made a faux pas at the party, confusing one Cannon executive with another and Victor Norman (Mailer) made him painfully aware of his mistake.

> I noticed Victor Norman staring at me. I figured he would let up in a while. When I looked again, Victor was still staring. He was looking at me as if he couldn't believe his eyes.
>
> 'All right, Victor,' I said loudly, 'so I shit my pants! Want to make a World War out of it?'

The story was true, as Mailer remembers.

'You know, Norman, you and me may have to go outside to fight,' said Bukowski.

Mailer says he felt a rush of adrenaline as he contemplated flying at Bukowski with murderous intent. 'It so happened that at the time I was in good shape and was still boxing, and Bukowski, by then, was in awful shape – huge belly, bad liver, all of it,' Mailer recalls. 'I remember that I felt such a clear, cold rage at the thought of what I'd be able to do to him – there are preliminaries to fights, mental preliminaries, where sometimes you think you're going to win and sometimes you think you're in trouble, and once in a while you think you have no chance. But this was one occasion when I felt a kind of murderous glee because I knew he had no chance. I was ready to go.'

He leaned forward and said: 'Hank, don't even think about it.'

Now that Cannon were behind the project, it was easier getting name actors interested in *Barfly* and it was soon decided that *9 ½ Weeks* star Mickey Rourke would play Henry Chinaski, although he was initially reluctant to take the part because of the subject matter. 'All the men in my family for a lot of generations were alcoholics,' he explains. 'It was sort of a disgusting character for me to play because a lot of the men in my family have never hit fifty, so I don't really have a lot of respect for boozers.'

Mickey Rourke had never read Bukowski's work and was not particularly impressed with the screenplay when he saw it, or the low budget. 'It was nothing at first that turned me on as an actor, but once I saw the package being put together, and I saw the meticulous dedication that was surrounding this project, that stimulated me more.'

Mickey Rourke suggested Faye Dunaway for the part of Chinaski's girlfriend, Wanda Wilcox, the character based on Jane Cooney Baker. Several years had passed since Faye Dunaway's great success in *Bonnie and Clyde* and her career had declined to the point where she was being offered television work and second-rate films. She felt that, because of her age, she was 'becoming invisible' as she wrote in her autobiography, *Looking for Gatsby*, and that *Barfly* was the chance of a comeback.

Then Cannon unexpectedly pulled the plug on the deal, saying there was no money to finance the picture. They also set a prohibitive turnaround fee, the price another movie company would have to pay to take over the project. Schroeder responded with one of the most bizarre bargaining tactics in the history of Hollywood. He bought a Black & Decker circular saw, took it into Menahem Golan's office, plugged in, switched on and held the blade over his left hand, threatening to slice his finger off unless the film went into production. When Golan saw that he was serious, he told him he had a deal. Bukowski reflected that his past life seemed tame in comparison with this sort of madness.

When Mickey Rourke visited San Pedro for tips on playing his part, he noticed that although Bukowski lived comfortably, his typing room 'looked like a boarding house, like a piece of shit dive. It was very suburban except for the room that he wrote in.' He got another insight into how he would play the character by listening to Bukowski talk. 'He spoke in a very peculiar way, almost like he was speaking to himself where he didn't really give a fuck if anybody else understood him.' Bukowski boasted about the fights with Frank McGilligan in Philadelphia, but Rourke didn't take the posturing seriously. 'You can't be any sort of physical specimen if you live out of a beer can,' he says. 'I saw him as a man who was more physical with his mouth than his fists.'

Filming began in a bar in Culver City with genuine barflies as extras, although Bukowski didn't know them. Mickey Rourke invited Bukowski into his trailer on the first day and poured him a large whiskey. He was most hospitable, saying Bukowski was welcome to stay as long as he liked. 'OK, I'll stay forever,' Bukowski replied, having lived in smaller apartments.

Mickey Rourke was thirty-two, just a little older than Bukowski had been when he lived in Philadelphia. He came on the set unshaven, wearing dirty clothes, shuffling and talking in an approximation of Bukowski's peculiar voice, drawing words out for emphasis. It was a fairly good immitation. 'The guy was great,' Bukowski said of the actor's performance, although he later modified his praise. 'He really became this barfly. He added his own dimension, which at first I thought, this is awful, he's overdoing it. But as the shooting went on, I saw he'd done the right thing. He'd created a very strange, fantastic lovable character.'

They also filmed at a bar on the outskirts of downtown, around 6th and Kenmore, where Bukowski worked as a stock room boy in the early '50s. Bukowski had a cameo part as a barfly in the scene where Wanda and Chinaski meet. There was real booze in the bottles and Mick Collins, who played the barman, began fixing drinks for everybody, getting himself and Bukowski loaded. He recalls how important a figure Bukowski was on set, unusually so for a screen-writer in a Hollywood film (Schroeder didn't change a word of dialogue unless Bukowski agreed). 'Barbet, Mickey, Faye, everybody took second place. They all respected him,' says Collins.

The exterior shots for Wanda's apartment were filmed at the Maryland Royal Palms, a rooming house at 360 S. Westlake Avenue next door to the Aragon where Bukowski had lived with Jane. In one scene, Faye Dunaway and Mickey Rourke walk down the hill outside the building. She is going to look for a job, and he wants her to come back and drink with him. If they had kept going to 6th, turned right and walked another block, they would have been on Alvarado Street where Bukowski met Jane. The memories all came back as Bukowski watched the filming of his life, amazed at how his fortunes had changed.

Faye Dunaway tried to make herself like Wanda, described in the screenplay as '. . . once quite beautiful but the drinking is beginning to have its effect: the face is fattening a bit, the slightest bit of a belly is beginning to show, and pouches are forming under her eyes.' But the actress was still beautiful. Bukowski didn't like her at all. In *Hollywood*, he described Chinaski's irritation when a scene had to be rewritten so the actress playing Wanda could show off her legs.

Filming continued for six weeks, and Bukowski spent much of that time hanging around the set. Linda Lee had taken acting lessons, and was given a small part but, unlike Bukowski, didn't make it into the final cut. David Lynch and his girlfriend, Isabella Rossellini, visited the set and chatted to Bukowski about *Eraserhead*. Helmut Newton photographed Bukowski with Faye Dunaway on his knee. Having a movie made about his life was a heady experience, and Bukowski was not so cool that he failed to get excited by it. He found himself watching the dailies and wondered aloud whether *Barfly* would win an Oscar, an institution he had once mocked in his poem, 'Another Academy'.

While *Barfly* was being edited, yet another film adaptation of Bukowski's work was released. Directed by Belgian film-maker Dominique Deruddere, *Crazy Love (aka Love is a Dog From Hell)* was premièred in Los Angeles in September, 1987. Bukowski watched it with Linda Lee and his new celebrity friends – Sean Penn and Madonna, and Elliott Gould and his wife. Although he had nothing to do with the making of the movie, and it remains an obscure art house work, Bukowski came to regard this adaptation

Barman Ruben Rueda who for many years served Bukowski drinks at the Musso & Frank Grill on Hollywood Boulevard. *(picture taken by Howard Sounes)*

'beer / rivers and seas of beer,' Bukowski wrote, 'beer is all there is.' *(picture by Richard Robinson. Courtesy of Special Collections, The University of Arizona Library. The quotation from the poem, 'beer', appears courtesy of Black Sparrow Press)*

The Seven-G's bar in downtown Los Angeles was one of the places Bukowski drank when he was living with Jane Cooney Baker and working as a shipping clerk at an art supply store. *(picture taken by Howard Sounes)*

The Frolic Room on Hollywood Boulevard was a favorite bar with Bukowski in the early 1970s. *(picture taken by Howard Sounes)*

Bukowski proudly poses, in February, 1971, with the head sculpted by Linda King and presented to him as a gift. Their love affair was at its height. When they fell out, as they regularly did, Bukowski would return the head to Linda. *(courtesy of Linda King)*

Linda King, the young sculptress Bukowski met and fell in love with in 1970 shortly after he quit his post office job. *(courtesy of Linda King)*

Relaxing in Barnsdall Park,
Hollywood, in 1972, aged fifty-two
and free from the post office at last.
(courtesy of Linda King)

In July, 1972, Bukowski went on a
rare vacation to the island of
Catalina, just off the coast of
California. With him was record
company executive Liza Williams
whom he was dating after a break-up
with Linda King.
(courtesy of Liza Williams)

Bukowski in the room at the hotel on the resort island of Catalina where he was staying with Liza Williams on vacation. Note the caged bird bought to keep him company. *(courtesy of Liza Williams)*

THE WRITER

In Santa Barbara with his editor-publisher John Martin and John's wife, Barbara, who designed Bukowski's Black Sparrow Press books. *(courtesy of John Martin)*

Bukowski is beginning to enjoy modest success in 1974 when this picture was taken at his Carlton Way apartment during a magazine interview. On the shelves behind him are some of the many chapbooks and small literary magazines his work had already appeared in. *(picture taken by William Childress)*

THE WOMEN ...

(Left) Linda King at Flo's Place, a bar she worked in on Sunset Boulevard. (courtesy of Linda King)

Joan Smith, a former go-go dancer friend of Bukowski's. She is also a poet, and published a tribute book to Bukowski after his death called Das ist Alles. (courtesy of Joan Smith)

Amber O'Neil cleverly got her own back on Bukowski for what he wrote about her in his third novel, Women, by writing a hilarious roman-a-clef of her own called Blowing My Hero. (courtesy of Amber O'Neil)

Joanna Bull felt so ill after having sex with Bukowski she threw up. (courtesy of Joanna Bull)

Poet Ann Menebroker, a close female friend and long-term correspondent of Bukowski's. He wanted her to leave her husband and come to live with him in LA. *(courtesy of Ann Menebroker)*

Jo Jo Planteen, a young fan whom Bukowski tried to seduce in the late 1970s. *(courtesy of Jo Jo Planteen)*

Pamela Miller, *aka* Cupcakes, the redhead Bukowski fell madly in love with when he met her in 1975. *(picture taken by Howard Sounes in 1997)*

With Georgia Peckham-Krellner, Cupcakes' best friend, in Bukowski's kitchen at Carlton Way.
(© Joan Levine Gannij)

With Brad and Tina Darby, Bukowski's neighbors at Carlton Way. Tina worked as an exotic dancer at a go-go club and Brad managed a sex shop. They spent many evenings together. *(courtesy of Linda King)*

William and Ruth Wantling.
Poet William Wantling drank himself to death after his friend Bukowski published a sarcastic short story about him. Bukowski tried to seduce his grieving widow, Ruth, who has never forgiven him for his behavior.
(courtesy of Ruth Wantling)

The artist R. Crumb drew this brilliant portrait of Bukowski after referring to photographs taken on his wedding day in August, 1985. Bukowski was marrying his second wife, Linda Lee Beighle, and wore a pin-stripe suit, snake skin shoes and a floral tie for the occasion, presenting a considerably smarter appearance than friends were used to.
(Portrait by R. Crumb, © 1986, Water Row Books. Used with permission of Water Row Books.)

Bukowski at work *(©Joan Gannij)*

In August, 1985, when Bukowski was sixty-five, he married for the second time. His bride, Linda Lee Beighle, was forty-one and had been running a health food restaurant in Redondo Beach. They set up home together in a detached house in the port town of San Pedro, south of Los Angeles.

(picture taken by Eric Sander, © Frank Spooner Picture Agency)

When the actor Mickey Rourke visited Bukowski's San Pedro home to talk about making the movie, *Barfly*, he noted that the house was very neat and suburban except the upstairs work room where Bukowski wrote his stories. The work room was like a 'piece of shit dive'. Here Bukowski is seen at his deak, kissing his typewriter for luck. *(picture taken by Eric Sander, © Frank Spooner Picture Agency)*

With his friend John Thomas, and John Thomas' wife Philomene Long.
(courtesy of John Thomas/photo credit: Sheri Levine)

Bukowski relaxes at home in San Pedro in the summer of 1987. His books were selling well and he was working with film director Barbet Schroeder on the script for the movie, *Barfly*.
(picture taken by Eric Sander, © Frank Spooner Picture Agency)

THE MOVIE: "BARFLY"

CHARLES BUKOWSKI

In the movie *Barfly*, which was released in 1987, Mickey Rourke played the Bukowski-like character of Henry Chinaski and Faye Dunaway was Wanda Wilcox, a character based on Bukowski's former girlfriend, Jane Cooney Baker. The book of the screenplay was illustrated with a photograph of Bukowski and the two stars. He liked Mickey Rourke but was less keen on Faye Dunaway, damning her performance with faint praise. *(The Movie: "Barfly" published by Black Sparrow Press, 1987)*

Reunited with his cousin Katherine Wood (left) and her sister Eleanor (right) at his San Pedro home in August, 1988, just as his health was beginning to fail. *(courtesy of Katherine Wood).*

Bukowski's grave at the Green Hills Memorial Park, south of Los Angeles. *(picture taken by Howard Sounes)*

In July, 1997, three years after Bukowski's death, Marina gave birth to her first child, Bukowski's grandson. He was named Nikhil Henry Bukowski Sahoo and is seen here with Marina at her home in Northern California. *(courtesy of FrancEyE)*

of three of his short stories as the most successful attempt to bring his work to the screen.

The theatrical release of *Barfly* was heralded by a publicity campaign and, for the first time in his career, Bukowski was sought after by the mainstream American media. It turned out he was a natural story for journalists: the bum they made a movie about. A question and answer session conducted by Sean Penn was given a spread in Andy Warhol's *Interview* magazine, illustrated with pictures by the famous photographer Herb Ritts. Bukowski and Linda Lee were pictured outside their house for the *Los Angeles Times*. Bukowski was also profiled in the gossip magazine, *People*, which ran the headline:

BOOZEHOUND POET CHARLES BUKOWSKI WRITES A HYMN TO HIMSELF IN *BARFLY*, AND HOLLYWOOD STARTS SINGING

The article described him as a 'potbellied old boozer' and the mythology of his life was embellished with the story that Linda Lee fed him thirty-five different types of vitamins to keep him alive. It amused them both because *People* was one of the low-brow publications Bukowski sometimes bought when he was shopping for beer.

He was also invited onto a number of television programs, including Johnny Carson's *Tonight Show*, but declined them all figuring his appearances on *Apostrophes* in France should be the beginning and end of his talk show career.

The finished film was a great disappointment. Bukowski thought Mickey Rourke quite good as Chinaski, but said he'd never looked *that* scruffy; no landlord would have rented a room to him if he had. Mickey Rourke defends himself, saying he looked as Schroeder directed him to and adds, probably with an element of truth: 'When you see yourself as you really are, sometimes that hurts.' Linda Lee thought the film awful, and Marina didn't think Mickey Rourke played anything that remotely resembled her father.

There was a party after the Hollywood première, with champagne served and photographers' flash lights popping. Mickey

Rourke and Faye Dunaway congratulated Bukowski on his screen-play and reporters from the daily newspapers made a note of every slurred word he uttered. He enjoyed the attention for a while and then the booze kicked in and the scene began to seem phony. 'I've got to get out of here,' he told Linda Lee. She suggested they stay a little longer, but he was adamant. 'This place stinks,' he said. 'It's making me sick.'

The reviews in the morning papers were mixed and *Barfly* did only fair business when it opened across the United States, although it proved more popular in Europe. Yet despite the lack of box office success, and although the film is not truly representative of Bukowski's work, it is *Barfly* more than anything that he became known for among the general public.

THE LAST RACE

15

Aside from almost bleeding to death when he was thirty-five, Bukowski had managed to abuse his body throughout his adult life with remarkably little ill-effect. He was certainly in bad shape – paunchy and unaccustomed to exercise, other than sporadically lifting barbells – but actual debilitating illness had not troubled him since that long ago hemorrhage after which, as he never tired of saying, the doctors warned he must never drink again. Of course, he had consumed rivers of alcohol since then. He had smoked heavily, used drugs, been beaten-up in bar fights and spent several nights in jail. And yet he did not appear significantly less healthy than most sixty-seven-year-old men.

But in the winter of 1987, following the première of *Barfly* and all the excitement and stress that went with the making of the film, Bukowski's health began to falter. At first he thought he simply had flu, but then weeks went by without him feeling better. On 17 January, 1988, he wrote to John Martin that he'd only drunk one bottle of wine since Christmas, a sure sign he was not himself. Blood tests showed him to have been run-down throughout the previous year, but no specific illness was identified and his doctor wanted to carry out further tests. In the meantime, he was forbidden from drinking, and he had little energy for writing the novel he had recently begun, *Hollywood*, which was based on his experiences making *Barfly*.

Luckily, Bukowski and John Martin had already decided that

their next book would be a collection of early poems from obscure chapbooks and literary magazines, some dating back to the 1940s. It was published later that year as *The Roominghouse Madrigals*. As Bukowski wrote in the foreword, the poems were quite different from the anecdotal style he had developed in later years, 'more lyrical than where I am at now', but he did not agree with those who said the early work was better.

There was another reminder of the past when he received a telephone call from his cousin Katherine Wood, daughter of Bukowski's happy-go-lucky Uncle John. Bukowski had gone to the trouble of mailing a German language edition of his travelogue, *Shakespeare Never Did This*, to his Aunt Eleanor in Palm Springs. She thought little of the book and gave it to Katherine, who could not make out what it was about as the text was in German. She tried to guess by looking at Michael Montfort's photographs. 'In almost every picture he has a bottle of wine in his hand so I thought he was a wine salesman,' she says. When *Barfly* came out, she wondered if cousin Henry was the author and, after contacting Black Sparrow Press, she was invited to tea at San Pedro. 'He was a little hung-over,' she says. 'You could see he had a pretty darn rough life with the drinking and the smoking. He wasn't in very good shape.'

'You probably wouldn't like my books,' said Bukowski, who had not seen Katherine since they were children.

Katherine agreed she probably would not. She did not want to learn about the 'seamy side of life'.

Bukowski finished *Hollywood* late one Saturday night in the early fall of 1988, despite his poor health. It is perhaps surprising what an upbeat and funny book it is, describing a domesticated and financially secure Henry Chinaski laughing at a world crazier than anything he had experienced in the factories, bars and apartment courts of *Post Office*, *Factotum* and *Women*.

The following morning he awoke with a blazing fever of 103 degrees which continued for a week. He could not eat or sleep and shivered until the bed shook, convinced he was dying. The fever stopped only to return a few weeks later, and then there was another attack – three debilitating fevers in succession. His weight fell to 168 lbs.

He consulted some of the best doctors in Beverly Hills, telling them his symptoms: he had no appetite and had lost weight; he was dizzy; he could not sleep; he was anemic and had a hacking dry cough. He felt so weak in the mornings, he had trouble walking to the toilet. The doctors told him he had a low hemoglobin count and an iron deficiency, for which he could take pills, but they couldn't say exactly what was wrong with him.

The mystery was solved when Bukowski took one of his cats to the vet, and the vet suggested he get checked for TB. 'He had gone to all these Beverly Hills doctors who were unable to diagnose what was wrong,' says John Martin. 'They said he was just run down, and they gave him pills and told him to take it easy, and not to drink. He had tuberculosis! But none of these highly paid practitioners had seen a case of tuberculosis in their lives because the rich don't get tuberculosis very often.' Bukowski probably contracted the disease as a child from Uncle John, who died of consumption in 1933. It had been dormant and surfaced because he was run-down. A six-month course of antibiotics was prescribed and a complete recovery expected.

One thing the illness taught him, although the lesson came somewhat late in life, was that he could live perfectly well without alcohol. He had been sober on and off since the illness began and became practically teetotal by necessity during the course of antibiotics. 'I didn't even feel like lifting a bottle,' he told a German interviewer who came to the house. 'I had no feeling for drinking. It was no great sacrifice.' Apart from the occasional lapse, his hard-drinking days were behind him.

The illness left him looking very much older: he had lost a lot of weight, making his face gaunt; his nose seemed more prominent; there were unsightly growths around his eyes; his silver hair now receded right back to the crown of his head; and his beard grew white around a ruination of yellow teeth. He moved differently, too, walking cautiously as if scared of falling. As official confirmation that he had entered an irreversible state of decrepitude, the government informed him, in August, 1990, that he was now eligible for his old age pension.

The reviews for *Hollywood* were good and John Martin was able to sell foreign rights around the world. Writing in the *Toronto*

Star, Jim Christy described it as a great book about the making of a mediocre movie. The critic from the *Los Angeles Times* liked it, too. Even *The Times* in Britain, where Bukowski had never enjoyed the same success he had in continental Europe, gave grudging praise to his account of the vanities of movie stars, saying the prose displayed 'a mean clarity of description'.

His next book also enjoyed a warm reception. *Septuagenarian Stew* was published in 1990 to coincide with Bukowski's seventieth birthday, a collection of poetry and prose which showed him still raging at the world. The short stories were the particular strength, and *The Life of a Bum* is one of his best ever, demonstrating a mastery over the form he had been practicing since adolescence. He drew from a lifetime of experience to create a vivid and sympathetic character in Harry, the bum who rejects the 8 to 5 routine, preferring to drink and sleep in the park.

Bukowski's critique of society had special resonance as America entered the recession of the early 1990s, with workers being laid off to face credit card debts and repayments on over-valued homes. He even anticipated the 'slacker' culture that emerged in college society as a reaction to the decade of greed, using the term in *The Life of a Bum* when a troop of soldiers yell at Harry:

> The convoy moved slowly. The soldiers saw Harry sitting on the park bench. Then it began. It was a mixture of hissing, booing and cursing. They were screaming at him.
> 'HEY, YOU SON OF A BITCH!'
> 'SLACKER!'
> As each truck of the convoy passed, the next truck picked it up:
> 'GET YOUR ASS OFF THAT BENCH!'
> 'COWARD!'
> 'FUCKING FAGGOT!'
> 'YELLOW BELLY!'
> It was a very long and a very slow convoy.
> 'COME ON AND JOIN US!'
> 'WE'LL TEACH YOU TO FIGHT, FREAK!'

The faces were white and brown and black, flowers of hatred.

In the story, Harry knows something the soldiers do not, or chooses to face a reality they would rather not think about: that they are marching towards death, and for no good reason, so they might as well get off the truck and join him on the bench. It is a philosophy of non-participation that runs through Bukowski's work and is one of the reasons he appeals to the young and disaffected.

Attendances were down at the race track and Bukowski noticed the punters did not spend money drinking like the old days, when everybody was out to have fun. The change in the times was brought home to Bukowski when Marina and her husband, Jeffrey Stone, whom she had married the previous fall, both of them college-educated, intelligent people working as engineers in the aerospace industry, lost their jobs on the same day. It seemed like the depression all over again with jobless men, 'failures in a failing time' and now jobless women, too.

When Marina visited San Pedro for Christmas, Linda Lee told her she was thinking of giving Bukowski a computer. He had changed from a manual to an electric typewriter, finding it easier and quicker, and without telling him her plans she'd ascertained he would be willing to try a word processor. Marina knew something about the technology and convinced Linda Lee she should buy an Apple Macintosh, because it was designed for people who knew little or nothing about computers. 'I had a feeling that, whatever it was, it had to be something he could mostly teach himself,' says Marina. Linda Lee was disconcerted by how bulky the box, screen, keyboard and printer were after the simplicity of a typewriter, and the price was a not inconsiderable $5,000 for what they wanted, but they bought it.

'Oh, shit,' said Bukowski, when he opened his gift on Christmas Day. 'I'm going to lose my soul.'

They took the computer up to his room and Marina began explaining how it worked. 'Just as I expected, he would listen to me, but it was really obvious he wanted to play with it and try it out and learn how things worked himself,' she says. He experimented most of the day, reluctant to go down-stairs to eat.

'Oh this is a miracle!' he said. 'Look, it's correcting my mistakes. I don't know how to spell. I know what the words are, but I don't know how to spell them, and look what it's doing!'

The Apple Mac reinvigorated Bukowski as a writer. He liked the way his words appeared on the screen – on a throne, as he put it – and enjoyed printing in different fonts and sizes of type. But the greatest benefit was that he could write more. His routine had been to type at night, when he was drinking and listening to the radio, and go back the following evening to correct by hand, discarding poems he didn't like and laboriously re-typing those he did. Errors of spelling, syntax and fact still crept into the typescripts, mistakes which always embarrassed him. Now he could correct his work on screen and the poems slid from the printer exactly as he wanted.

He had always been prolific, unusually so with more than forty books to his name, most published within the past twenty years, but after getting the computer he more than doubled his output, work he mailed to John Martin's new office in Santa Rosa, Northern California.

At Martin's suggestion, Bukowski also began a journal on the Apple Mac, posthumously published, in 1997, with illustrations by R. Crumb, as *The Captain is Out to Lunch and the Sailors Have Taken Over the Ship*. In the entry of 22 November, 1991, Bukowski explains how the computer aided his work:

Well, my 71st year has been a hell of a productive year. I have probably written more words this year than any year of my life . . . This computer that I started using on Jan. 18 has had much to do with it. It's simply easier to get the word down, it transfers more quickly from the brain (or wherever this comes from) to the fingers and from the fingers to the screen where it is immediately visible – crisp and clear. It's not a matter of speed per se, it's a matter of flow, a river of words and if the words are good then let them run with ease.

There were problems, of course: nights when he had not

correctly saved what he had written and lost everything, although he reflected this was a petty thing compared with knocking over a good bottle of wine; and one of the cats sprayed the disk drive, necessitating the return of the computer to the shop for repairs. In future he would put a beach towel over it when he went to bed. Despite these set-backs, the work piled up, masses of poems for John Martin to make into books.

Approximately half the material Bukowski mailed to Santa Rosa was set to one side as unpublishable. John Martin describes the rejected work as not poems, but 'just some words on a page' and a good proportion of Bukowski's unpublished poetry is bad. Sometimes it is gratuitously offensive, without the saving grace of being funny, like a poem he wrote stating that Greek people stink. Leafing through what soon amounted to a sizable stack of rejected poems, Martin was forced to conclude that many were simply gibberish. Bukowski realized this, too. In 'as the poems go' he observed that the best writers have said little and the worst far too much, but he knew he became blocked if he tried to be perfect so it was better for him to keep writing and leave the editing to others.

Despite the uneven quality, much of this late outpouring of work was among the best poetry Bukowski ever wrote. And the first book he wrote using the Apple Mac, the 1992 anthology *The Last Night of the Earth Poems*, is one of his finest collections. Partly because he was turning out so much work, *The Last Night of the Earth Poems* is the longest Bukowski book published by Black Sparrow Press. He liked his poetry anthologies to be large and John Martin agreed, believing the poems worked better when they were gathered together in a substantial volume. *War All the Time* (1984) and *You Get so Alone at Times That it Just Makes Sense* (1986) had both been long books. But *The Last Night of the Earth Poems* was over four hundred pages, 159 new poems, more than the collected works of some poets.

The method of editing *The Last Night of the Earth Poems* was the same as with all the other Bukowski books published by Black Sparrow. He gave John Martin carte blanche to choose what he wanted to publish. 'He didn't even know what I was going to put in, and then he never went back to look at his early work so he didn't know what I left out. He didn't care,' says John Martin, who usually arranged the poems in chronological order so the later anthologies start with poems about Bukowski's childhood, a subject he never tired of writing about, and end with him contemplating death. *The Last Night of the Earth Poems* is divided into four roughly chronological sections, each introduced with a phrase taken from one of the poems or from a poem Martin rejected as substandard but which had one striking stanza.

The book includes many wonderful poems, like 'we ain't got no money, honey, but we got rain', a supremely effective recreation of childhood containing a wealth of striking images, like the passage describing the downpours Bukowski remembered from when he was young, and the sounds after the rain stopped:

> and then, at once, it would
> stop.
> and it always seemed to
> stop
> around 5 or 6 a.m.,
> peaceful then,
> but not an exact silence
> because things continued to
> drip
> > drip
> > > drip
> and there was no smog then
> and by 8 a.m.
> there was a
> blazing yellow sunlight,
> Van Gogh yellow –
> crazy, blinding!
> and then
> the roof drains
> relieved of the rush of
> water

began to expand in
the warmth:
PANG! PANG! PANG!

The style he had been working at for years, writing one simple line after another with as little ornamentation as possible, was perfectly achieved.

There were poems that consisted of words arranged one, two or three to a line, like a list, but Bukowski chose the line breaks carefully and managed to convey interesting images and ideas. They were often funny as well. In 'pulled down shade' for example, a woman reflects upon the failings of her partner:

. . . I've
known you for
6 months
but I have
no idea
who you are.
you're like
some
pulled down shade
. . .
a woman can
drop
out of your
life and
forget you
real fast.
a woman
can't go anywhere
but UP
after
leaving you,
honey.

There is also an apocalyptic feeling pervading *The Last Night of the Earth Poems*. It is signalled by the title, which Bukowski feared might be mistaken for having a wholly ecological meaning, and is present in all the vignettes of Los Angeles life, whether writing about the depression era with nightmare visions of his uncle 'running down the street with a knife in his back'; about his father, saying for the first time that he must have been insane; or modern Los Angeles: crime-ridden, divided by racial conflict and economic inequality, choked with pollution, its citizens 'slapped silly' by heat waves, frustrated to the point of violence by traffic congestion, and all to pay taxes to a government drowning in debt. When Angelenos rioted that year following the acquittal of four white policemen for attacking a black man, Rodney King, Bukowski's vision became terribly real. In 'Dinosauria, we', he wrote that, 'there will be open and unpunished murder in the streets.' In real life, fifty-eight people were killed, many beaten to death in broad daylight.

In the poem, 'transport', he allowed himself a rare late use of (mixed) metaphor, reviewing his life in terms of successive modes of travel: the railway journeys of his youth, the junk-yard cars he drove when he lived at De Longpre Avenue, and the foreign automobiles of his later success, like the Acura he bought for cash after the BMW. The poem ends with a vision of the future when people will be able to fly like birds. Another poet, especially one of Bukowski's mature years, might have used this image to sentimental effect, as an ascension to heaven perhaps, but Bukowski liked to subvert expectations:

> one night not so long
> ago
> I had a dream that I
> could fly.
> I mean, just by working
> my arms and my legs
> I could fly through the
> air
> and I did.
> there were all these people
> on the ground,
> they were reaching up their

arms and trying to pull me
down
but
they couldn't do
it.

I felt like pissing on
them.
they were so
jealous.

all they had to do was
to work their way
slowly up to it
as I had
done.

such people think
success grows on
trees.

you and I,
we know
better.

The San Pedro house had been further improved with expensive furniture, an elaborate security system in case they were burglarized, even a lap pool to go with the jacuzzi. Bukowski found a swim and a plunge in the tub was relaxing when he came home from the track, and he had no compunction about enjoying his wealth in this way. 'I have nothing against money; give me all the money you want. I will not refuse it,' he said. 'Because I've been dead broke so many times, I've been so dead broke, starved so long, I realize the value of money. It's tremendous. Money is magic. I'll take all I can get. I hope I never miss a meal again.'

He enjoyed picking up the check when he went out for dinner with friends, paying with one of his various gold cards, although he was disgruntled about paying for one particularly expensive evening with Sean Penn and Madonna considering they were a 'couple of millionaires'.

After the divorce of his celebrity friends, Bukowski's sympathies remained with Sean Penn and he turned Madonna down when her agent asked if he would pose with the star for her book, *Sex*. He told friends she behaved like she'd discovered the subject.

He refused other offers of work that would bring in big money, but which would inconvenience him in some way, including $25,000 to make a television programme with PBS and $10,000 to give two readings in Holland. He said he didn't want to travel, and was now rich enough not to.

A producer wrote to Bukowski, asking to talk to him about a television series. He attached two $100 bills to the first page of the letter and a third $100 bill to the second page, to hold his interest. Bukowski took the $300 to the track and, when he returned home, he called the producer's number. The idea was to make a sit-com based on the life of a disreputable old writer, someone like Bukowski, with Harry Dean Stanton starring. Bukowski knew the actor, so he called and asked what he thought. Stanton said he didn't know anything about the project, but would like to see Bukowski anyway so it was arranged that they would meet the producer for a drink at the house in San Pedro.

Bukowski got in early from the track and relaxed in the hot tub before receiving his guests, already having doubts about the project:

> My work was finally getting recognized. And I was still writing the way I wanted to and felt that I had to. I was still writing to keep from going crazy, I was still writing, trying to explain this god-damned life to myself. And here I was being talked into a tv series on commercial tv. All I had fought so hard for could be laughed right off the boards . . .

> (From: *The Captain is Out to Lunch and the Sailors Have Taken Over the Ship*)

When they met that evening, Harry Dean Stanton warned Bukowski that network sit-coms used canned laughter, which sounded bad, and the content was inevitably censored because of the sponsors. Maybe if they could take the project to Home

Box Office, where they would have more freedom to portray Bukowski's work honestly, it might work. The talking went on for several hours and finally the producer lost his temper, muttering it wasn't fair the way movie actors had a downer on television. *They* made plenty of lousy films. 'I remember saying that in that format, network television, there is no way you could do Hank's work or do anything about Hank,' says Harry Dean Stanton. 'Actually the producer wasn't all that happy about it. But I think I was dead right.'

Another evening Bukowski, Linda Lee and Harry Dean Stanton went out on the town with Sean Penn. They had tickets for a concert by the rock band U2 and made the trip to the show by limousine.

Dodger Stadium was pulsating with light and sound when they took their seats in the VIP section. The lead singer, Bono, was a fan of Bukowski's work and the group had recorded a tribute song, 'Dirty World', using words from *The Days Run Away Like Wild Horses Over the Hills*.

'This concert is dedicated to Linda and Charles Bukowski!' Bono shouted, and the multitude roared their approval as if they knew who Bukowski was. It made him laugh.

There was a vibrancy there but it was short-lived. It was fairly simplistic. I suppose the lyrics were all right if you could understand them. They were probably speaking of Causes, Decencies, Love found and lost, etc. People need that – anti-establishment, anti-parent, anti-something. But a successful millionaire group like that, no matter what they said, THEY WERE THE ESTABLISHMENT.

(From: *The Captain is Out to Lunch and the Sailors Have Taken Over the Ship*)

They went to the bar afterwards and Bukowski got loaded on vodka-7s. He nodded hello to celebrities he had come to know since *Barfly*, although he worried about hanging out with film directors, pop singers and actors. He mostly disliked their work and, after years of being true to his art, he hoped he wasn't being sucked into the show business maw. The only solution was to have another vodka-7. He ended up having so many he couldn't remember a word Bono said to him, and Bukowski later collapsed drunk on the front steps of his house.

He decided to cut back on schmoozing with celebrities, everyone except Sean Penn whom he felt close to. 'Most of these people have pretense and Hank was not somebody who accepts pretense,' says Linda Lee.

If he had to, he was ready to give it all up and go back to the tar paper shack in Atlanta and live on candy bars, so long as he could write the way he wanted, without selling out. And he kept writing, turning out five hundred poems a year. He also began thinking about a new novel, something different. After all, he had exhausted the events of his life. It would be a detective story, of sorts, *Pulp* – a homage to bad writing.

He was still not wholly well, complaining of occasional pains in his head, stiffness in his back and neck and, in the summer of 1992, he underwent an operation to remove cataracts which seriously impaired his vision.

There were other irritants, too: readers he called 'Chinaski freaks'. They turned up at his door demanding autographs, giggling on his porch while he explained he did not receive uninvited visitors. One group of fans parked a camper van in the street and had a party so they could say they had been drunk at Bukowski's house. It drove him half-mad. 'He hated people coming round and just sitting there wanting to have beers with Charles Bukowski,' says Linda Lee. 'It horrified him to think about doing something like that.'

Although these people said they had read his work, they seemed to have no understanding of who he was. Several wrote to say they liked his books so much they stole them from public libraries, as if that was something he would approve of. Bukowski was disgusted. If it hadn't been for the public library system, he might never have discovered *Ask The Dust*.

Fans who approached him with consideration, and did not impose on his privacy, were often rewarded with letters, poems and sometimes drawings. He also continued to support small magazines by submitting work to editors across America and also

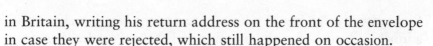

in Britain, writing his return address on the front of the envelope in case they were rejected, which still happened on occasion.

Book dealer Ed Smith wrote asking if he could publish a Bukowski news letter, which he wanted to call *Sure*, a word Bukowski often used when he signed off at the end of his letters. Bukowski agreed so long as he didn't have to contribute anything. The news letter's circulation grew until there were hundreds of subscribers around the world, a cross-section of society ranging from laborers to doctors, but with an emphasis on white collar workers, 'people who were the exact opposite of him', as Smith says.

At times, Bukowski became irritated by Linda Lee's sociability and the people she wanted them to entertain at the house. Linda's mother visited several times and stayed for Christmas causing Bukowski to reflect upon the best Christmas he ever had. It was in Philadelphia. He saw no one, pulled the shades down and went to bed.

The date he looked forward to each year was 2 January, the anniversary of his $100 a month deal with John Martin. It was the luckiest break of his life. Twenty-three years later Martin gave Bukowski his latest raise, bringing the pay check to $7,000 a month. Nineteen of his books were in print, each title selling at least ten thousand copies a year in America, and new markets were opening up around the world all the time with his books being translated into more than a dozen languages, including French, German, Spanish, and even Japanese.

Black Sparrow printed a Bukowski poem in a booklet each New Year, as a gift for friends. The 1993 poem was 'those marvelous lunches' and Bukowski sat down to sign the series of 226, making them worth several hundred dollars each. It was only a couple of years since he had staggered drunk into Book City on Hollywood Boulevard and offered to sign any of his books in exchange for the price of a beer.

'Those marvelous lunches' recalls school days during the depression when Bukowski's parents gave him peanut butter sandwiches for lunch, because they were short of money. Bukowski had been so hungry he forced himself to make friends with

Richardson, a fat 'sissy' whose parents sent him to school with a lunch pail stocked with ham sandwiches, beef sandwiches, fruit, and a thermos of chocolate milk. Richardson gave Bukowski potato chips and, in exchange, Bukowski kept him company on the way home.

> . . . I would
> carry the pail as
> I walked Richardson
> back to his
> house.
>
> we never spoke.
>
> as we got to his door
> I would hand him
> the lunch
> pail.
>
> then the door would
> close and he would
> be gone.
>
> I was the only friend
> he had.
>
> sissies live a hard
> life.

It rained that afternoon as Bukowski autographed the books, adding a drawing of a man with a bottle of booze. When he was finished, he wrote a covering letter to John Martin sincerely thanking him for the raise to $7,000 a month which he considered an astonishing amount of money especially as they had not set out to become rich, but to publish books that they liked. He had lived through the depression and now they had both made it through the recession and were still on top of their game. Maybe better than ever. He warned he was getting old and might slip in the future, but believed that, even with slippage, they would continue to have luck so long as the gods remained kind.

END OF THE NIGHT

16

Pulp was the first novel Bukowski had written which was not explicitly autobiographical, or even addressed his usual interests. Indeed, it broke all his rules, being conceived as a pastiche of a Mickey Spillane crime story. The plot, such as it is, concerns down-at-heel private eye Nicky Belane who is hired by two clients to investigate cases that are semi-surreal and also have metaphorical meaning. Lady Death asks him to find the writer Louis-Ferdinand Céline, whose melancholy novel *Journey to the End of the Night* was one of Bukowski's favorite books. The second client, John Barton (a character based on John Martin) asks Belane to find The Red Sparrow.

'The Red Sparrow? What the hell is that?'
'I'm sure it exists, I just want to find it, I want you to locate it for me.'
'Any leads for me to go on?'
'No, but I'm sure the Red Sparrow is out there somewhere.'
'This Sparrow doesn't have a name, does it?'
'What do you mean?'
'I mean, a name. Like Henry. Or Abner. Or Céline?'
'No, it's just the Red Sparrow and I know that you can find it. I've got faith in you.'
'This is going to cost you, Mr Barton.'

'If you find the Red Sparrow I will give you one hundred dollars a month for life.'

Belane starts his search for Céline at a Hollywood book store run by Red, a character based on Bukowski's friend, Sholom 'Red' Stodolsky. When Belane walks into the store, Red tells him he has just missed 'that drunk Chinaski' and that Céline is in back. Belane goes over to talk to him and Red, a crusty old fellow in real life, also the proprietor of a Hollywood book store, gets upset and shouts at them:

'HEY YOU!' he yelled, 'GET THE HELL OUT OF HERE!'
We were the only two in there.
'Which one to get the hell out?' I asked.
'THE ONE THAT LOOKS LIKE CÉLINE! GET THE HELL OUT OF HERE!'
'But why?' I asked.
'I CAN TELL WHEN THEY'RE NOT GOING TO BUY!'

Even though he was apparently writing a crime story and had dispensed with the character of Henry Chinaski, Bukowski was still writing about his own life, and *Pulp* is full of in-jokes that only really make sense to those readers who are familiar with both his previous books, and something of his life story. He had been working sporadically at this peculiar project since 1991 and it was not going smoothly. A crime story, even one as unorthodox as *Pulp*, has to be plotted and Bukowski kept writing his hero into corners. When this happened, he abandoned the novel and wrote poems, which he said kept coming like 'hot turds'. By the spring of 1993, two years after starting *Pulp*, he was still only three quarters of the way through, and then he fell ill again.

He had myelogenous leukemia. A white blood cell had mutated and replicated itself, spreading the disease throughout his body. Cancer was another word for it. The doctor told him the bleak truth was that, without treatment, he might only live six months. Or they could try chemotherapy, which often had unpleasant side effects and still might not save him. Bukowski said he would do whatever they suggested and checked into the San Pedro Peninsula Hospital, a place he had driven by many times.

> . . . I sat there and watched the cars
> pass on the street and I thought,
> those lucky sons of bitches don't
> know how lucky they
> are
> just to be dumb and driving through
> the air
> while I sit here on top of my
> years
> trapped,
> nothing but a face in the window
> that nobody ever
> saw.
>
> ('the observer')

He must have dropped off to sleep because, when he opened his eyes, he saw yellow flowers. Bukowski once wrote he liked yellow so much he could eat it.

'Frances?' he asked, focusing on the mother of his child. He had never got used to her new name, FrancEyE. 'Frances, what are you doing here?'

'I just thought you should have some flowers,' she said. Marina had told her he was sick and she caught the bus from Santa Monica, wanting to see him before the chemotherapy started.

'Well, you know, I don't want visitors.'

'I know. I just thought you should have some flowers . . . and I love you,' she said. She patted his hands, the hands which had held their daughter, and said good-bye to him.

A catheter was inserted into a main vein and the chemotherapy started. Bukowski lost his strength and his hair fell out in long silvery strands on the pillows. Linda Lee brought food from home each day and hugged and kissed him. She often stayed through the night watching the IV lines to make sure there were no air bubbles, calling the nurses when he wanted help. Bukowski was bleeding from different parts of the body, the strangest parts, including his forehead. He spent sixty-four days in hospital over the following months, going home between treatments. Then the doctors said the cancer was in remission.

Taylor Hackford was in New York producing a movie when he called home to Los Angeles to get his messages. 'Hello, Taylor Hackford, you don't know me,' said a man's voice on his answer machine, 'but I'm a friend of Hank's and I just thought you should know Hank died tonight at 8.05.' The caller hung up without leaving his name.

Not sure quite what to do, Hackford called Bukowski's number and, when the answer machine clicked on, he left a cautious message.

'Linda, this is Taylor. I'm in New York. I just got a really horrible message about Hank. I'm not going to say what it is, but I would appreciate you calling me back . . .'

'Taylor, baby, what's happening?'

'Shit! Hank?' asked Hackford.

'Yeah, baby.'

'You won't believe this, but some guy called my house and left a message on the machine you died tonight.'

'What an aaaasss-hole,' said Bukowski.

'I sat on the bed and I just wept.'

'I'm touched, baby. I'm touched.'

Rumors of Bukowski's death had gone round on four occasions in recent months. Nobody knew for certain how it was happening, but Bukowski believed it to be malicious and wrote a poem about the jealous, failed writers he presumed were responsible for upsetting his family and friends.

> your cowardice will
> not be
> missed
> and you were
> dead
> long
> before
> me.
>
> ('an answer')

It was a long time since Hackford had seen Bukowski, and the sorrow he felt when he heard he might be dead reminded him how much he cared, so they arranged to meet at San Pedro. 'He had cancer. He talked about that,' says Hackford. 'He had been in the hospital once. He said, "It's slow-moving and I'm writing every day."' Hackford brought champagne and two bottles of red wine over to the house and introduced Bukowski and Linda Lee to his girlfriend, the actress Helen Mirren, whom Bukowski had watched in Peter Greenaway's sexually explicit movie, *The Cook, The Thief, His Wife & Her Lover*.

'Yeah, I saw you taking it all . . .' he said mischievously as he greeted her, 'lying there in that freezer . . .'

She laughed and they were soon emptying bottles like old times. They went out for Thai food, drinking beer at the restaurant, and came back to the house for more wine. 'I stumbled out of there at a quarter to six in the morning,' says Hackford. 'Helen and I and Hank had drunk seven bottles of wine – Linda had stayed on rum and coke – seven bottles of regular wine and a bottle of champagne.'

After the initial euphoria of being in remission, Bukowski gave up alcohol altogether and drank only herbal tea and mineral water. He had been cutting back ever since his bout of TB and found that he didn't miss the booze at all. He quit smoking, too.

An emaciated old man, invalided out of the struggle of life, he spent the days quietly in the garden sitting under the walnut tree. He took up transcendental meditation, at Linda Lee's suggestion, and agreed to try the alternative healing treatments of the self-help guru, Deepak Chopra: mind over matter and rubbing oil into the body to remove impurities. He had always scoffed at New Age ideas in the past, but with 'the dark angel' of death hovering, he was willing to try anything, as he wrote in 'decline':

> sitting naked behind the house,
> 8 a.m., spreading sesame seed oil
> over my body, jesus, have I come
> to this?

> I once battled in dark alleys for a
> laugh,
> now I'm not laughing.

He decided to complete *Pulp* while he could, knowing in his heart it would probably be his last book, and killed off Nicky Belane with four gun shots to the gut. Bukowski then wrote an ending which was partly a contemplation of his own death. As the detective lays dying, the Red Sparrow appears before him like a vision of God, metaphorically recalling the Black Sparrow which had transformed his own life.

> Then, as I watched, the Sparrow slowly opened its beak.
> A huge void appeared. And within the beak was a vast yellow
> vortex, more dynamic than the sun, unbelievable.
> This isn't the way it happens, I thought again.
> The beak opened wide, the Sparrow's head moved closer
> and the blaze and the blare of yellow swept over and enve-
> loped me.

Bukowski was proud of all his books, but *Pulp* had a unique place in his affections and those close to him draw attention to its metaphysical aspects. 'To me, it was incredible,' says Linda Lee, 'funny and poignant, sort of surrealistic.' But aside from addressing impending death, it is hard to find much to commend *Pulp*. In abandoning the subject matter he knew about and could write convincingly about – low-paid work, relationships between men and women, and the predicament of the urban under-class – he seemed lost. It is significant that such a fluid writer, who did not like revising his manuscripts, had so much trouble getting the book how he wanted it. 'He completely rewrote it after he finished the first draft,' reveals John Martin. 'He just didn't like it. He said it was bad writing.'

There was little to do after the book was finished, 'horse-less days', not particularly uncomfortable but without action. He listened to Linda Lee vacuuming, the telephone ringing. A salesman called, trying to sell them the *Encyclopaedia Britannica*. He watched his cats basking in the sun on the red brick patio. The fattest, Craney, lay with its paws in the air oblivious to danger and its master's illness. Bukowski followed shadows as the sun moved round the house, and he drank gallons of water to try and wash away the metallic taste that had stayed with him from chemotherapy.

In the evenings, when he had enough strength, he went upstairs and wrote contemplative end-game poems:

> it's a cool summer night.
> hell trembles nearby,
> stretches.
> I sit in this chair.
> my 6 cats are
> close by.
>
> I lift the bottle of water,
> take a large
> swallow.
>
> things will be far worse than
> they are
> now.
> and far
> better.
>
> I wait.
>
> ('this night')

In August, Bukowski and Linda Lee drove down to a San Pedro store, Vinegar Hill Books, where Bukowski was presented with an elaborate birthday cake. He signed books and allowed himself to be the center of attention as his fans made speeches in his honor and fussed over him. It was peculiar to have become respectable at last. But never wholly so. As he prepared to leave, Bukowski froze the smile on the face of a newspaper journalist, saying: 'I can see your headline: "Old man of seventy-three signs his last books."'

When Michael Montfort visited the house, Bukowski spoke to him about *Pulp*, which John Martin was planning to publish after a volume of letters. 'I finally finished it,' he told Montfort and Montfort's friend, Gundolf S. Freyermuth, who had come to interview him, revealing his doubts about the work. 'It's going to ruin my reputation. Lot of bad stuff in it. I hope I've done it on purpose,' he said. 'I don't know what made me write it. I guess I got tired of writing about myself, about what happened to me. So I wrote this entirely fictional thing about this fifty-five-year-old detective. Of course, part of the way he acts and talks is also me. I couldn't get away from it.'

Montfort had heard the doctors thought Bukowski might make a sustained recovery, but it didn't seem possible. 'I thought their view was way too optimistic. So I had kind of mixed feelings meeting my best friend, kind of knowing he is dying, and the doctor says he is not.'

'Michael, we haven't paid the hospital bills yet,' said Bukowski.

'You are insured, Hank. What's the problem? Even if it's $100,000, you've got the money.'

Bukowski agreed, but he still seemed worried, never having come to terms with the fact he would not have to think about money again, with the house and cars paid for, and hundreds of thousands in the bank. If he sold everything and pooled his capital, he would have the best part of a million dollars.

The remission lasted into the fall of 1993 when the cancer returned and Bukowski went back to hospital. He knew he was dying, but refrained from speaking about it with Linda Lee unless he had a particular concern to discuss. 'In his writing he talks about that. I would never intrude,' she says. He kept within himself, a tough guy who felt that showing emotion was to make himself vulnerable.

It was decided he would be more comfortable at home in San Pedro. A nurse came in each day and Dr Dick Ellis, a friend he made at hospital, sometimes joined them for dinner. Marina, who came to stay, says her father faced death with the same phlegmatic attitude which had helped him through his twisted childhood, his difficult early life, the factory jobs and relationships. The recent years at San Pedro with Linda Lee had been comfortable, but most of his life had been hard and there were many times when he despaired of the future and wished himself dead. 'In a way, it was just another hard time. Starting off from being a child, he was used to having a tough life and he wasn't that much different in some ways. It was just another hard knock. It turned out to be the hardest one, I guess, but it didn't change him.'

In the meantime, it was a case of getting through the days as comfortably as possible. He got a fax machine and found this new form of technology pleased him, just as the Apple Mac had.

On 18 February he sent John Martin what he called 'my first FAX POEM':

> it's too late:
> I have been
> smitten.

Then there was no more strength to write. 'That was terrible to see – the mind was there, but he couldn't do anything because the body gave up,' says Linda Lee. 'The body shut down.' The chemotherapy that was attacking the corrupted blood cells had also destroyed his immune system. Bukowski contracted pneumonia and returned to hospital for treatment. 'Within about five days, they got rid of the pneumonia, but he still had an infection and they couldn't locate it,' says Linda Lee, who was at the bedside with Marina. 'They kept him in there. They kept him alive, injecting this stuff with catheters sticking in all over the place. Dreadful! Horrible! And he was the bravest soldier.' At 11.55 a.m. on Wednesday 9 March, 1994, Bukowski died. He was seventy-three.

John Martin was one of the first to be told. 'At that point you can't even believe a person is gone,' he says.

Because of the earning power of Bukowski's books, Black Sparrow Press had grown from nothing into a company which turned over more than a million dollars a year, a remarkable collaboration started on Bukowski's coffee table at De Longpre Avenue with the signing of a set of broadsides. 'I was thinking what life would be without him. We'd been intimately engaged in one very purposeful and single-minded pursuit: him to write and me to publish him and others for thirty years. I knew I had enough material for a number of books after he was gone, but that wasn't much consolation. I couldn't talk to him every day.'

The bond between Marina and her father had been extremely close. 'I always knew that if anything was wrong all I had to do was get hold of him and he would fix it,' she says. 'Even as an adult who had been taking care of myself for many years, and doing just fine, I noticed, aside from missing him after he died, I was also left with a feeling of missing that security in the back of my mind, just knowing that everything would always be OK, but if it wasn't I could call him and he would make it OK somehow.'

Although Bukowski had maintained he was a loner, some one who did not need or want many close friends, there were a number of men and women for whom his death was a great loss, people like Carl Weissner who had been ready to come over from Germany at a moment's notice; people like Michael Montfort, Sean Penn, Steve Richmond and John Thomas. In the early hours of the morning, John Thomas was unable to sleep and turned on the local twenty-four-hour news station. Bukowski's death was announced in one of the bulletins and Thomas found himself weeping.

It was not until three days later that Linda King discovered Bukowski had died. Her nephew told her after reading about it in a magazine. Linda and Bukowski had been apart for almost twenty years, but the memory of love endured, as she writes:

> the bright pleasantness of that bedroom
> on Edgewater Terrace will forever live
> in my memory with pure pleasure
> the laughter and the witty stories
> the art, the sculpture, the reading
> the laughter, the love, the laughter

At Bukowski's favorite Hollywood restaurant, Musso & Frank, barman Ruben Rueda cancelled the order for sweet German white wine, Rieslings and Liebfraumilch. Bukowski had frequently drunk two bottles at the bar before sitting down to eat and had been such a good customer the restaurant stocked it especially for him.

The newspaper obituaries concentrated on Bukowski's low-life image. He was the 'bard of the bar room', an unsophisticated writer with an inexplicable cult following. Aside from the occasional good review for his novels, and the attention paid to *Barfly*, the mass media had always treated him in this dismissive way.

Yet Bukowski stands alone in modern American literature, unclassifiable and much imitated. His simple prose and poetry style stemmed from common ideas: he was initially influenced by reading Hemingway and Fante, but, as he said, there weren't many laughs in Hemingway, so he added humor. Everyday life was Bukowski's chosen subject matter, not heroic deeds or glamorous people, but the experience of less successful Americans living in cheap apartments and working at menial jobs. He wrote convincingly about this world, although he exaggerated and edited his own life story. He also addressed human relationships with honesty: the relationship between a child and his parents, and between men and women.

Because of his fondness for writing about drinking, his willingness to sensationalize his life and to be gratuitously vulgar, Bukowski laid himself open to critics. He also probably published too much, certainly too much poetry. But if one reads his work carefully – the six novels, the dozens of short stories, the screenplay and numerous books of poetry – there is an uncompromising personal philosophy running through that is convincing, if challenging: a rejection of drudgery and imposed rules, of mendacity and pretentiousness; an acceptance that human lives are often wretched and that people are frequently cruel to one another, but that life can also be beautiful, sexy and funny.

Many critics say that he is a cynical writer, but maybe he simply had a realistic view of how people behave, and didn't feel the need to give them the benefit of the doubt. 'He is not a mainstream author and he will never have a mainstream public,' says John Martin. 'The kind of writing he does offends too many people. It's too honest and too direct.'

It was a typically hot, smoggy Los Angeles afternoon when Bukowski's friends gathered at Green Hills Memorial Park for his funeral. Monday 14 March, 1994. His body had been dressed in a plaid shirt and wind-breaker with pens in his breast pocket, as if he were on his way to Hollywood Park, and sealed within a casket made from poplar wood.

Apart from Linda Lee and Marina Bukowski, the mourners included John and Barbara Martin, Sean Penn, Red Stodolsky and his wife, Mina, John Thomas and his wife, Philomene Long, and Carl Weissner, together with friends and neighbors from San Pedro and Dr Dick Ellis from the hospital. Shortly before 3 p.m., they filed into the chapel, a nondescript building looking like a suburban bungalow, with the distinction of stained glass over the door. 'There was a smell of a skunk going in there,' says John Thomas. 'I remember thinking that was appropriate.' There was no minister, although Bukowski had been christened a Catholic. Instead, Linda Lee had arranged for Buddhist monks to conduct the service, with friends invited to give personal eulogies.

John Martin said Bukowski had been a great writer and certainly somebody he would never forget. Carl Weissner tried to speak, but was too upset to say much. Sean Penn said a few words about their friendship. When the chief monk got up, many in the congregation found him unintelligible. 'The one who gave the speech kept saying seven. I think he thought the body was seven years old,' says Thomas. 'You could almost feel Hank smiling from inside the coffin at how absurd that funeral was.'

The mourners got back in their cars and drove up Bay View Drive, past the serried stone tablets, turned left on Avalon Drive and parked on the side of a hillock known as Ocean View where Bukowski was to be buried in a grave dug next to a young tree. One of the monks placed a rose on the casket. Bukowski's friends tapped the lid for luck and walked away.

and to think, after I'm gone,
there will be more days for others, other days,
other nights.
dogs walking, trees shaking in
the wind.

I won't be leaving much.
something to read, maybe.

a wild onion in the gutted
road.

Paris in the dark.

('A New War')

ACKNOWLEDGMENTS

From Andernach, Germany, to Los Angeles, California, more than a hundred people who knew Charles Bukowski were interviewed for this biography over a period of two years. Others contributed by correspondence and many granted me access to previously unpublished letters, manuscripts and photographs. I am grateful to everyone who gave of their time, but would like to thank the following individuals by name:

My greatest debt is to Bukowski's publisher/editor, John Martin, of Black Sparrow Press. Both John and his wife, Barbara, who designs the Black Sparrow books, were most helpful and hospitable. I am particularly grateful to John for allowing me access to his previously unpublished personal correspondence with Bukowski which covers a period of twenty-seven years and was an invaluable source of information.

Of the members of Bukowski's family, special thanks to Bukowski's widow, Linda Lee Bukowski, and his only child, Marina Bukowski. Also thanks to Marina's mother, FrancEyE; and to Bukowski's cousins, Katherine Wood, in California, and Karl and Josephine Fett in Andernach, who granted me access to the family archive of previously unpublished letters and photographs. I am also grateful to the following relations of Bukowski's first wife, Barbara Nell Frye: Tom Frye of Wheeler, Texas, and Sunny Thomas and Leah Belle Wilson of California. Leah Belle Wilson provided the photograph of Bukowski and Barbara Frye which is the first ever to be published. In Andernach, Matthew Davis was a skillful and patient translator.

For Bukowski's school days, thanks to the following alumni of Los Angeles High School, graduating class of summer, 1939: Roger Bloomer, Stephen Cavanaugh, John Corbeil, Fred Merrill, Robert Merryman, Mark Morton and Barbara Purdy. Thanks to the principals and staff at the following institutions: Virginia Road Elementary School, Mount Vernon Junior High School, Susan Miller Dorsey High School, LA High School and Los Angeles City College. Also thanks to Los Angeles Unified School District for supplying details of Bukowski's education history.

The staff at the Selective Service System at Arlington, Virginia, helped locate Bukowski's draft record. Brenda Galloway of Temple University, Philadelphia, helped research the period Bukowski spent in the city, doing field work on my behalf around Fairmount Avenue.

Most of the new material about Jane Cooney Baker came from Roswell, New Mexico, and thanks are due to friends and acquaintances of the Cooney family who still live in Roswell, including: Richard G. Bean, Orville Cookson, Lavora Fisk, Jean Rockhold and John H. Wyley. Thanks also to the Historical Society of Roswell, Roswell Library, the *Roswell Daily Record* and Roswell High School, the principal of which supplied the photograph of Jane which is the first ever to be published. I am also grateful to Céline Sanchez at the State of New Mexico Department of Health for helping me research Jane's family history.

I am grateful to the United States Postal Service for giving me copies of Bukowski's personnel file and to Bukowski's former co-workers at the Terminal Annex in Los Angeles: David Berger, Johnny Moore and Grace Washington.

Of Bukowski's literary associates, several of whom were close friends of Bukowski, thanks to the following: John Bennett, Douglas Blazek, John Bryan, Neeli Cherkovski, Judson Crews, Lawrence Ferlinghetti, the late Allen Ginsberg, E.V. Griffith, Jack Hirschman, Philomene Long, Norman Mailer, Gerard Malanga, the late Marvin Malone, Ann Menebroker, the late Jack Micheline, Barry Miles, Harold Norse, Ben Pleasants, Al Purdy, Steve Richmond, Kevin Ring, Jory Sherman, Ed Smith, Joan Smith, Nikos

Stangos, John Thomas, Gypsy Lou Webb, Miller Williams, A.D. Winans, Carl Weissner and Leslie Woolf Hedley. Special thanks to Gerard Malanga, Steve Richmond and Nikos Stangos for giving me copies of their previously unpublished correspondence with Bukowski. Thanks also to the following: Raymond Carver's widow, Tess Gallagher; John William Corrington's widow, Joyce Corrington; John Fante's widow, Joyce Fante; and William Wantling's widow, Ruth Wantling. Joyce Corrington kindly gave me copies of her husband's voluminous correspondence with Bukowski.

Several of Bukowski's former girlfriends were brave enough to talk about their relationships with him and I am grateful to the following: Joanna Bull, Linda King, Amber O'Neil, Jane Manhattan, Pamela Miller (aka Cupcakes), Jo Jo Planteen, Claire Rabe and Liza Williams. Special thanks are due to Linda King for allowing me to read and print her previously unpublished love letters, and also to Ruth Wantling for talking about her encounter with Bukowski.

Thanks to the following film actors who knew Bukowski: Ben Gazzara, Elliott Gould, Sean Penn, Mickey Rourke and Harry Dean Stanton. My special thanks to film director Taylor Hackford who arranged for me to view his documentary, *Bukowski*, at his home in Hollywood.

Other friends and associates of Bukowski who were helpful include the following: Sheila Applebaum, whose late husband, Arthur, was Bukowski's attorney; Jefferson Airplane singer-songwriter, Marty Balin; photographer Sam Cherry and his grand-son, Dani Tull; *Barfly* actor Mick Collins; Bukowski's former De Longpre Avenue landlord, Francis Crotty, and Bukowski's former De Longpre Avenue neighbors, Paul Jenson and Sina Taylor; the artist R. Crumb; Bukowski's friends when he lived at Carlton Way, Brad Darby, Tina Darby and George Di Caprio; Rolf Degen who met Bukowski in Germany; Linda King's sister, Gerry; the singer-songwriter, Bob Lind; photographer Michael Montfort; artist Spain Rodriguez; author and journalist Lionel Rolfe; Ruben Rueda, who served Bukowski drinks at The Musso & Frank Grill in Hollywood; the late Sholom 'Red' Stodolsky of Baroque Books, Hollywood; Ben C. Toledano who met Bukowski in New Orleans; and the cartoonist Robert Williams. Thanks also to Henry Bukowski's former Temple City neighbors, Irma Billie and her late husband, Francis.

Al Berlinski of Sun Dog Press, Michigan; New Orleans book dealer Ed Blair; and Seattle book dealer, Ed Smith, supplied invaluable background information. Al Berlinski and Ed Smith also gave me copies of rare books as well as putting me in contact with people I might not otherwise have found.

I am grateful to Black Sparrow Press, to Ed Blair, Linda King, Ed Smith, Joan Smith and Jeffrey H. Weinberg of Sudbury, Massachusetts, for the Bukowski line drawings used to illustrate the chapters.

I visited and corresponded with the special collections libraries of several universities and I am grateful to staff at the following institutions: the University of Arizona at Tucson; Brown University, Rhode Island; Centenary College, Louisiana; Mainz University, Germany; the State University of New York at Buffalo, with particular thanks to Michael Basinski; the University of California at Los Angeles (UCLA); the University of California at Santa Barbara (UCSB), with particular thanks to Yolanda Blue; Temple University, Philadelphia, and to Brenda Galloway; and the University of Texas at Austin, with particular thanks to Bill Fagelson.

Also thanks to Jamie Byng at Canongate Books, Kevin Williamson at Rebel Inc., and the staff of Grove Press.

Finally, thank you to my agents: Jane Bradish-Ellames at Curtis Brown, London, and Russell Galen at Scovil Chichak Galen, New York.

SOURCE NOTES

General note: Most extracts from Bukowski's poems and prose works appear courtesy of Black Sparrow Press. See Selected Bibliography for details. All interviews are dated unless the interviews are too numerous to list, or because the dates have already been given.

PROLOGUE

The 1972 San Francisco poetry reading was based on my interviews with the following people who were at the reading and/or the party afterwards: Marty Balin (2 Feb, 1997); John Bennett (28 Sept, 1997); Douglas Blazek (7 June, 1997); Lawrence Ferlinghetti (14 Jan, 1997); Taylor Hackford (5 Feb, 1997); Linda King (various dates in 1996 and 1997); and Harold Norse (13 Dec, 1996 & 15 Jan, 1997). Taylor Hackford screened his documentary, *Bukowski*, for me; Linda King gave me access to her unpublished correspondence with Bukowski; Marty Balin gave me a copy of the film script he wrote for the proposed Bukowski movie. I also referred to an audio tape of the reading, *Poems and Insults!*; and to stories and articles by John Bennett.

Bukowski's height is taken from a June, 1965, letter he wrote to Steve Richmond, published in *Screams from the Balcony*.

The poem, 'the rat', appears in *Mockingbird Wish Me Luck*.

1   TWISTED CHILDHOOD

The statement that ninety-three per cent of what Bukowski wrote is autobiographical is from a December, 1976, interview Bukowski gave to *Hustler* magazine.

In Andernach, Germany, Bukowski's cousins, Karl and Josephine Fett, granted me access to the previously unpublished family archive of letters, postcards and photographs which is the primary source for the meeting of Bukowski's parents, their background and early life together. Karl Fett was also a helpful interviewee and guide to Andernach (11–13 April, 1997). Matthew Davis translated. I also interviewed Bukowski's cousin Katherine Wood (12 & 29 Jan, 16 June, 1997) who allowed me access to her archive of family documents and photographs in California. The third main source of information about Bukowski's German ancestry was the reminiscences of Bukowski's late uncle Heinrich Fett as quoted in *Shakespeare Never Did This*.

Additional background information on family history came from the following sources: Andernach's registry of births, deaths and marriages – which proves he was born legitimately; the report of Bukowski's birth to the United States Consulate in Coblenz, Germany (courtesy of John Martin); the death certificates of Henry Charles Bukowski, Henry Charles Bukowski Jnr, Katharina Bukowski, Leonard Bukowski and Emilie Olga Bukowski, all held by the State of California; the records of the Mountain View Cemetery, Altadena, California, where several members of the family are buried; the Military Personnel Records of Henry Bukowski, held at the National Personnel Records Center in St Louis, Missouri; and the Los Angeles City Directories held at Los

Angeles Public Library. I am grateful to Rolf Degen of Mendig, Germany, and to Ben Pleasants of Los Angeles, both of whom interviewed Heinrich Fett and Charles Bukowski in the 1970s, and to the library staff at Mainz University, Germany. Henry and Kate Bukowski's stay with the Gerhardt family, including information about Henry's collection of pornographic photographs, and Kate Bukowski's vulgar jokes, are from a previously unpublished letter Erwin Gerhardt wrote to Bukowski (16 Dec, 1977) that is part of the Bukowski archive at the University of Arizona, Tucson.

Bukowski's widow, Linda Lee Bukowski, was helpful on the subject on Bukowski's youth and his feelings for his parents (25 Oct, 1996). Linda King allowed me access to her unpublished correspondence, which reveals details of how children treated him at school.

Bukowski's quotes about being beaten are from the autobiographical essay he wrote for *Adam* magazine in 1971. Details of beatings at Longwood Avenue are drawn from numerous interviews he gave throughout his career, especially those filmed by Barbet Schroeder for *The Charles Bukowski Tapes*, and also from the *Adam* magazine essay. I quote from Bukowski's remarks in both the film and the essay. The quoted remark about his 'twisted' childhood is from an August, 1987, interview with Chris Hodenfield for *Film Comment* magazine. I also referred to *Ham on Rye*, which Bukowski said was autobiographical, other than two minor scenes.

Details of Bukowski's education are taken from the following sources: Los Angeles Unified School District records; Mount Vernon Junior High School's *Minute Man* magazine; the staff of Susan Miller Dorsey High School; and the principal of LA High School, Dr Anne Falotico, who let me consult the school archive of year books. I also spoke and corresponded with many former students of LA High who were at school with Bukowski, including the following: Roger Bloomer (12 Feb, 1997); Stephen Cavanaugh (14 Feb, 1997); John Corbeil (27 Feb, 1997); Fred Merrill (6 Jan, 12 Feb, 22 April, 1997); Robert Merryman (14 Feb, 1997) and Barbara Purdy (6 June, 1997). I also visited Virginia Road Elementary School and am grateful to the principal, Jacklyn Thompson.

Additional background came from: *Europe Since Napoleon* (Pelican, 1966) by David Thomson; *The Fragmented Metropolis* (University of Califonia Press, 1967) by Robert M. Fogelson; *Hank* by Neeli Cherkovski; *The Charles Bukowski Tapes*; *Halliwell's Film Guide* (Grafton Books, 1987); Los Angeles City Directories held at LA Public Library; and Bukowski's US Postal Service records which include details of where he lived as a child.

The poem, 'education', appears in *You Get So Alone at Times That It Just Makes Sense*; 'we ain't got no money, honey, but we got rain' is from *The Last Night of the Earth Poems*. I also referred to poems in *Bone Palace Ballet*, and *War All the Time*.

2   THE BARFLY YEARS

Bukowski's discovery of John Fante's *Ask the Dust* is based on the foreword Bukowski wrote for the Black Sparrow edition of the novel published in 1980, and I quote from the foreword. I also interviewed John Fante's widow, Joyce (3 June, 1997).

Background information on downtown Los Angeles came from the books, *Downtown Los Angeles* (City Vista Press, 1997) by Robert D. Herman, and *The Fragmented Metropolis* (University of California Press, 1967) by Robert M. Fogelson.

Bukowski's employment with Sears Roebuck is based on his writings in *Ham on Rye* and on interviews with former store worker, Fred Merrill (12 Feb & 22 April, 1997), who helped establish that Bukowski worked at the Pico Boulevard store and not the store on Olympic Boulevard, as has previously been supposed.

The staff of Los Angeles City College made Bukowski's college records available and supplied background information about the college's history. Bukowski's espousal of Nazism is based on his various writings, particularly in *Ham on Rye* and *Bone Palace Ballet*. I also interviewed FrancEyE (3 Jan, 1997) and consulted Kate

Bukowski's previously unpublished correspondence. The quote 'all us working class' is from a letter Kate Bukowski wrote to her parents at Christmas, 1936.

Details of Bukowski's subsequent employment history is based on his United States Postal Service file which includes a detailed account of all the places he lived and worked after leaving school. For this, and his travels around America, I also consulted his autobiographical writings in the following books: *Betting on the Muse, Factotum, Mockingbird Wish Me Luck, Notes of a Dirty Old Man* and *Tales of Ordinary Madness*. Additional background information came from *The Charles Bukowski Tapes*, and *Hank* by Neeli Cherkovski.

Bukowski's remarks about sending '8 or 10' stories a week to the New York magazines is from a letter he wrote to Douglas Blazek published in *Screams from the Balcony*. I also referred to *Aftermath of a Lengthy Rejection Slip (Story*, 1944).

For draft records, I am grateful to Barbi Richardson at Selective Services in Arlington, Virginia, who located Bukowski's file.

The staff at Temple University, Philadelphia, found newspaper reports of Courtney Taylor's court appearances which outline his criminal record and prison record. Bukowski's US Postal Service file also included specific information about the date of Bukowski's arrest for draft dodging. These new sources of information fix the date of the arrest as 22 July, 1944, two years after it was previously thought to have happened. Bukowski's US Postal Service file gave additional detail on where in Philadelphia he lived and Brenda Galloway conducted local research on my behalf. She found city records relating to Fairmount Motor Products and to bar man Frank McGilligan. The Philadelphia Historical Society supplied background information about Moyamensing Prison, and I am also grateful to the Pennsylvania prison authorities. Additional information about Bukowski's stay in prison is taken from his autobiographical writings and interviews as previously described. The quotes from Bukowski about the bar on Fairmount Avenue are from his interview with Chris Hodenfield published in *Film Comment* magazine (August, 1987).

Bukowski's claim that he gave up writing for ten years is based on various interviews he gave, particularly one to William

Childress for *Poetry Now* magazine in 1974 in which he said: 'I call it my ten years off with no writing phase . . . I was terrified at the thought that I might have to enter the drab world of 9 to 5.'

The quote, 'poetry is the shortest . . .' is from Len Fulton's essay, 'See Bukowski Run' (*Small Press Review*, May, 1973).

I consulted an original copy of *Portfolio III* at the University of Arizona, Tucson, and original copies of *Matrix* magazines at the University of California at Santa Barbara (UCSB).

The photographs of Bukowski in his suit and tie, and letters explaining the photographs, are courtesy of the Fett family in Andernach (translations by Matthew Davis). The anecdote about Henry Bukowski posing as his son is based on a letter Bukowski wrote to Jim Roman (26 Sept, 1965) published in *Screams from the Balcony*. I also consulted staff at Los Angeles County Museum.

Biographical information about Jane Cooney Baker is based primarily on interviews and correspondence with friends of the Cooney family in Roswell, New Mexico: Richard G. Bean (28 Mar & 6 April, 1997); Orville Cookson (6 April, 1997); Lavora Fisk (5 & 13 May 1997); Jean Rockhold (8 April, 1997); and John H. Wyley (6 April, 1997). The principal of Roswell High School allowed me access to the school year books from which the photograph of Jane, which is the first published, is taken. Members of the Roswell Historical Society researched back issues of the *Roswell Daily Record* and found reports of the deaths of Dr Cooney and Mary Cooney as well as the marriage of Jane Cooney to Craig Baker. Céline Sanchez, Registrar of the State of New Mexico Department of Health, was very helpful in locating birth, death and marriage certificates relating to the Cooney family. I also consulted Jane Cooney Baker's California death certificate. I referred to the screenplay of *Barfly*; the movie, *Barfly*; and *The Charles Bukowski Tapes*. The date of Bukowski's meeting with Jane – different from what has previously been thought – was fixed by cross-referencing Bukowski's correspondence about the meeting, his US Postal Service record and information from friends in Roswell.

The 'Notice to Quit' is from *The Outsider* magazine (Vol. 1, No.3, Spring, 1963).

Details about Bukowski having anal sex with a male friend are from the following sources: his short story about the incident, published in *Notes of a Dirty Old Man*; a tape-recorded conversation with John Thomas reprinted in *Bukowski in the Bathtub*. This is the source of the Bukowski quote: 'You know . . .' (In correspondence with me on 10 Nov, 1997, John Thomas writes: 'Yes, Hank meant it. He thought it was funny, but he told the anecdote as a real one.') Neeli Cherkovski also told me that Bukowski claimed to him that the story was true.

Bukowski's arrest record is taken from his US Postal Service personnel file as are details of his employment with the post office as Christmas temporary carrier and then permanent carrier.

The date of Bukowski's illness was pinpointed by his US Postal Service record and from an unpublished letter to Bukowski from Los Angeles County demanding payment for his treatment. Additional information on the illness comes from Bukowski's own writings and interviews, as already described.

The quote from Linda King is from my 4 Jan, 1997, interview with her. I also referred to my 1996 interview with Linda Lee Bukowski.

Additional background information for this chapter came from Bukowski's previously unpublished correspondence with the following: John Bennett, courtesy of Brown University, Rhode Island; John William Corrington, courtesy of Joyce Corrington; Linda King and John Martin. I also referred to the University of Arizona archive; *The Charles Bukowski Tapes* (the conversation between Bukowski and Jane); and *Film Comment* magazine (August, 1987).

Details of how Bukowski came to take up horse racing are based on his book, *Horsemeat*, and his comments in *The Charles Bukowski Tapes*. The quotes about why he gambled, 'I piss away . . .' are from a conversation with John Thomas transcribed and reprinted in *Bukowski in the Bathtub*.

The poem, 'Sparks', is from *A New Year's Greeting from Black Sparrow Press* (1983); 'fire station' is from *Play the Piano Drunk/Like a Percussion Instrument/Until the Fingers Begin to Bleed a Bit*; 'drink' is from *Betting on the Muse*; 'what will the neighbors think?' is from *Bone Palace Ballet*. 'Soft and fat like summer roses' is from *Matrix* magazine (Vol.9.No 2, Summer, 1946), and has never previously been published in any book.

3   DEATH WANTS MORE DEATH

Details of Bukowski's relationship with Barbara Frye is based on interviews and correspondence with Barbara's relations: Tom Frye (28 Oct, 1996); Sunny Thomas (3 Dec, 1996) and Leah Belle Wilson (19 Oct, 1996/2 Jan & 21 Feb, 1997). I referred to my interviews with Pamela Miller (25 June & 6 July, 1997), whom Bukowski spoke to about his divorce. I consulted Bukowski's unpublished correspondence with Linda King; his unpublished correspondence with John William Corrington; and general correspondence published in *Screams from the Balcony*. I also consulted Bukowski's college record courtesy of Los Angeles City College; his 1955 Las Vegas marriage certificate; his US Postal Service personnel file; the autobiographical story, *Confessions of a Coward*, published as *A New Year's Greeting from Black Sparrow Press (1995)*; and Bukowski's books *Notes of a Dirty Old Man* and *Post Office*.

The description of Bukowski's home on North Mariposa Avenue is drawn from interviews with visitors: Sam Cherry (31 Dec, 1996); FrancEyE (3 Jan, 1997); and Jory Sherman (28 Dec, 1996). I also referred to a contemporaneous description published in the *Literary Times* (Mar, 1963). The quotes from Bukowski about his neighbors are from his introduction to *The Roominghouse Madrigals*. I also referred to *The Charles Bukowski Tapes*.

Information about the deaths of Henry and Kate Bukowski came primarily from interviews with their former Temple City neighbors, Francis and Irma Billie (3 Jan & 1 May, 1997); from Katherine Wood; from unpublished correspondence between Henry Bukowski and his parents-in-law which is part of the Fett family archive in Andernach; and from Bukowski's unpublished correspondence with John William Corrington. I also consulted the death certificates of Henry and Kate; legal papers relating to Henry Bukowski's estate; the records of the Mountain View Cemetery, Altadena; the records of Los Angeles County Museum of Art; and *Notes of a Dirty Old Man*.

The Linda Lee Bukowski quote is from an interview conducted on 25 Oct, 1996.

The Bukowski quote, 'he's dead . . .' is from a 26 Sept, 1965, letter to Jim Roman published in *Screams from the Balcony*.

Bukowski's publishing history in small poetry magazines is based on interviews with Judson Crews (31 Mar, 1997) (including the threat to commit suicide if Crews did not publish him, which was made in a letter from Bukowski to Crews in June, 1953), and Leslie Woolf Hedley (21 & 22 July 1997); and by referring to original copies of the following small magazines: *Epos, Existaria, Harlequin, Matrix, Naked Ear, Quixote, Semina* and *Trace*. These are at the University of Arizona, Tucson; UCLA; and UCSB.

The John Martin quote is from an interview conducted on 13 Nov, 1997.

For the publication of *Flower, Fist and Bestial Wail*, I corresponded with E.V. Griffith (31 Mar, 1997); I consulted the correspondence between Bukowski and Griffith published in *Screams from the Balcony*; and documents relating to Hearse Press held at UCSB. I also referred to an original copy of *Flower, Fist and Bestial Wail* at UCSB.

The section concerning Jane Cooney Baker's latter years, and her death, is taken from Bukowski's unpublished correspondence with John William Corrington, and from my interviews with Jory Sherman. I also referred to Jane's death certificate. The pathology department at Guy's Hospital, London, helped decipher her cause of death. I consulted the records of the San Fernando Mission where her body is buried, and referred to Bukowski's comments in *The Charles Bukowski Tapes* together with his writings in the following books: *The Days Run Away Like Wild Horses Over the Hills, Post Office* and *The Roominghouse Madrigals*.

The history of the Loujon Press is based primarily on my interviews with Louise 'Gypsy Lou' Webb (various dates between 1996 and 1997). I also referred to interviews and correspondence with Webb family friend Ed Blair (various dates from 1996 to 1997) who supplied valuable background information, including his article, 'How to Start an Outsider' (*Louisiana Literature*); and interviews with Jory Sherman; original copies of *The Outsider* and related papers at UCSB; unpublished correspondence between

Bukowski and the Webbs, held at UCSB and the University of Arizona; and the tenth issue of *Sure* (Ed Smith, 1994).

The poems, 'The Day I Kicked Away a Bankroll', 'A Nice Place', 'old man dead in a room' and 'Soirée' are from *The Roominghouse Madrigals*. 'The Tragedy of the Leaves' appears in *Burning in Water, Drowning in Flame*. 'for Jane, with all the love I had, which was not enough –' appears in *The Days Run Away Like Wild Horses Over the Hills*. I also quote from letters published in *Screams from the Balcony* and *Living on Luck*.

4   CONVERSATIONS IN CHEAP ROOMS

Bukowski's depression following the death of Jane Cooney Baker is based on his unpublished correspondence with John William Corrington; my 9 Feb, 1997, interview with Ann Menebroker; interviews with Jory Sherman (various dates); letters published in *Outsider 3* (the burlesque show and the death of Jane's fish); and letters published in *Screams from the Balcony*, including the Dec, 1962, letter to Ann Menebroker about his arrest.

Background information about Bukowski's relationship with his Aunt Eleanor and Uncle Jake Hostetter are from interviews with Katherine Wood.

Additional background information about Bukowski's grieving for Jane comes from his comments in *Bukowski in the Bathtub*.

John Bryan described his association with Bukowski in interviews (13 Jan & 6 June, 1997). I referred to original copies of rare Bukowski publications and literary magazines at the libraries of UCSB and the University of Arizona. I also studied correspondence held at these universities which relates to the publication of his work in the little magazines.

The description of Bukowski's post office work is based primarily on my interviews with his former co-workers: David Berger (4 Mar & 24 April, 1997); Johnny Moore (6 Mar, 1997); and

Grace Washington (14 May, 1997). I also consulted the novel *Post Office* and Bukowski's US Postal Service personnel file.

Bukowski's relationship with FrancEyE, and her personal history, is based on my interviews with FrancEyE (3 Jan & 30 May, 1997); her birth certificate; her unpublished correspondence with Bukowski held at UCSB; and Bukowski's unpublished correspondence with John William Corrington.

Bukowski's relationship with Sam Cherry and his family is based on interviews with Neeli Cherkovski (various dates) and Sam Cherry (31 Dec, 1996).

The publication of *It Catches My Heart in Its Hands* is based on interviews with Gypsy Lou Webb and Ed Blair on various dates. I also consulted the Bukowski/Webb correspondence, published and unpublished; original copies of the various editions of *It Catches My Heart in Its Hands* at UCSB; and letters in *Outsider 3*. The quoted writings of Jon Webb are from the colophon of *It Catches My Heart in Its Hands*, and Bukowski's quoted reaction to the book is from letters in *Screams from the Balcony*. I further referred to *A Bibliography of Charles Bukowski*, by Stanford Dorbin. Bukowski's quotes about Robinson Jeffers are from a 1 April, 1960, letter to Jory Sherman printed in *Screams from the Balcony*.

The poem, 'an empire of coins', is from *Betting on the Muse*; 'I thought of ships, of armies, hanging on . . .' is from *The Days Run Away Like Wild Horses Over the Hills*. The letters between Bukowski and his neighbor appear in *Screams from the Balcony*. The poem, 'the biggest breasts', is from *Renaissance* magazine, 1962, and has never previously been published in book form.

The chapter title is adapted from Bukowski's poem, 'conversation in a cheap room', originally published in *It Catches My Heart in Its Hands*.

5 FAMILY LIFE AT DE LONGPRE AVENUE

FrancEyE described her pregnancy, the birth of Marina and her relationship with Bukowski (interviews dated: 3 Jan & 30 May, 1997). I consulted Marina's birth certificate, and my interviews with Neeli Cherkovski and Jory Sherman.

The description of the De Longpre Avenue court is based on interviews with Neeli Cherkovski (various dates); Francis Crotty (4 Jan, 1997); FrancEyE (3 Jan & 30 May, 1997); Paul Jenson (31 Dec, 1996); Steve Richmond (8 Nov, 1996); and Sina Taylor (31 Dec 1996). I also referred to 'Grip The Walls' (*The Wormwood Review*, No.16, 1964); to my interview with Al Purdy (27 Dec, 1996); and to the book, *The Bukowski/Purdy Letters 1964–1974*.

Bukowski's meeting and dealings with the Webbs were described by Gypsy Lou Webb and by FrancEyE.

His quote about Marina, 'The girl-child . . .' is from a 1 Mar, 1965, letter to John William Corrington, published in *Living on Luck*.

Concerning the meeting between Bukowski and Corrington and the making of the second Loujon book, I interviewed Ed Blair (various interviews and correspondence between Dec 1996 and June 1997); Joyce Corrington (9 Dec, 1996); Ben C. Toledano (1 July, 1997); and Miller Williams (18 Feb, 1997). I also consulted the following sources: the Bukowski–Webb correspondence collected at UCSB, and at the University of Arizona; Bukowski's unpublished correspondence with Corrington; Bukowski's unpublished correspondence with Steve Richmond; Bukowski's correspondence with the Webbs collected in the books, *Living on Luck* and *Screams from the Balcony*; Bukowski's correspondence with Al Purdy published in *The Bukowski/Purdy Letters 1964–1974*, in which he writes about letting everybody down (14 Mar, 1965) and describes drinking with Jon Webb (23 Mar, 1965); Bukowski's introduction to *Burning in Water, Drowning in Flame* in which he describes the process of making *Crucifix in a Deathhand*, and conversations with Webb; the essay 'Corrington, Bukowski, and the Loujon Press' (*Louisiana Literature*) by Lloyd Halliburton; original copies of *The Outsider* magazine, *It Catches My Heart in Its Hands*; and *Crucifix in a Deathhand* – all held at UCSB; the book, *John William Corrington/Southern Man of Letters* (UCA Press, 1994) edited by William Mills; and various background letters, photographs and documents kindly supplied by

Ed Blair. I consulted Henry Miller's unpublished correspondence with Bukowski at UCSB.

FrancEyE told me about Bukowski's admiration for Dorothy Healey. Bukowski's comments, 'What I've tried to do . . .', are from his interview with Sean Penn printed in *Interview* magazine (Sept, 1987); and the quote 'I am not a man who . . .' is from an interview with William Packard published in the book, *The Poet's Craft* (Paragon House Publishing, 1987). I also consulted the books *Crucifix in a Deathhand* and *Burning in Water, Drowning in Flame*.

Douglas Blazek described his association with Bukowski (7 June, 1997). I also consulted the unpublished Bukowski–Blazek correspondence collected at UCSB; the published correspondence in *Screams from the Balcony* and original copies of *Ole* magazine at UCSB.

FrancEyE described her break-up with Bukowski and their life at De Longpre Avenue (3 Jan & 30 May, 1997). I interviewed Marina Bukowski about her childhood (21 July, 1997); I referred to letters from Bukowski to his friend William Wantling; correspondence published in *Screams from the Balcony*; and to Bukowski's unpublished correspondence with Steve Richmond.

The poem, 'the new place', appears in *The Roominghouse Madrigals*. The poem, 'something for the touts, the nuns, the grocery clerks and you . . .', appears in *Burning in Water, Drowning in Flame*; *Confessions of a Man Insane Enough to Live with Beasts* appears in *South of No North*. FrancEyE's poem, 'Christ I feel shitty', is from *Das ist Alles*.

6 BLACK SPARROW, AND THE SIXTIES

John Martin described his personal background, his first meeting with Bukowski and the launch of Black Sparrow Press. I spoke to Barbara Martin about the design of the sparrow logo (13 Jan,

1997). I interviewed Gerard Malanga (18 Dec, 1996). I consulted interviews with John Martin and Charles Bukowski that appeared in the *Boston Review* (Nov/Dec issue, 1992). In his interview, Bukowski described their meeting and first conversations. I also looked at previously unpublished letters from Martin to Bukowski that are held at UCSB, together with the first Black Sparrow Press broadsides, and the introduction to *The Charles Bukowski Papers* (Department of Special Collections, UCSB). Extracts from John Martin's unpublished letters to Bukowski are courtesy of John Martin.

I interviewed Lawrence Ferlinghetti about Bukowski's poetry (14 Jan, 1997). The quotes from Bukowski on his writing style are from *The Charles Bukowski Tapes*.

For Bukowski's involvement and attitudes to the sixties drug culture, I interviewed the following: John Bryan (13 Jan & 6 June, 1997); Steve Richmond (various dates between 1996 & 1997); and John Thomas (1 Jan & 26 June, 1997). I also consulted the following: *Screams from the Balcony*, including Bukowski's 2 Feb, 1966, letter to Steve Richmond, 'LSD, yeah . . .'; the unpublished correspondence of Bukowski and Steve Richmond; *Bukowski in the Bathtub*, including Bukowski's conversation with John Thomas about LSD; and publications by Steve Richmond including: *Earth Rose* (Earth Rose 1/undated); *Hitler Painted Roses* (Earth Books and Sun Dog Press, 1994); and *Spinning Off Bukowski* which I referred to for the description of Bukowski's clothing and his visits to Richmond's store. For Bukowski's negative views on drugs, I referred to his comments in *The Charles Bukowski Tapes*.

John Bryan described Bukowski's association with *Open City* (13 Jan & 6 June, 1997). Bukowski's opinion of the newspaper's staff, 'scummy Commie . . .', was reported to me by Bryan. I interviewed Jack Micheline (15 Jan, 2 June & 20 Sept, 1997) and quote from his prose-poem, 'Long After Midnight', published in *Sixty-Seven Poems for Downtrodden Saints* (FMSBW, 1997). Bukowski's quote, 'The crew did not . . .', is from the autobiographical essay he wrote for *Adam* magazine (1971). I consulted Bukowski's preface to the City Lights edition of *Notes of a Dirty Old Man*, taking the quote 'Think of it yourself . . .'; and consulted copies of *Open City* at UCLA. I interviewed John Thomas (1 Jan,

1997) about Bukowski's working methods. Bukowski's former De Longpre Avenue neighbors, Sina Taylor and Paul Jenson, told me he used to read his copy to an elderly woman who lived next door (31 Dec, 1996).

Details of Bukowski's trip to see the Webbs in Tucson, Arizona, are primarily taken from my interviews with Gypsy Lou Webb. I also referred to Bukowski's unpublished correspondence with John William Corrington; to letters published in *Screams from the Balcony*; and to Bukowski's short story, *My Stay in the Poet's Cottage*, published in *Tales of Ordinary Madness*. Background information came from the *Tucson Daily Citizen* (15 July, 1967); the periodical, *Book Production History* (Feb, 1967); and correspondence from Ed Blair.

The history of the thirteenth Penguin Modern Poets book is taken principally from interviews with Harold Norse (13 Dec, 1996 & 15 Jan, 1997); and my interview with Nikos Stangos (29 Jan, 1997). Nikos Stangos kindly made available his unpublished correspondence with Bukowski. Further background information came from Harold Norse's book, *Memoirs of a Bastard Angel* (Bloomsbury, 1990); and from the unpublished correspondence of Bukowski and John William Corrington.

Douglas Blazek described his meeting with Bukowski and gave opinions of his work (7 June, 1997). I also consulted letters from Bukowski to Blazek published in *Screams from the Balcony*.

Details of Bukowski's problems with the US Postal Service are based on interviews with his former union representative, David Berger (4 Mar, 1997); with FrancEyE (3 Jan, 1997) and Bukowski's former landlord, Francis Crotty (4 Jan, 1997). I also consulted Bukowski's Feb, 1967, letter to Steve Richmond for the exchange with the angry postal worker. This letter is published in *Screams from the Balcony*. Additional background came from the archive of Bukowski letters at Brown University, Rhode Island; and the letters to the Webbs published in *Screams from the Balcony*.

For Bukowski's relationship with the beat writers, I referred to my interviews with Lawrence Ferlinghetti (14 Jan, 1997); Jack Micheline (various dates in 1997); and Harold Norse (13 Dec, 1996 & 15 Jan, 1997). The description of Bukowski's meeting with Neal Cassady is taken from my (6 June, 1997) interview with John

Bryan; Allen Ginsberg's quotes are from my correspondence with Allen Ginsberg (28 Sept, 1996). Bukowski's conversation with Cassady, and their car ride, is based on Bukowski's contemporaneous *Open City* column published in *Notes of a Dirty Old Man*; Bukowski's Feb, 1968, letter to the Webbs, published in *Screams from the Balcony*; and my interviews with John Bryan. Background details about the life of Neal Cassady came from the following books: *Ginsberg* (Viking, 1989) by Barry Miles; *Jack's Book* (Penguin, 1979) by Barry Gifford and Lawrence Lee; and *Kerouac* (Picador, 1978) by Ann Charters.

Harold Norse's comments about Bukowski's sexuality come from interviews with Norse conducted on 13 Dec, 1996 & 15 Jan, 1997. I also quote from Norse's autobiography, *Memoirs of a Bastard Angel*. I consulted Bukowski's correspondence at UCSB and referred to my interviews with Neeli Cherkovski. The anecdote about Bukowski inviting Cherkovski into his bed comes from an interview with Cherkovski on 16 Dec, 1996. I also interviewed John Martin and Jack Micheline.

Details of the publication of *Notes of a Dirty Old Man*, details of the *Skinny Dynamite* case and the demise of *Open City* are from my interviews with John Bryan (13 Jan & 6 June, 1997); and Jack Micheline (15 Jan, 2 June & 20 Sept, 1997). I also consulted the following sources: the biographical note, letters and *LA Free Press* extract published in Jack Micheline's book, *Sixty-seven Poems for Downtrodden Saints* (FMSBW, 1997); *Skinny Dynamite* (Second Coming Press, 1980); Bukowski's book, *The Most Beautiful Woman in Town*; and Bukowski's letters in *Screams from the Balcony*.

Bukowski's involvement with Zapple was described for me by Barry Miles in an interview (12 Feb, 1997). I spoke to former Apple executive Tony Bramwell (4 Feb, 1997); I referred to Bukowski's unpublished correspondence at UCSB; and Bukowski's unpublished correspondence with John Bennett held at Brown University, Rhode Island.

John Martin described Bukowski's opinion of the Black Mountain poets in an interview on 20 July, 1997. Neeli Cherkovski described the history of *Laugh Literary and Man the Humping Guns*. I interviewed Sam Cherry (1 Jan, 1997) and consulted original copies of *Laugh Literary and Man the Humping Guns* courtesy of Neeli Cherkovski's nephew, Dani Tull.

Sam Cherry and Neeli Cherkovski described the taking of the box car photograph. I interviewed John and Barbara Martin about the design of *The Days Run Away Like Wild Horses Over the Hills* and referred to my interviews with Harold Norse. I also referred to *Whitman's Wild Children* (Lapis Press, 1988) by Neeli Cherkovski.

The poem, 'a little atomic bomb', appears in *Play the Piano Drunk/Like a Percussion Instrument/Until the Fingers Begin to Bleed a Bit*; 'traffic ticket' and 'true story' appear in *Burning in Water, Drowning in Flame*. 'The Genius of the Crowd' appears in *The Roominghouse Madrigals*. The extract from 'Long After Midnight' appears by kind permission of Jack Micheline. Extracts from *Notes of a Dirty Old Man*, copyright 1969, are reprinted by permission of City Lights Books.

7 POST OFFICE

Details of how Bukowski left the post office are primarily taken from my interviews with John Martin, and from Bukowski's United States Postal Service personnel file. John Martin described the breakdown of the $100-a-month in an interview on 21 July, 1997.

Bukowski's attitude to money is based on interviews with Neeli Cherkovski; FrancEyE (3 Jan & 30 May, 1997); Harold Norse (15 Jan, 1997); Steve Richmond (8 Nov, 1996); and John Thomas (1 Jan, 1997).

Bukowski's Bridge reading was described in interviews with: Neeli Cherkovski, Jack Micheline, Harold Norse, Steve Richmond and John Thomas, who kindly supplied a list of the poems read on 19 December, 1969. I also consulted Thomas's review of the reading which appeared in the *LA Free Press* on 6 Feb, 1970.

Johnny Moore described the night Bukowski left the post office (6 Mar, 1997). I also referred to, and quote from, *Post Office*.

For the writing of *Post Office*, I consulted the original manuscript of the novel which is held at UCSB. I referred to the 25th Black Sparrow Press imprint of the novel; and to my interviews with John Martin. I quote from Russell Harrison's book, *Against The American Dream* (BSP, 1994). Bukowski's quote, 'I was concerned . . .', is from an article in the periodical, *LJ* (1 Feb, 1971). The Bukowski quote 'for laughs' is from a 23 Feb, 1970, letter from Bukowski to Carl Weissner published in *Living on Luck*.

The anecdote about Bukowski throwing forty paintings away is from an unpublished letter (dated 17 April, 1970) from Bukowski to Harold Norse. The letter is part of the Bukowski archive at Temple University, Philadelphia. I further consulted my 20 July, 1997, interview with John Martin in which he described Bukowski's artwork and interest in art.

Details of Bukowski's readings in New Mexico and Seattle, Washington, are from the following sources: unpublished correspondence between Bukowski and Linda King; the video film, *Bukowski at Bellevue*. The quote 'a drunken half-fuck' is from a June, 1970, letter from Bukowski to Sanford Dorbin published in *Living on Luck*.

I interviewed and corresponded with Ann Menebroker about her visit to De Longpre Avenue (interviews: 9 Feb & 6 July, 1997) and quote from her letters to Bukowski held at UCSB, with her kind permission.

Details of Bukowski's problems with his De Longpre neighbors are from various unpublished letters he wrote to Harold Norse. The letters are at Temple University, Philadelphia.

I referred to original copies of the pornographic magazines Bukowski wrote for. They are at the University of Arizona, Tucson. The archive at UCSB contains a letter from the editor of *Fling* to Bukowski (26 June, 1971).

I interviewed Carl Weissner (7 Mar & 10 Aug, 1997) regarding the translation of *Notes of a Dirty Old Man* and its publication in Germany. The section about the fake Henry Miller quote, and the quoted Bukowski letter, is from *Living on Luck*.

Details of Bukowski's applications to the National Endowment for the Arts are from correspondence at UCSB. The quote, 'I thought the life of a writer . . .', is from a 1 Sept, 1970, letter from Bukowski to Neeli Cherkovski, published in *Living on Luck*.

The extract from 'Another Academy' is from *A New Year's Gift for the Friends of Black Sparrow Press*.

8 LOVE LOVE LOVE

Bukowski's relationship with Linda King is primarily based on my interviews with Linda King conducted on various dates in 1996 and 1997, and our correspondence. Linda kindly made available her previously unpublished correspondence with Bukowski, her collection of artwork, magazines, and photographs. Extracts from her love letters to Bukowski appear with her permission. (*NB*: The letter from Bukowski to Linda about picking up a man on the way home has been lost, but Linda's reply of 7 May, 1971, reads, in part: 'I hope you had a good time with your homosexual pick-up . . .')

For additional background, I consulted the previously unpublished Bukowski–King correspondence at UCSB; and the article, 'Bukowski', written by Linda King and published in *Small Press Review* (May, 1973). The reference to the unpublished Bukowski poem, 'I have eaten your cunt like a peach', is from this article. I also referred to my interviews with Neeli Cherkovski, John Martin and Steve Richmond; to Bukowski's unpublished correspondence with Richmond; and to a previously unpublished letter dated 14 June, 1976, from Linda King to John Martin listing all the times Bukowski had been violent towards her.

For additional background information for the early part of the chapter, I referred to *An Anthology of LA Poets* (Laugh Literary/Red Hill Press, 1972); *Me and Your Sometimes Love*

Poems; *Women*; and back issues of *Open City* and the *LA Free Press* which are on microfiche at UCLA.

The Gerald Locklin review of *Post Office* was published in the *Long Beach Press-Telegram* on 18 Mar, 1971.

The poem by Linda King, 'How Long (for C.B.)', appears with her kind permission.

9 WOMEN

Bukowski's relationship with Liza Williams is based on my interviews with Liza conducted on 22 Feb & 25 June, 1997. Liza made available a photograph album of the Catalina holiday, which provided useful background information. Additional background came from Bukowski's unpublished letters to Linda King, and letters published in *Living on Luck*.

The primary source for the death of Jon Webb were my interviews with Gypsy Lou Webb. Ed Blair supplied useful background information and a copy of the June and Clyde story which appeared in the *LA Free Press* on 14 April, 1972. The Gypsy Lou quotes about Jon's ashes are from an article by Liza Williams published in the *LA Free Press* in 1972, later reprinted in *Sure* magazine (No. 2, Aug, 1991).

For details about Liza Williams' party, I interviewed guests: Spain Rodriguez (19 July, 1997); Robert Williams (3 April, 1997); and corresponded with R. Crumb (19 Jan & 10 Mar, 1997).

All quotes from Linda King are from my interviews conducted on various dates in 1996 and 1997, and these are the primary sources of all passages relating to Bukowski's relationship with Linda. She also made available her unpublished correspondence with Bukowski and the extracts from the following letters: the letter beginning 'I was so happy . . .' is dated 21 May, 1972; and the letter beginning 'Bastard Bukowski' is dated 30 May, 1972.

Quotes from Marina Bukowski are from my interview with her on 21 July, 1997.

The section about the Silver Lake party is based on my interviews with Linda King, and the following guests: John Bennett and Marty Balin (as detailed in the Source Note to the Prologue); Brad Darby (13 Feb & 28 April, 1997); and Tina Darby (7 July, 1997). I also referred to John Bennett's short story, *The Party to End All Parties*, which appears in *The Moth Eaters* (Anglefish Press, 1997).

John Martin told me the story about Bukowski and the police who turned out to be fans (21 July, 1997). I spoke to Linda King about the fight which preceded the arrest.

Bukowski's relationship with Joanna Bull was described by Joanna Bull in interviews and correspondence (7, 15 & 27 Mar, 1997). Joanna also made available her unpublished correspondence with Bukowski.

Bukowski's trip to Utah is based on my interviews with Linda King and her sister, Gerry King (5 Jan, 1997). I also referred to Bukowski's published letters in *Living on Luck* and his writings in *Women*.

The screening of Taylor Hackford's documentary, *Bukowski*, was based on my interviews with Neeli Cherkovski; Taylor Hackford (5 Feb, 1997); Linda King; and Jory Sherman. Taylor Hackford was kind enough to screen the film for me at his home in Hollywood. For additional background, I referred to Jory Sherman's chapbook, *Friendship Fame and Bestial Myth*; and Steve Richmond's book, *Spinning Off Bukowski*.

Ruth Wantling described Bukowski's visit to Normal, Illinois, the death of William Wantling and her trip to Los Angeles (interviews on various dates in 1996 and 1997). I also spoke with her friend, Victoria Harris (4 Dec, 1996), and interviewed the following: Brad Darby (13 Feb, 1997); Tina Darby (7 July, 1997); and Steve Richmond (8 Nov, 1996). Additional information is from Bukowski's unpublished correspondence with William and Ruth Wantling, held at UCSB, and Bukowski's unpublished correspondence with John Bennett, held at Brown University, Philadelphia. I also referred to microfiches of the *LA Free Press* at UCLA; and to A.D. Winans' book, *The Charles Bukowski/Second Coming Years*.

The poem, 'cooperation', is from *Play The Piano Drunk/Like a Percussion Instrument Until/The Fingers Begin to Bleed a Bit*. The poem, 'trouble with spain', is from *Burning in Water, Drowning in Flame*. The poem, 'the icecream people', was first published in the *New York Quarterly* (No. 14/Spring, 1973) and has never previously been published in a book. The extract appears here by permission of Black Sparrow Press.

10 GETTING FAMOUS

The Santa Cruz reading is based on my correspondence with the late Allen Ginsberg (23 Sept, 1996), and on an article by Ric Reynolds in the 6 Dec, 1974, issue of the *Berkeley Barb*.

The information that Bukowski was invited to the Naropa Institute comes from a 18 Oct, 1978, letter from Ginsberg to Bukowski which is held at UCSB, and Bukowski's reply declining the invitation. Harold Norse told me about Bukowski's meeting with William Burroughs (13 Dec, 1996).

Regarding the Sartre/Genet quotation about Bukowski being the best poet in America, John Martin initially referred me to *Esquire* magazine where he believed it first appeared. I also referred to the 17 June, 1976, issue of *Rolling Stone* magazine, where the claim was made. The staff at *Esquire* searched their archives, but found nothing. I then contacted international Sartre and Genet scholars starting with Professor Malcolm Bowie at Oxford University, England, who consulted his colleagues in Britain and the United States, none of whom knew about the quotation. Dr Jean-Pierre Boulé, secretary of the UK Society for Sartrean Studies, took my enquiry to the 1997 Sartre convention in Paris, France, but no one was aware of a connection between Sartre and Bukowski. Edmund White, author of *Genet*, knew nothing about an association with Genet. Albert Dichy, director of the Genet archive in Paris, was firmly of the opinion Genet had said no such thing (11 June, 1997). In an interview with John Martin in Santa Rosa on 21 July, 1997, he agreed the quotation was no more than apocryphal.

The Bukowski quote, 'I look around . . .', and details about Bukowski's meeting with Raymond Carver are from Donald McRae's interview with Bukowski published in the *Guardian* newspaper, London, on 14 Dec, 1991. I also corresponded with Carver's widow, Tess Gallagher (18 Dec, 1997). Lines from 'You Don't Know What Love Is' come from *Fires: Essays, Poems, Stories* by Raymond Carver, first published in Great Britain in 1985 by Collins Harvill, copyright 1968, 1969, 1970, 1971, 1972, 1973, 1974, 1975, 1976, 1977, 1978, 1979, 1980, 1981, 1982, 1983, 1984 by Tess Gallagher. Reproduced by permission of The Harvill Press.

Bukowski's Santa Barbara reading was described by John Martin (21 July, 1997) and club owner Claire Rabe (6 & 22 Mar, 1997). I also referred to an article in the *Santa Barbara News & Review* (24 Oct, 1975).

Bukowski's comments about the inspiration for *Factotum* are from an interview he gave to Robert Wennersten of *London* magazine, reprinted in *Zoot* magazine (June, 1996). I also quoted from Richard Elman's review of *Factotum* which appeared in the *New York Times* on 8 Aug, 1976; and referred to the 1989 Penguin edition of George Orwell's *Down and Out in Paris and London*.

The Bukowski quote, 'My writing has no meaning . . .', is from Bukowski's interview with *Hustler* magazine (Dec, 1976), as are his comments about *The Fiend*.

Details about Bukowski's payment by *Hustler* is from a 18 May, 1976, letter from the managing editor of *Hustler* to Bukowski. It is on file at UCSB. All comments from John Martin are from interviews with the author.

Tina and Brad Darby described life at Carlton Way in interviews on various dates between Feb and July, 1997. I also corresponded with Bob Lind (1 June, 1997) and interviewed Bob Lind (8 Oct, 1997).

The section about Bukowski's friendship with George Di Caprio is from my 28 July, 1997, interview with George Di Caprio.

Linda King described her break-up with Bukowski in interviews and correspondence on various dates in 1996 and 1997. I referred to her previously unpublished 14 June, 1976, letter to John Martin. I also spoke to Tina Darby; referred to *Women*; and Bukowski's letters in *Living on Luck*.

The primary source for the section about Pamela Miller (aka Cupcakes) are my interviews with Pamela (6 & 25 July, 1997). I also referred to letters published in *Living on Luck*.

The poems, 'one for the shoeshine man', 'how come you're not unlisted?', and 'huge ear rings' are from *Love Is a Dog from Hell*. *The Fiend* is from *The Most Beautiful Woman in Town*: copyright 1967, 1968, 1969, 1970, 1972, 1983 by Charles Bukowski. Reprinted by permission of City Lights Books.

11 RED DEATH SUNSET BLOOD GLORY GALS

Pamela Miller (aka Cupcakes) described her meeting with Bukowski and their subsequent affair (25 June & 6 July, 1997). The notes Bukowski left at her apartment are taken from *Living on Luck*. I referred to Pamela's original inscribed copy of *Scarlet*; to *Women* and *Love Is a Dog From Hell*.

The New York reading was described by Pamela Miller. I also consulted my interview with Gerard Malanga (18 Dec, 1996). Additional background came from reviews of the reading that appeared in *Dodeca* magazine (Aug, 1976) by Tom Jackrell, and *The Drummer* magazine (6 July, 1976) by Louise Simons; and from Bukowski's own writings in *Love Is a Dog from Hell* and *Women*.

Background about Bukowski's other affairs and correspondence with women fans are from the following sources: my interview with Amber O'Neil (23 Mar, 1997); interviews and correspondence with Jane Manhattan (7 & 14 Mar, and 14 Aug, 1997); and interviews and correspondence with Jo Jo

Planteen (4–23 Mar, 1997). Amber O'Neil allowed me to quote from her self-published chapbook, *Blowing My Hero*. I also referred to her unpublished correspondence with Bukowski. Jo Jo Planteen allowed me to read her unpublished correspondence with Bukowski. I consulted Bukowski's general correspondence on file at the University of Arizona; and letters in *Living on Luck*.

Bukowski's relationship with A.D. Winans' girlfriend is based on details that appear in Winans' book, *The Charles Bukowski/Second Coming Years*; from my 7 July, 1997, interview with Winans; and from Bukowski's unpublished correspondence with Winans, collected at Brown University, Philadelphia.

All quotes from John Martin, including the story about the two Dutch girls, are from my interviews with Martin.

The exchange between Bukowski and his mail man is from Barbet Schroeder's *The Charles Bukowski Tapes*.

All quotes from Linda Lee Bukowski (nee Beighle) are from my 25 Oct, 1996, interview with Linda Lee. I also interviewed Joan Smith (26 July, 1997). Background information on Linda Lee's early relationship with Bukowski is taken from the following sources: Bukowski's published correspondence in *Living on Luck*; his correspondence with Amber O'Neil, published in *Blowing My Hero*; his unpublished correspondence with a confidential source; his unpublished correspondence with Jo Jo Planteen, Linda Lee's contribution to the documentary *The Ordinary Madness of Charles Bukowski*; Linda Lee's 1985 Certificate of Registry of Marriage; pages 253–254 of *Hank* by Neeli Cherkovski; my interviews with Pamela Miller; the unpublished Beighle–Bukowski correspondence at the University of Arizona; and, at Linda Lee's suggestion, Bukowski's fictionalized account of their meeting as published in *Women*.

I am grateful to the staff of The Musso & Frank Grill in Hollywood, and especially to barman Ruben Rueda whom I interviewed there on 2 Jan, 1997.

Details of Bukowski's last meeting with Linda King are based on my interviews with Linda King on various dates between 1996 and 1997.

I also consulted Thomas Schmitt's 1976 documentary, *Charles Bukowski – East Hollywood*.

The extracts from Bukowski's letters to Cupcakes and Carl Weissner are from *Living on Luck*.

The poems, 'i made a mistake', 'liberty', 'a stethoscope case' and 'the retreat' are published in *Love is a Dog from Hell*. The poem, 'i am a reasonable man', appears in *Dangling in the Tournefortia*. The poem, 'the shower', appears in *Mockingbird Wish Me Luck*.

12 EUROPEAN SON

Bukowski's publishing history in Germany was described by Carl Weissner in interviews (5–6 Mar & 10 Aug, 1997).

I interviewed Michael Montfort on 23 July, 1997, and referred to his limited edition book, *Bukowski (Photographs 1977–1987)*.

Montfort and Weissner described the Hamburg reading. For additional background, I referred to *Shakespeare Never Did This*, and to audio and video recordings of the Hamburg reading.

I visited Andernach, Germany, in April, 1997, and interviewed Heinrich Fett's son, Karl Fett, and Heinrich Fett's daughter-in-law, Josephine Fett, about Bukowski's return to the town. Matthew Davis translated.

I interviewed Rolf Degen (23–25 Mar, 1997) and am grateful to the library staff at Mainz University in Germany for finding a contemporaneous article Degen wrote about his meeting with Bukowski in Andernach.

Additional information came from *Shakespeare Never Did This* and interviews with Linda Lee Bukowski (25 Oct, 1996), Michael Montfort and Carl Weissner.

The account of Bukowski's business affairs, and his relationship with John Martin, is based primarily on Bukowski's unpublished 1978 correspondence with John Martin. I also referred to my interviews with John Martin; and a 6 June, 1978, letter from Bukowski to Carl Weissner, published in *Living on Luck*.

Details of the purchase of the San Pedro house are taken

from Bukowski's unpublished correspondence with John Martin; and from Bukowski's books, *Dangling in the Tournefortia* and *Hollywood*.

Background about Barbet Schroeder is from *The Biographical Dictionary of Film* by David Thomson. I also consulted *Hank* by Neeli Cherkovski; and *Living on Luck*.

Linda Lee Bukowski described her 1978 trip to France with Bukowski and his appearance on the *Apostrophes* television program. I also referred to video film of the show and to *Shakespeare Never Did This*. The quote from Barbet Schroeder is from his contribution to the documentary, *The Ordinary Madness of Charles Bukowski*.

The poem, 'Looking for a Job', appears in *Burning in Water, Drowning in Flame*.

13   CHINASKI IN SUBURBIA

Reaction to *Women* by Bukowski's girlfriends, and female acquaintances, is from interviews as previously listed. I also referred to and quoted from *Women*.

Bukowski's association with John Fante is primarily based on my correspondence and 3 June, 1997, interview with Joyce Fante, and on my interviews with John Martin. Ben Pleasants, who interviewed Bukowski and Fante in the 1970s, told me Bukowski was worried about meeting Fante because he felt he had taken the idea of short chapters from him. For additional background material, I referred to the following sources: an article about John Fante, written by Frank Spotnitz, which appeared in *American Film* magazine in July, 1989; Bukowski's unpublished correspondence with John Martin; an audio tape of a reading Bukowski gave at Redondo Beach, California, in April, 1980, during which he urged the crowd to buy Fante's books and called him 'my buddy . . .'; the Bukowski preface for the 1980

Black Sparrow Press edition of *Ask the Dust*; and Black Sparrow editions of Fante's novels, *Wait Until Spring, Bandini* (1983) and *Full of Life* (1988). The dialogue between Bukowski and Fante is partly based on an essay by Bukowski about John Fante, which is part of John Martin's archive in Santa Rosa. I also referred to a 27 Jan, 1990, letter from Bukowski to Kevin Ring, editor of *Beat Scene* magazine, in which Bukowski relates the dialogue between him and Fante.

Bukowski's lifestyle at San Pedro, and the purchase of his BMW, is based on my interview with Linda Lee Bukowski; interviews with John Martin; Bukowski's unpublished correspondence with John Martin; and correspondence in *Living On Luck*. I also referred to poems published in *Dangling in the Tournefortia*. Details of the *Barfly* deal are from letters in *Living on Luck*; Bukowski's unpublished correspondence with John Martin; Bukowski's novel, *Hollywood*; and an interview with Bukowski by Chris Hodenfield published in *Film Comment* (Aug 1987).

Linda Lee Bukowski described the background to the making of *The Charles Bukowski Tapes*, Bukowski's return to Longwood Avenue and the circumstances surrounding the occasion when he kicked her off the sofa. I also referred to an essay Barbet Schroeder wrote for the *Elms Lesters Celebrates Charles Bukowski* exhibition, in London, in 1996. The quoted exchanges between Bukowski, Linda Lee and Schroeder are taken from *The Charles Bukowski Tapes*.

The primary source for the making of the film, *Tales of Ordinary Madness*, was my 21 June, 1997, interview with Ben Gazzara. I also referred to the following: my 14 Jan, 1997, interview with Lawrence Ferlinghetti; Bukowski's unpublished correspondence with John Martin; Bukowski's books *The Most Beautiful Woman in Town* and *Tales of Ordinary Madness*; *Halliwell's Film Guide* (6th edn), *Adam* magazine (Feb 1972 edn); and the film itself. Details of the Los Angeles première are from my interviews with: Linda Lee Bukowski; Lionel Rolfe (3 June, 1997); and Gene Vier (3 June, 1997). Details of Bukowski's behavior after the première are from Rolfe's book, *In Search of Literary LA*. Details of Bukowski's drunk driving arrest are from my interview with Linda Lee Bukowski; from Bukowski's poem, 'the star', published in *War All the Time*; and his short story, *Mad Enough*, published in *Septuagenarian Stew*.

All comments by Linda Lee Bukowski on Bukowski's alcoholism, and their relationship, are from my interview with her. I referred to my interviews with John Martin and Joan Smith, both of whom allowed me to see their unpublished correspondence with Bukowski. I also referred to *Play the Piano Drunk/Like a Percussion Instrument/Until The Fingers Begin to Bleed a Bit*, and Joan Smith's book, *Das ist Alles*.

For the publication of *Ham on Rye*, I referred to my interview with Linda Lee Bukowski; to Bukowski's unpublished correspondence with A.D. Winans, held at Brown University, Rhode Island; to the 3 Oct, 1982, edition of the *Los Angeles Times* and to *Ham on Rye*. Derivations of the *Ham on Rye* title are from the book, *Das war's*, by Gundolf S. Freyermuth; and from John Martin comments in the documentary, *The Ordinary Madness of Charles Bukowski*. I also referred to the book, *Charles Bukowski*, by Gay Brewer. Regarding the writing of *Women*, Bukowski wrote to John Martin on 13 Sept, 1976, that, 'my nose might be too close to the mirror at the moment'. The letter is published in *Living on Luck*.

Extracts from Bukowski's introduction to *Ask the Dust* appear courtesy of Black Sparrow Press. The poems, 'the film makers' and 'the secret of my endurance', are from *Dangling in the Tournefortia*. The poem, 'the star', is from *War All the Time*. The poems, 'blue moon, oh bleweeww mooooon, how I adore you!' and 'mermaid', are from *Play the Piano Drunk/Like a Percussion Instrument/Until the Fingers Begin to Bleed a Bit*.

14   HOLLYWOOD

The description of Bukowski at the track is taken from the many poems and prose pieces he wrote about the subject, particularly from the following books: *Horsemeat*, *Bone Palace Ballet* and *The*

Captain is Out to Lunch and the Sailors Have Taken Over the Ship. I also discussed the subject with friends who accompanied him to the track, including FrancEyE, Linda King, Taylor Hackford, Michael Montfort and Liza Williams.

Details of Bukowski's income in the 1980s comes from Bukowski's tax records and calculations for the Internal Revenue Service. Details of the changes to his will are from his unpublished correspondence with a confidential source.

Bukowski's splits with Linda Lee are based on Bukowski's unpublished correspondence with Linda King, a confidential source, Joan Smith and A.D. Winans; from my interviews with Linda Lee Bukowski, and John Martin; and from *The Charles Bukowski Tapes*. I also interviewed Joan Smith (26 July, 1997).

The publication of *War All the Time* was described by John Martin.

I corresponded with R. Crumb in March, 1997, about the books *Bring Me Your Love* and *There's No Business* and quote from the latter.

The circumstances of Bukowski's proposal of marriage to Linda Lee are from Bukowski's unpublished correspondence with a confidential source; from interviews with the confidential source and Arthur Applebaum's widow, Sheila (5 April, 1997); and from Bukowski's book, *The Wedding*. Linda Lee also described her decision to marry Bukowski. Details about the preparation for the wedding are taken primarily from *The Wedding*. I also interviewed guests: John Martin, Michael Montfort (23 July, 1997), and Steve Richmond, and further consulted Bukowski's unpublished correspondence with Steve Richmond. For additional background material I consulted Richmond's book, *Spinning off Bukowski*; Gerald Locklin's book, *Charles Bukowski: A Sure Bet*; Neeli Cherkovski's *Hank*; and the marriage certificate.

The events surrounding the death of Barbara Frye are based on interviews with her cousins, Tom Frye (28 Oct, 1996), and Sunny Thomas (3 Dec, 1997); correspondence and interviews (1996–1997) with her aunt, Leah Belle Wilson; and with Linda Lee Bukowski. I also referred to Barbara Frye's unpublished correspondence with Bukowski, held at UCSB.

The section on the making of *Barfly*, and Bukowski's involvement with the film industry, is based on my interviews with the following: Linda Lee Bukowski (25 Oct, 1996); Mick Collins (18 Aug, 1996); Elliott Gould (27 June & 7 July, 1997); Taylor Hackford (5 Feb, 1997); John Martin; Michael Montfort (23 July, 1997); Mickey Rourke (16 Dec, 1996); Harry Dean Stanton (31 July, 1997); and John Thomas (1 Jan, 1997).

I corresponded with Norman Mailer (27 Nov, 1996). I referred to Bukowski's unpublished correspondence with John Martin. I also corresponded with Sean Penn, 'I loved the guy' (21 Oct, 1997).

Secondary sources for the making of *Barfly* were as follows: the Sean Penn quotes 'Everybody was excited . . .' are from the documentary *The Ordinary Madness of Charles Bukowski*; the Faye Dunaway quotes are from her autobiography, *Looking for Gatsby* (HarperCollins, 1995); Bukowski's encounter with Arnold Schwarzenegger is from *Das war's* by Gundolf S. Freyermuth and Michael Montfort. I also referred to the following newspaper and magazine articles: an interview with Charles and Linda Lee Bukowski by Chris Hodenfield published in *Film Comment* (Aug, 1987); Sean Penn's interview with Bukowski published in *Interview* (Sept, 1987); the *Los Angeles Times Magazine* interview with Linda Lee and Bukowski by Paul Ciotti (22 Mar, 1987); the (London) *Guardian* (31 Jan, 1987); *People* magazine (16 Nov, 1987); the (London) *Evening Standard* (Feb, 1988); and an interview with Menahem Golan published in the (London) *Independent* (15 May, 1997).

I also referred to the film, *Barfly*; and the books: *The Movie 'Barfly'*; *Hollywood*; *Madonna* (Sidgwick & Jackson, 1989) by Robert Matthew-Walker; *Charles Bukowski: A Sure Bet* by Gerald Locklin; and the *Time Out Film Guide* (Penguin, 1989).

The poem, 'horse fly', appears in *Bone Palace Ballet*.

15 THE LAST RACE

Bukowski's bout of tuberculosis is recorded primarily in his unpublished correspondence with the following friends: John Bennett, John Martin, Steve Richmond, Ed Smith and A.D. Winans. The Bukowski quotes about the illness are from Thomas Schmitt's 1990 documentary, *I'm Still Here*; and I referred to a 1990 Danish documentary made by the Mette Fugl company. Both were viewed at *Elms Lesters Celebrates Charles Bukowski*, and I am grateful to the organizers of this exhibition. I also referred to my interviews with Linda Lee Bukowski, Michael Montfort and John Martin.

John Martin discussed his working relationship with Bukowski and the publication of *The Roominghouse Madrigals*.

Michael Montfort told me the story about Bukowski and the vet (23 July, 1997).

Katherine Wood (née Bukowski) described her 1988 reunion with Bukowski (29 Dec, 1996 & 12 Jan, 1997).

Bukowski's use of the Apple Macintosh computer was described for me by Linda Lee Bukowski (25 Oct, 1996); Marina Bukowski (21 July, 1997); Neeli Cherkovski and John Martin. I also referred to Bukowski's unpublished correspondence with John Martin; and *The Captain is Out to Lunch and the Sailors Have Taken Over the Ship*. John Martin discussed Bukowski's less successful poems and showed me the archive of unpublished work.

For the passage about the completion and publication of Bukowski's fifth novel, *Hollywood*, I consulted the following sources: his unpublished correspondence with John Martin and other friends (as listed above); the novel itself and articles in the *Los Angeles Times* (4 June, 1989); *The Times* (8 July, 1989); and the *Toronto Star* (undated cutting).

Details of Bukowski's success, his attitude to money and his income from royalties are primarily taken from his unpublished correspondence with John Martin and others. I also interviewed Linda Lee Bukowski, Neeli Cherkovski, John Martin and Michael Montfort. I referred to a 27 Jan, 1990, letter from Bukowski to *Beat Scene* editor Kevin Ring which reveals he had turned down $10,000 to read in Amsterdam. The quote, 'I have nothing against money . . .', is from *The Charles Bukowski Tapes*.

The story about the proposed Bukowski sit-com, and the U2 concert, is based on *The Captain is Out to Lunch and the*

Sailors Have Taken Over the Ship and my interview with Harry Dean Stanton (31 July, 1997). I also consulted *Zooropa* by U2 (Island, 1993).

Bukowski's attitude to his fans is drawn from my interview with Linda Lee Bukowski; from Bukowski's unpublished correspondence with John Martin; and from *The Captain is Out to Lunch and the Sailors Have taken Over the Ship*. I also interviewed Ed Smith (8 Jan, 1997), who allowed me to read his unpublished correspondence with Bukowski. I further consulted *Sure, the Charles Bukowski Newsletter* (issues 1 to 10). Special thanks are due to Ed Smith for giving me a copy of *A New Year's Greeting from Black Sparrow Press* (1993). The Bukowski autograph at the start of the chapter is from the book, which he signed on the day described at the end of the chapter.

The story, *The Life of a Bum*, is from *Septuagenarian Stew*. The poems, 'Dinosauria, we', 'pulled down shade', 'transport' and 'we ain't got no money, honey, but we got rain' are from *The Last Night of the Earth Poems*.

16 END OF THE NIGHT

Details about Bukowski's leukemia, and treatment, are taken primarily from my 25 Oct, 1996, interview with Linda Lee Bukowski and my 15 Oct, 1997, interview with Marina Bukowski. I also referred to my interviews with Michael Montfort (23 July, 1997); FrancEyE (3 Jan, 1997); and Carl Weissner (6 Mar, 1997). Additional information came from Bukowski's unpublished correspondence with John Martin, Steve Richmond and Ed Smith, together with letters from Bukowski to Kevin Ring which were later published in *Beat Scene* magazine (issue 20). I also consulted Bukowski's death certificate. For background information on leukemia I am grateful to the forensic pathology department of Guy's Hospital, London.

Taylor Hackford described his last meeting with Bukowski and Bukowski's meeting with Helen Mirren (5 Feb, 1997).

Details of Bukowski's seventy-third birthday are drawn from the German book, *Das war's*. Bukowski's comments about *Pulp* are also from *Das war's*, as are details of how Bukowski's body was dressed for burial. All quoted exchanges between Bukowski and Michael Montfort are from my interview with Michael Montfort.

Reaction to Bukowski's death are from my interviews with the following: Marina Bukowski (21 July & 15 Oct, 1997); FrancEyE (3 Jan, 1997); Linda King (4 Jan, 1997); Philomene Long (1 Jan, 1997); John Martin; Michael Montfort (23 July, 1997); Ruben Rueda (2 Jan, 1997); John Thomas (1 Jan, 1997) and Carl Weissner (6 Mar, 1997). I am also grateful to Sholom 'Red' Stodolsky of Baroque Book Store, Hollywood.

For details of Bukowski's funeral, I referred to the above individuals, and consulted the order of service; the records of Green Hills Memorial Park; its funeral director, Ernesto Alonzo; and the book, *Charles Bukowski: A Sure Bet* by Gerald Locklin.

The Linda King poem is from a 25 Feb, 1997, letter to the author.

The poems, 'decline', 'the observer' and 'this night', are from *Betting on the Muse*. The poem, 'an answer', is from *Bone Palace Ballet*. The extract from the Fax poem has never previously been published and appears here courtesy of Black Sparrow Press.

SELECTED BIBLIOGRAPHY

Charles Bukowski was an extraordinarily prolific writer who published not only in conventional book form, but in chapbooks, broadsides, illustrated special editions, and in numerous small literary magazines.

In this selected bibliography I have listed Bukowski's main publications in the United States together with some curiosities. Early chapbooks and limited editions are included (although many are so rare they can be found only in university libraries) because they are significant in terms of his career and/or they have been mentioned in the text. I have also listed posthumous publications, of which there will be more in years to come; Black Sparrow Press has a great number of unpublished poems and some short stories, although there will be no more novels. I have not listed broadsides, magazine appearances, or foreign editions (with one or two exceptions, as explained below). Nor have I mentioned all the special edition books Black Sparrow Press prints each year as gifts for friends, opting to note a few interesting examples only. To list everything Bukowski published in every format would require a book in itself and, indeed, there have been attempts at this including *A Bibliography of Charles Bukowski* by Sanford Dorbin. Furthermore, although Bukowski's complete work is scattered through many obscure publications, the best material has generally been collected in the main Black Sparrow editions which are widely available.

THE NOVELS

There are six, the last published shortly after Bukowski died.

Post Office (Black Sparrow Press, 1971)
Factotum (Black Sparrow Press, 1975)
Women (Black Sparrow Press, 1978)
Ham on Rye (Black Sparrow Press, 1982)
Hollywood (Black Sparrow Press, 1989)
Pulp (Black Sparrow Press, 1994)

BOOKS OF POETRY

Several of these titles are chapbooks which were published in small editions, and are long out of print. But the main Black Sparrow Press anthologies – which contain the bulk of Bukowski's best poetry – are widely available.

Flower, Fist and Bestial Wail (Hearse Press, 1960)
Longshot Pomes for Broke Players (7 Poets Press, 1962)
Run with the Hunted (Midwest Press, 1962)
It Catches My Heart in Its Hands (Loujon Press, 1963) *Note*: The first Bukowski book printed by Jon and Gypsy Lou Webb in New Orleans. It has long been out of print.
Crucifix in a Deathhand (Loujon Press, 1965)
Cold Dogs in the Courtyard (Literary Times-Cyfoeth, 1965)
The Genius of the Crowd (7 Flowers Press, 1966)
2 Poems (Black Sparrow Press, 1967)
The Curtains are Waving and People Walk Through/The Afternoon/Here and in Berlin and in New York City and in Mexico (Black Sparrow Press, 1967)
At Terror Street and Agony Way (Black Sparrow Press, 1968)
Poems Written Before Jumping out of an 8-Storey Window (Poetry X/Change, 1968)
The Days Run Away Like Wild Horses Over the Hills (Black Sparrow Press, 1969) *Note*: The first substantial poetry anthology printed by Black Sparrow Press, it is still available and is one of Bukowski's greatest books.

Penguin Modern Poets 13 – Charles Bukowski/Philip Lamantia/ Harold Norse (Penguin Books, London, 1969) *Note*: This is the only foreign publication of Bukowski's poetry included in the selected bibliography. I have listed it because it was Bukowski's first book with a major publishing house, and because it was also sold in the United States. It is no longer in print.

If We Take – (Black Sparrow Press, 1970) *Note*: This was printed as a New Year gift.

Fire Station (Capricorn Press, 1970) *Note*: A limited edition of one poem.

Me and Your Sometimes Love Poems (Kisskill Press, 1972) *Note*: A book of poems by Bukowski and Linda King, self-published when they were both living at De Longpre Avenue in Hollywood. It was reprinted in 1994 by Linda who incorporated comic drawings by Bukowski which they had meant to use in the first edition. Although not available in book stores, it is a fascinating account of a relationship.

Mockingbird Wish Me Luck (Black Sparrow Press, 1972)

Burning in Water, Drowning in Flame: Poems 1955–1973 (Black Sparrow Press, 1974) *Note*: This anthology collects poems from the two Loujon Press books, together with later work, in a modestly priced and widely available edition.

Tough Company (Black Sparrow Press, 1976) *Note*: Printed as a New Year gift.

Scarlet (Black Sparrow Press, 1976) *Note*: This is the limited edition of poems Bukowski wrote about his girlfriend, Pamela Miller (aka Cupcakes). All the poems were later reprinted in *Love Is a Dog from Hell.*

Art (Black Sparrow Press, 1977) *Note*: A single poem elaborately printed as a New Year gift for friends of Black Sparrow Press.

Love Is a Dog from Hell: Poems 1974–1977 (Black Sparrow Press, 1977) *Note*: This has proved the most popular of all Bukowski's poetry books and is widely available in paperback. Most of the poems concern Bukowski's complicated love life in the mid-1970s.

A Love Poem (Black Sparrow Press, 1979) *Note*: Printed as a New Year gift.

Play the Piano Drunk/Like a Percussion Instrument/Until the

Fingers Begin to Bleed a Bit (Black Sparrow Press, 1979)
Note: This book is made up of poems originally featured in
a monthly magazine, *Sparrow*, which was used by John Martin
as a way of showcasing the work of poets he was publishing in
more substantial editions. Despite its off-putting title, it contains
some of Bukowski's best poetry, including 'fire station'.

Dangling in the Tournefortia (Black Sparrow Press, 1981)

War All the Time: Poems 1981–1984 (Black Sparrow Press, 1984)

The Last Generation (Black Sparrow Press, 1982) *Note*: Printed
as a New Year gift.

Sparks (Black Sparrow Press, 1983) *Note*: Printed as a New
Year gift.

You Get So Alone at Times That it Just Makes Sense (Black
Sparrow Press, 1986) *Note*: One of the large late anthologies
of Bukowski's poetry.

The Roominghouse Madrigals: Early Selected Poems 1946–1966
(Black Sparrow Press, 1988) *Note*: John Martin trawled through
the little literary magazines Bukowski had first published in to
compile this book of very early poems.

In the Shadow of the Rose (Black Sparrow Press, 1991) *Note*: A
limited edition dedicated to Bukowski's friend, Sean Penn.

Three by Bukowski (Black Sparrow Press, 1992) *Note*: A limited
edition.

The Last Night of the Earth Poems (Black Sparrow Press, 1992) *Note*:
The last full-length poetry book published during Bukowski's
lifetime, and one of his best.

Those Marvelous Lunches (Black Sparrow Press, 1993) *Note*: A
New Year gift to friends of the press.

Heat Wave (Black Sparrow Graphic Arts, 1995) *Note*: A limited
edition illustrated by artist, Ken Price, and sold to collectors. It
was produced in a regular edition priced $1,250 and an even
more expensive de luxe edition priced $3,500. The book comes
in a Perspex box together with a CD.

A New War (Black Sparrow Press, 1997) *Note*: A booklet of five
poems published as a New Year gift to friends of the press. The
poem which appears at the end of chapter sixteen is from this
booklet.

Bone Palace Ballet: New Poems (Black Sparrow Press, 1997) *Note*:

A large anthology of previously unpublished work selected and published by John Martin after Bukowski's death. John Martin chose the title.

POETRY AND PROSE IN A SINGLE VOLUME

Horsemeat (Black Sparrow Press, 1982) *Note*: A limited edition with photographs by Michael Montfort of Bukowski at the race track.

Septuagenarian Stew: Stories and Poems (Black Sparrow Press, 1990) *Note*: One of Bukowski's great late books, published in the year of his seventieth birthday. This is widely available in paperback.

Betting on the Muse: Poems and Stories (Black Sparrow Press, 1996) *Note*: Previously unpublished work selected by John Martin and published after Bukowski's death. Many of the poems address the subject of impending death.

SHORT STORIES

Confessions of a Man Insane Enough to Live with Beasts (Mimeo Press, 1965) *Note*: This is a very early chapbook published in a small edition and no longer in print, but the story can also be found in *South of No North*.

All the Assholes in the World and Mine (Open Skull Press, 1966) *Note*: As above.

Notes of a Dirty Old Man (Essex House, 1969) *Note*: A collection of stories written by Bukowski as his weekly column for the underground newspaper, *Open City*. It was later reissued by City Lights Books and is still widely available in paperback.

A Bukowski Sampler (Quixote Press, 1969)

Erections, Ejaculations, Exhibitions and General Tales of Ordinary Madness (City Lights Books, 1972) *Note*: In 1983 this very large book was reissued in two volumes, *Tales of Ordinary Madness* and *The Most Beautiful Woman in Town*, both of which are still available in paperback.

South of No North (Black Sparrow Press, 1973)

Bring Me Your Love (Black Sparrow Press, 1983) *Note*: A special edition of a single short story, illustrated by R. Crumb.

Hot Water Music (Black Sparrow Press, 1983)

There's No Business (Black Sparrow Press, 1984) *Note*: Another special edition of a single short story, illustrated by R. Crumb.

Confession of a Coward (Black Sparrow Press, 1995) *Note*: This autobiographical short story concerns Bukowski's marriage to Barbara Frye and was printed as a New Year gift for friends of Black Sparrow Press after Bukowski's death.

MISCELLANEOUS PUBLICATIONS

There are a large number of Bukowski curiosities that cannot be classified as poetry, novels or short stories. Many are illustrated limited editions. Book dealers commonly charge in excess of $500 for such rarities, and prices can go over $1,000 if the books are signed by Bukowski (*Note*: 1998 prices). Obscure though most of these publications are, several deserve mention:

Dear Mr Bukowski (Garage Graphics, 1979) *Note*: A series of cartoon drawings by Bukowski, with a brief explanatory text, printed on cards and gathered within an envelope as a collector's item. Only fifty copies were made.

The Day it Snowed in LA (Paget Press, 1986) *Note*: A series of cartoons by Bukowski and a brief text, 'The Adventures of Clarence Hiram Sweetmeat', which recounts a day when snow falls on Los Angeles and everyone goes crazy. Clarence's father smiles for the first time in ten years.

The Wedding (Brown Buddha Books, 1986) *Note*: This is a very rare limited edition printed to celebrate Bukowski's marriage to Linda Lee Beighle in August, 1985. The text is by Bukowski and there are photographs by Michael Montfort.

The Movie: Barfly (Black Sparrow Press, 1987) *Note*: Bukowski's screenplay to the Barbet Schroeder film starring Mickey Rourke and Faye Dunaway. It contains photographs taken on the set.

Run with the Hunted: A Charles Bukowski Reader (HarperCollins, 1993) *Note*: Not to be confused with the 1962 poetry chapbook of the same name. A reader edited by John Martin, and arranged so that it tells the story of Henry Chinaski's life in roughly chronological order.

Shakespeare Never Did This (Black Sparrow Press, 1995) *Note*: A travelogue describing Bukowski's two trips to Europe in 1978, illustrated with black and white photographs by Michael Montfort. First published by City Lights Books in 1979, it was reissued in an augmented edition by Black Sparrow Press, in 1995, and contains both poetry and prose. It is widely available.

The Captain is Out to Lunch and the Sailors Have Taken Over the Ship (Black Sparrow Graphic Arts, 1997) *Note*: A limited edition of Bukowski's daily journal in the last years of his life, costing $650 when first published in April, 1997. It is illustrated by R. Crumb, and has since been issued as a more affordable Black Sparrow Press paperback.

BOOKS OF LETTERS

Three volumes of letters have been published to date, but Bukowski was such an enthusiastic correspondent that hundreds of letters remain uncollected.

The Bukowski/Purdy Letters: 1964–1974 (Paget Press, 1983) *Note*: Selected correspondence of Bukowski and the Canadian poet, Al Purdy, whose work Bukowski greatly admired. The two men never met.

Screams from the Balcony: Selected Letters 1960–1970 (Black Sparrow Press, 1993) *Note*: The first of two substantial volumes of letters published by Black Sparrow Press.

Living on Luck: Selected Letters 1960s–1970s, Volume 2 (Black Sparrow Press, 1995)

FILM/VIDEO

There have been numerous television documentaries about Bukowski and a handful of feature-length films based on his work. These are the most notable examples:

Bukowski at Bellevue (Black Sparrow Press/Visionary, no date) *Note*: Although not released until the 1990s, this is a video film of one of Bukowski's earliest public readings recorded by students at Bellevue College, Washington State, in 1970. Technical quality is very poor.

Bukowski (KCET, 1973) *Note*: A black and white documentary directed by Taylor Hackford. It features Bukowski reading in San Francisco and includes footage of rival girlfriends, Linda King and Liza Williams. The film was made for Los Angeles public television station, KCET.

Charles Bukowski – East Hollywood (Thomas Schmitt, 1976) *Note*: A black and white documentary film featuring rare footage of Bukowski with his girlfriend, Cupcakes, whom he dated after splitting with Linda King.

Tales of Ordinary Madness (23 Giugno/Ginis Film Paris, 1981) *Note*: Directed by Marco Ferreri and starring the American actor Ben Gazzara, this European art house film is based on short stories by Bukowski. He took no part in the making of the film, and did not like it.

Crazy Love (Mainline Pictures, 1987) *Note*: A Belgian-made movie directed by Dominique Deruddere and based on three short stories by Bukowski who had nothing to do with its making. However, he considered it the best adaptation of his work.

The Charles Bukowski Tapes (Les Films du Losange, 1987) *Note*: Made by Barbet Schroeder while trying to raise money to make *Barfly*, this fascinating video tape documentary consists of Bukowski talking directly to camera about his life and work. It is divided into fifty-two short sequences, most filmed at Bukowski's house in San Pedro, California, but there is also footage of Bukowski touring his old haunts in East Hollywood and revisiting the house on Longwood Avenue where he was brought up. Copies are hard to locate and cost in the region of $100.

Barfly (Cannon, 1987) *Note*: The motion picture starring Mickey Rourke and Faye Dunaway, and directed by Barbet Schroeder. Bukowski wrote the screenplay and makes a non-speaking cameo appearance as a barfly in the scene when Chinaski meets Wanda.

I'm Still Here (Tag/Traum, 1990) *Note*: A German television documentary filmed in color by Thomas Schmitt. It includes footage of Bukowski at home in San Pedro following his bout of tuberculosis.

The Ordinary Madness of Charles Bukowski (British Broadcasting Corporation, 1995) *Note*: A documentary film made as part of the BBC's *Bookmark* series on modern authors. It was first broadcast in the United Kingdom after Bukowski's death.

There are plans for further film adaptations of Bukowski's work. Taylor Hackford owns the rights to *Post Office*, and has talked to Sean Penn about playing Henry Chinaski. The director, Paul Verhoeven, owns film rights to *Women*.

AUDIO RECORDINGS

Several of Bukowski's public readings were recorded and have been marketed on audio cassette, LP and CD. Bukowski also recorded at home and some of these sessions have been packaged for sale. Unfortunately, tapes have been re-edited and bootlegged over the years and tapes with different titles often contain the same material. As a result, I have listed only a few:

Bukowski/Poems & Insults! (City Lights Books, 1972) *Note*: A recording of Bukowski's appearance at the Poet's Theater in September, 1972.

Hostage (Rhino Records/1994) *Note*: This is a recording of a reading at Redondo Beach, California, in 1980. It has also been packaged and sold as *Absolutely Live in Redondo Beach!*

Bukowski Reads his Poetry (Black Sparrow Graphic Arts, 1995)

BOOKS ABOUT CHARLES BUKOWSKI

Several of these are memoirs published in small editions.

A Bibliography of Charles Bukowski by Sanford Dorbin (Black Sparrow Press, 1969)

Charles Bukowski: A Critical and Bibliographical Study by Hugh Fox (Abyss Publications, 1969)

Bukowski: Friendship, Fame and Bestial Myth by Jory Sherman (Blue Horse Publications, 1981)

All's Normal Here edited by Loss Pequeno Glazier (Ruddy Duck Press, 1985) *Note*: A collection of work about Bukowski by his friends. It also includes letters and some original work by Bukowski.

The King of San Pedro by David Barker (Richard G. Wong & Co, 1985) *Note*: A curious miniature book, it gives the basic facts of Bukowski's biography.

Bukowski (Photographs 1977–1987) by Michael Montfort (Graham Mackintosh, 1987) *Note*: Printed for an exhibition of Michael Montfort's photographs in Hamburg, Germany.

The Poet's Craft edited by William Packard (Paragon House, 1987) *Note*: Chapter twenty-three reprints an interview Bukowski gave to the *New York Quarterly* about his method of writing.

Whitman's Wild Children by Neeli Cherkovski (The Lapis Press, 1988) *Note*: The first chapter, 'Notes on a Dirty Old Man', is about Bukowski.

Sure edited by Ed Smith (published by Ed Smith, 1991–1994) *Note*: The ten volumes of the news letter, *Sure*, published by Ed Smith between 1991 and 1994, include a wealth of information.

In Search of Literary LA by Lionel Rolfe (California Classics Books, 1991) *Note*: This contains one chapter about Bukowski, 'Tales of an Extraordinary Madman', based on the evening of the première of *Tales of Ordinary Madness*.

Hank by Neeli Cherkovski (Random House, 1991) *Note*: Later re-issued by Steerforth Press.

Bukowski by Michael Montfort (Michael Montfort, 1993) *Note*: A limited edition of photographs.

Against the American Dream: Essays on Charles Bukowski by Russell Harrison (Black Sparrow Press, 1994) *Note*: A critical study of Bukowski's work.

Blowing My Hero by Amber O'Neil (Amber O'Neil Productions, 1995) *Note*: Amber O'Neil is a pseudonym for one of Bukowski's former girlfriends who self-published this memoir after reading what he wrote about her in *Women*. The title relates to Amber giving Bukowski oral sex. Amber was obliged to withdraw *Blowing My Hero* from sale after a complaint from Bukowski's estate that she did not have permission to reprint letters from Bukowski.

Das ist Alles: Charles Bukowski Recollected edited by Joan Jobe Smith (Pearl Editions, 1995) *Note*: A collection of poems by friends and admirers of Bukowski published following his death. FrancEyE and Linda King are among the contributors.

Das war's by Gundolf S. Freyermuth with photographs by Michael Montfort (Rasch und Röhring, 1996) *Note*: Published in Germany, this book contains the last interview Bukowski gave and is illustrated with photographs by Michael Montfort.

Spinning off Bukowski by Steve Richmond (Sun Dog Press, 1996) *Note*: An engaging memoir by Bukowski's friend of many years, it is widely available.

Charles Bukowski: A Sure Bet by Gerald Locklin (Water Row Press, 1996)

The Charles Bukowski/Second Coming Years by A.D. Winans (The Beat Scene Press, 1996)

The Buk Book Text by Jim Christy with photos by Claude Powell (ECW Press, 1997) *Note*: This features photographs of Bukowski groping his former neighbor, Tina Darby.

Charles Bukowski by Gay Brewer (Twaynes United States Authors Series, 1997) *Note*: An excellent critical study of Bukowski's work.

Sixty-Seven Poems for Downtrodden Saints by Jack Micheline (FMSBW, 1997) *Note*: An anthology of Jack Micheline's writings over the years, it contains various pieces about Bukowski including the prose-poem, 'Long After Midnight'.

Bukowski in the Bathtub edited by Philomene Long (Raven of Temple of Man, 1997) *Note*: Transcripts of conversations between Bukowski and his friend, John Thomas.

INDEX